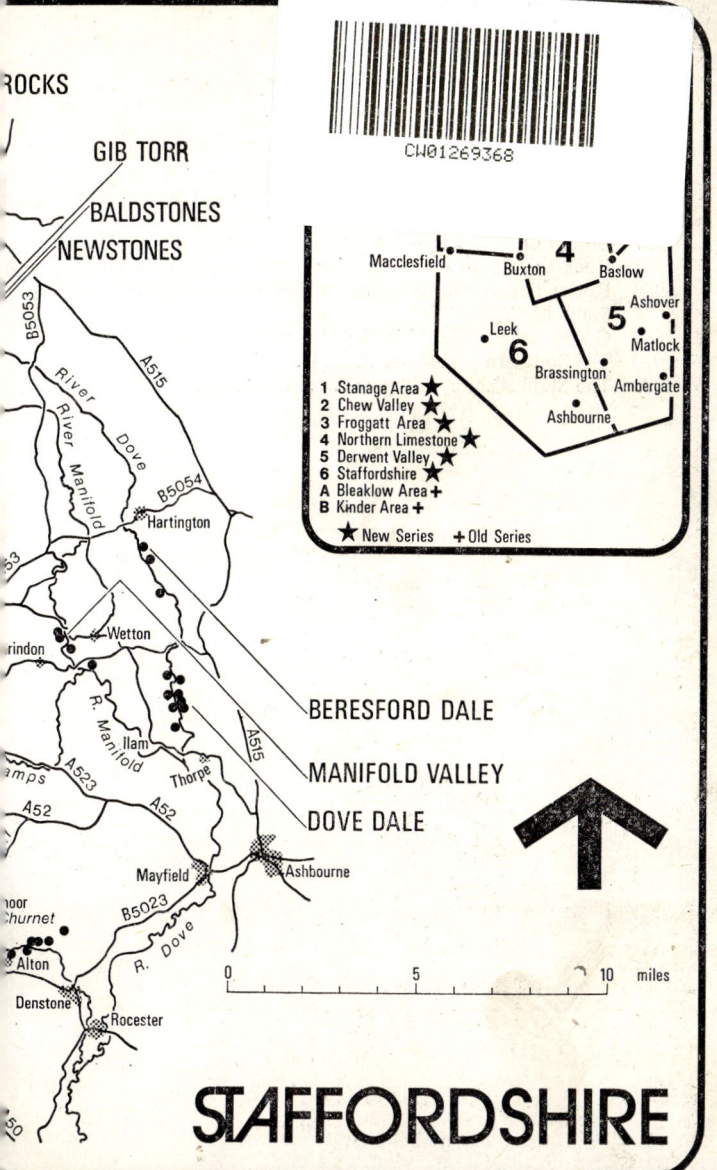

## PREVIOUS EDITIONS

| | |
|---|---|
| 1913 | Some Gritstone Climbs. John Laycock |
| 1924 | Recent Developments on Gritstone. Fergus Graham, Morley Wood, etc. |
| 1951 | Climbs on Gritstone—Volume 3. Allan Allsopp |
| 1957 | Climbs on Gritstone—Volume 3 revised |
| 1957 | Climbs on Gritstone—Volume 4. Eric Byne and Wilf White |
| 1961 | Rock Climbs on the Mountain Limestone. Graham West |
| 1968 | Rock Climbs on the Roaches and Hen Cloud. North Staffs M.C. |
| 1968 | Guide to the Staffordshire Roaches and Hen Cloud. J. Smith |
| 1970 | The Southern Limestone Area. Paul Nunn |
| 1973 | The Staffordshire Gritstone Area. David Salt |

ROCK CLIMBS IN THE PEAK
Volume 6

# STAFFORDSHIRE AREA

Series Editor: GEOFF MILBURN

Editors of this volume: MIKE BROWELL
BRIAN DALE
STEPHEN DALE
NICK LONGLAND

Produced for and by
THE PEAK COMMITTEE of the
BRITISH MOUNTAINEERING COUNCIL

Copyright: British
Mountaineering Council 1981

© Copyright British Mountaineering Council
   or individual authors
ISBN 0 903908 65 4

First Edition: New Series 1981

Cover Photographs:
Front Cover: Easter Island, Ilam Rock
   *Photo by Chris Jackson*

Rear Cover: Hawkwing, Roaches Lower Tier
   *Photo by Dave Jones*

Inside Rear Cover: Ramshaw Crack, Ramshaw Rocks
   *Photo by Tony Moulam*


Distributors:
Cordee
249 Knighton Church Road
Leicester
LE2 3JQ


Printed in Great Britain by
Joseph Ward, Wellington Road, Dewsbury, West Yorkshire

# CONTENTS

|  | page |
|---|---|
| Line Drawing list | 4 |
| Photograph list | 5 |
| Acknowledgements | 6 |
| Introduction | 7 |
| Access | 8 |
| Geology | 9 |
| Technical Notes | 13 |
| MOUNTAIN RESCUE | 14 |

THE CRAGS alphabetically in each area:

### LIMESTONE AREA:

| | |
|---|---|
| Baley Buttress | 21 |
| Beeston Tor | 70 |
| Celestial Twins, The | 53 |
| Chimney, The | 61 |
| Dovedale Castle | 50 |
| Dovedale Church | 45 |
| Dove Holes | 26 |
| Drabber Tor | 55 |
| Ilam Rock | 28 |
| Ossam's Crag | 63 |
| Pickering Tors | 30 |
| Pike Crag | 52 |
| Ravens Tor | 22 |
| Thor's Cave | 65 |
| Tissington Spires | 36 |
| Peakstone Inn Amphitheatre | 94 |
| Peakstone Rock | 98 |
| Rainroach Rock | 92 |
| Rakes Dale | 91 |
| Sharpcliffe Rocks | 111 |
| Stony Dale Quarry | 105 |
| Toothill Rock | 90 |
| Wootton Lodge Crags | 86 |
| Wright's Rock | 95 |

### CHURNET VALLEY AREA:

| | |
|---|---|
| Belmont Hall Crags | 114 |
| Castle Crag | 88 |
| Dimmings Dale | 99 |
| Flintmill Buttress | 125 |
| Garston Rocks | 123 |
| Harston Rocks | 116 |
| Ina's Rock | 85 |
| Oldridge Pinnacle | 122 |
| Ousal Dale | 103 |
| Park Banks Crags | 82 |

### GRITSTONE AREA:

| | |
|---|---|
| Back Forest | 239 |
| Baldstones | 235 |
| Bosley Cloud | 249 |
| Five Clouds | 183 |
| Gib Torr | 237 |
| Gradbach Hill | 245 |
| Hen Cloud | 192 |
| Knypersley Rocks | 256 |
| Mow Cop | 259 |
| Newstones | 231 |
| Nth Cloud (Roche End) | 190 |
| Ramshaw Rocks | 211 |
| Roaches, The: Lower Tier | 136 |
| Upper Tier | 148 |
| Rock End | 258 |
| Skyline Area, The | 167 |

# LINE DRAWINGS

| Staffordshire Area | | IFC |
|---|---|---|
| *No.* | | *page* |
| 1 | Dovedale | 16 |
| 2 | Ravens Tor | 23 |
| 3 | Dove Holes | 27 |
| 4 | Ilam Rock | 29 |
| 5 | Pickering Wall | 32 |
| 6 | Tissington Spires | 37 |
| 7 | South Gully Area | 42 |
| 8 | Dovedale Church Map | 46 |
| 9 | Dovedale Church | 47 |
| 10 | The Manifold Valley | 57 |
| 11 | The Chimney | 62 |
| 12 | Ossam's Crag | 64 |
| 13 | Thor's Cave | 67 |
| 14 | Beeston Tor | 71 |
| 15 | The Lower Churnet Valley | 79 |
| 16 | The Upper Churnet Valley | 109 |
| 17 | The Roaches Area | 129 |
| Lower Tier, Roaches: | | |
| 18 | Left of The Steps | 137 |
| 19 | Raven Rock | 141 |
| 20 | Righthand End | 145 |
| Upper Tier, Roaches: | | |
| 21 | Blushing Buttress | 150 |
| 22 | Great Slab | 154 |
| 23 | Boulder Plan | 157 |
| 24 | Central Massive | 159 |
| 25 | Maud's Garden | 162 |
| 26 | Chicken Run | 164 |

| | | *page* |
|---|---|---|
| Skyline Area | | |
| 27 | Condor Buttress | 168 |
| 28 | Tower Buttress | 171 |
| 29 | Skyline Buttress | 175 |
| 30 | Alpha Buttress | 178 |
| The Five Clouds: | | |
| 31 | The Third Cloud | 186 |
| 32 | The Fourth Cloud | 189 |
| Hen Cloud: | | |
| 33 | Lefthand Section | 196 |
| 34 | Central Buttress | 200 |
| 35 | Eliminate Area | 205 |
| Ramshaw Rocks: | | |
| 36 | Loaf and Cheese | 214 |
| 37 | Lower Tier | 217 |
| 38 | Ramshaw Crack Area | 221 |
| 39 | North End | 226 |
| 40 | Newstones | 232 |
| 41 | Baldstones | 236 |
| 42 | Bosley Cloud Plan | 250 |
| 43 | Mow Cop Pinnacle | 261 |
| 44 | Mow Cop Plan | 263 |

# PHOTOGRAPHS

| | page |
|---|---|
| Aquarius, Ravens Tor: Dave Jones climbing  *Photo by Mike MacDonald* | i |
| Fingerdrive, Left Celestial Twin: Dave Jones climbing  *Photo by Mike MacDonald* | ii |
| Dance of the Flies, Stony Dale Quarry: Steve Dale climbing  *Photo Steve Dale collection* | iii |
| Dust Storm, Rakes Dale: Brian Dale climbing  *Photo Steve Dale collection* | iv |
| Encouragement, Hen Cloud: Phil Gibson climbing  *Photo by Gary Gibson* | v |
| Slowhand, Hen Cloud: Mike MacDonald climbing  *Photo by Dave Jones* | vi |
| Hunky Dory, Roaches Lower Tier: John Regan climbing  *Photo by Simon Horrox* | vii |
| Appaloosa Sunset, Third Cloud: Mike MacDonald climbing  *Photo by Dave Jones* | viii |

# ACKNOWLEDGEMENTS

It is the field workers who initially get a guidebook (and occasionally an editor) off the ground. With one exception, who requested anonymity, their names head the sections describing the various crags. Without diminishing the efforts of all such individuals who have sacrificed time and freedom to go 'working on the guide' a particular debt is owed to Dave Jones who is responsible for the lion's share of the Roaches area and whose enthusiasm overcame many a sticky patch. Chris Calow provided a similar driving force for the Dovedale section. The credits to the cameramen are given in the photograph list. Chris Jackson has organised the various maps and diagrams; these were the excellent work of Phil Gibson, George Bridge, Mike Browell, Sue Lawty and Chris Butterfield. Jean Dale, Frances Fleming and Carol Tew transformed the often chaotic drafts into coherent typescript. Mike Browell, as Business Editor, liaised with the printer and, along with the Editors, Dave Gregory and the Guidebook Executive, read and corrected the proofs. The Peak District Guidebook Executive gave valuable advice and assistance on many problems on request, as have the mass rallies of the Guidebook Sub-Committee, on anything and everything, whether asked for or not!

A special acknowledgement is owed to the previous guidebook editors and their helpers.

Finally, Dave Gregory has recently announced his retirement from the somewhat hot seat of Series Editor. In addition to successfully steering the current series through a period of evolution to its present healthy state, he has over the last decade put in a vast amount of work, all too often taken for granted. Peak District climbers owe him a great deal both for his technical expertise in editing, proof reading and the difficult task of moulding multiform scripts into a consistent whole, and for the encouragement and assistance he has given to all involved in producing the Peak guides. This volume is dedicated to Dave.

# INTRODUCTION

This volume, the last of the second series of B.M.C. Peak District guidebooks, covers a varied area both in landscape and geology and the climber is offered a rich choice of limestone, sandstone and grit in surroundings to suit a diversity of tastes. Staffordshire has crags for all seasons and weathers and has the added bonus of an abundance of notable pubs, many with enlightened licensing laws.

All the major crags in this volume have seen much innovative activity in recent years but the limestone valleys in particular have received a complete face-lift since the previous guide. Extensive exploration and gardening has unearthed many hidden gems whose quality should prevent their disappearance with time, back into the undergrowth, as did certain routes of the late 60s. The modern free-climbing ethic, due in part to improved protection methods, has been applied here no less vigorously than elsewhere in the Peak; only a handful of artificial routes now remain. This trend has not however always been matched by an equal purity on the new route scene. The increasingly keen competition for first ascents and subsequent glory seems to have encouraged practices which can only harm the sport. False claims and dates and dubious first ascent ropework do not detract from the route invented; they merely indicate a growing unhealthiness and render the production of definitive guidebooks that much harder. Hold chipping and even wholesale attempts to destroy climbs, both of which have occurred in the Roaches area recently, do matter and it is hoped that anyone found perpetrating such selfish vandalism will be more than frowned upon. Good new route possibilities (as well as loads of rubbish) still exist and the old maxim 'If you can't climb it, leave it for someone who can' is still valid.

Access to crags is becoming increasingly difficult and this area is no exception despite the recent happy solution on the Roaches. It is important to appreciate that climbing on most of the crags is only possible because of the tolerance of the owners and that their surroundings are often highly valued as scenic resources or for other interests such as conservation. Continued access depends very much on us, as climbers, preserving our good name. In the long run, a 'try and stop me' attitude is less likely to work than patient negotiation.

The crags are covered by 1:50,000 O.S. Sheets 118 and 119 and except for Mow Cop and the Churnet areas, by the 1:25,000 map; The White Peak.

# ACCESS

Many of the crags in this guidebook, particularly those in the Churnet Valley, are outside the Peak District National Park. On several of them the access situation is quite sensitive and climbers should take care not to antagonise owners. The designation of an area as a National Park does not confer on any member of the public the right to have access to land unless access agreements have been made. Where access agreements have not been concluded it will generally be necessary to obtain permission from the owner. There is an obligation throughout the country to obtain permission to camp irrespective of the designation of an area within the Park as an access area. It is not permissible to light fires on campsites due to the very serious risk of causing extensive fires although the individual is free to discuss this point with the owner in question. The National Parks and Access to the Countryside Act 1949 and the Countryside Act 1968 give planning authorities powers to make access agreements and access orders. The intention of these agreements and orders is to provide the public with the facility to wander at will over land designated and signposted as open country. In general, such land, referred to as 'Access Land', is in the gritstone moorland regions of the Park and for many of the crags in the area of this guidebook it is technically necessary to obtain access permission from the owner or his agent. THE INCLUSION OF A CRAG OR THE ROUTES UPON IT IN THIS GUIDEBOOK DOES NOT MEAN THAT ANY MEMBER OF THE PUBLIC HAS THE RIGHT OF ACCESS TO THE CRAG OR THE RIGHT TO CLIMB UPON IT. The amicable future of the climbing on the crags in this guide is to a great extent in your hands. Climbers must at all times observe the highest standards of behaviour particularly in relation to litter, disturbance of stock, disturbance of plants and animals in conservation areas, lighting of fires and damage to walls and any other property.

Up to date information on camping arrangements or other access matters can be obtained from the National Park Office, Aldern House, Baslow Road, Bakewell, Derbyshire. Telephone Bakewell 2881, or from the following information centres:

Field Head, Edale. Telephone Hope Valley 70207.
Old Market Hall, Bakewell. Telephone Bakewell 3227.
Castle Street, Castleton. Telephone Hope Valley 20679.

# GEOLOGY AND GEOMORPHOLOGY
by R. D. Brown

The emergence of Britain from the Cretaceous (Chalk) sea 60 million years ago began a period of erosion which has continued to the present. During this time the Dane and Dove river systems have eroded thousands of feet of strata from the Derbyshire Dome, the southern culmination of the Pennine Anticline.
The oldest rocks exposed in the region, the Carboniferous Limestone Series, outcrop in the Dovedale-Manifold area in the core of the dome. Between Hollinsclough and Hartington the Dove occupies an open valley on shales of the Millstone Grit Series. The eastern valley-side is the edge of the limestone outcrop which here dips west beneath the shales. From Hartington to Thorpe the Dove has cut an impressive gorge across the limestone outcrop. The finest part of this gorge, Dovedale, is over 500 feet deep and contains most of the limestone crags. The gem of the limestone cliffs, Beeston Tor, is however in the gorge of the Manifold. In the hills just west of the Manifold gorge the limestones dip west beneath shales and the Millstone Grit outcrop extends to the Potteries Coalfield.
A major feature of the Millstone Grit outcrop is the Goyt Trough a tight syncline which runs from New Mills south to Leek. The southern part of this, the Goldsitch Syncline, has been deeply dissected by the Dane and Churnet headwaters. The topography produced by this dissection has been strongly controlled by the presence of a particularly massive sandstone, the Roaches Grit, in the folded sequence of sandstones and shales. The syncline is symmetrical and so the strata dip inwards on each side of the axis at 20-30°. On each limb of the fold the Roaches Grit forms a prominent escarpment facing outwards, away from the axis, and along which the major gritstone crags occur. Thus on the western limb at Hen Cloud, the Roaches and Back Forest, the Roaches Grit dips east-north-east, whereas on the eastern limb at Ramshaw, Newstones and Gib Torr the dip is west-north-west. The fold axis trends north-south through Upper Hulme and, since the fold plunges to the north, the Roaches Grit escarpments converge southwards. Just north of Upper Hulme, at the point of convergence, the Churnet has breached the grit by valley incision along the fold axis. The topographic form of this breached plunging syncline is visible from the Mermaid Inn.
In the core of the Goldsitch Syncline, between the gritstone outcrops, there is a small outlier of the Lower Coal Measures overlying the Millstone grit Series. The Coal Measures comprise shales with thin sandstone beds and a few coal seams. The upper

Dane and Black Brook have deeply dissected this outcrop of relatively weak strata.

The Carboniferous Limestones began to form 350 million years ago from the calcareous skeletal remains of the rich marine fauna of a sub-tropical sea. The Dovedale-Manifold area was a zone of transition between the massif, a relatively shallow stable area of sea floor in the north-east, and a deeper water basin of more rapid subsidence in the south-west. Between massif and basin a zone of greater turbulence provided an ideal environment for reef building algae and corals. Thus there were three distinct environments, the massif, the basin, and the reef, in each of which a different type of limestone was formed. In the clear water of the massif thick bedded pure limestones were deposited. These beds are exposed in Wolfscote Dale and at Iron Tors but, because of their uniform resistance to erosion, crags tend to be rather small. In the deep muddy water of the basin, thin beds of impure cherty limestone and shales were deposited. These beds are exposed in Milldale and in the Manifold Valley west of Beeston Tor. The basinal deposits are not massive enough to form good crags although there are numerous small outcrops. In the reef environment massive, poorly bedded, fossiliferous limestones were formed. All the good limestone crags are developed on the Dovedale Limestone, a reef deposit which attains a thickness of 500 feet. The Dovedale Limestone passes laterally into either basinal or massif limestones at the margin of the reef zone.

Major structures such as the Goyt Trough were created at the end of the Carboniferous Period by west to east compression during the Hercynian orogeny. This orogeny also produced numerous smaller folds and associated faults and joints which are best developed in the Millstone Grit sequence and in the well bedded limestones. The massive reef deposits, as at Beeston Tor, were much more resistant to deformation and so have few fault or joint structures. At Beeston obvious lines are therefore rather sparse; Beeston Eliminate and Ivy Gash exploit the only prominent bedding structures, The Thorn follows a major joint, and Bertram's Chimney is a fault. On steep walls climbing is made possible, as on Perforation, by small pockets developed from the abundant large pores. At Raven's Tor the passage from reef into basinal deposits is exposed in the north end of the crag. In such a transition zone the reef limestone is less massive than at Beeston Tor and many climbs follow either cracks, such as Aquarius, or grooves such as Venery. The cracks are joints and the grooves are formed by the intersection of joint planes. At Tissington Spires an intersecting network of minor faults and joints has been etched out into a unique group of pinnacles. Joints also provide some of Tissington's best lines such as George and John Peel. Around

Ecton Hill the joints and faults were mineralised by copper bearing solutions and the ores so formed have been extensively mined. Small caves and natural arches may follow cavities that were formed in the original reef; the larger caves, such as Thors Cave, are probably due to more recent chemical solution. Limestone formation ended 300 million years ago when a phase of uplift resulted in the emergence of the sea bed. After a period of erosion the land was submerged and buried beneath sediments derived from the south. So began the deposition of 2500 feet of Millstone Grit sediments. The first deposits were shales and silty sandstones and then a river delta brought in the Roaches Grit from the north. This grit comprises two beds of purple feldspathic sandstone separated by shales. The upper bed attains a thickness of 200 feet and it forms the majority of the gritstone crags. However, at Five Clouds and the Roaches the lower bed is very massive and forms a lower tier of crags below the main edge. Most grit crags have rounded faces split by vertical and horizontal cracks. The vertical cracks are joints, the faces are often joint plane surfaces, and the horizontal cracks are bedding planes. The flaring of cracks and the rounding and fluting of faces are the result of weathering processes such as frost heave and chemical decay. On the Roaches Lower Tier many routes, like The Mincer follow joint cracks up bulging walls of massive grit. As on Pebbledash, large quartz pebbles may provide the only means of progress across smooth faces. On the upper Tier, and at Hen Cloud, bedding and jointing are better developed and therefore routes are more abundant. The steep dip into the hillside results in inward sloping jugs and slab angled joint faces. Spectacular overhangs occur where large blocks have fallen leaving bedding plane roofs, as on The Sloth. The combination of steep dip and closely spaced jointing has resulted in parts of Ramshaw being etched into weird pinnacles.

The Alton crags comprise quarried and natural exposures of Triassic sandstones. These are red sandstones and conglomerates which were deposited in desert basins by flash floods. The variable strength of the iron oxide cement binding the sand and pebbles together makes this rock rather unreliable.

During the last glaciation of the Quaternary Ice Age the ice sheet which moved south from the Lakes and Scotland attained a depth of over 1000 feet on the Cheshire plain. The ice was prevented from moving into the Derbyshire limestone area by the south-west Pennine ridge and so glacial deposits of boulder clay and outwash gravel are found only in the west. The incursion of the ice sheet had the effect of diverting some pre-glacial drainage systems into new alignments. For example the Churnet formerly flowed into the Dane via the gap now occupied by Rudyard Reservoir. In the upland area beyond the ice limit freeze-thaw processes resulted in blockfields forming below gritstone crags and screes beneath limestone cliffs.

The Ice Age ended 10,000 years ago with the onset of a warm and wet climate. The wetter conditions triggered landslides on some steep hillslopes. For instance the Lud's Church ravine is a fissure in the Roaches Grit produced by a landslide on the underlying shales. During the transition to the drier climate of the present much of the drainage of the limestone area disappeared underground, in dry summers even the Manifold sinks into its bed near Wetton Mill. Unspectacular processes such as soil creep and chemical solution continue to modify the landforms, but by comparison with man's activities they are of limited significance.

# TECHNICAL NOTES

CLASSIFICATION
Adjectival Grades
These are subjective assessments of the overall difficulty of a route and the seriousness involved in doing it. They take into consideration the quality of the rock, the exposure, quantity of protection, technical difficulty, strenuousness and sustained nature of the route. They assume that climbers carry a comprehensive range of modern protection devices.
The grades are Moderate, Difficult, Very Difficult, Hard Very Difficult, Mild Severe, Severe, Hard Severe, Mild Very Severe, Very Severe, Hard Very Severe and Extremely Severe. This last category is open ended and indicated by E1, E2, E3, etc.

Technical Grades
The technical grade is an objective assessment of the cumulative difficulty of the pitch, and as such, considers the strenuousness and sustained nature of the climbing up to and after the hardest move. There is no definite relationship between the technical grade and the adjectival grade although in most cases climbs of a given adjectival grade are likely to cover a limited range of grades of technical difficulty. For the most part technical grades have only been given to climbs in or above the Very Severe categories. The grades usually used are 4a, 4b, 4c, 5a, 5b, 5c, 6a, 6b, etc.; the system being open ended.
The climbs have generally been graded for on-sight leads but it should be noted that many of the newer and harder climbs have not yet been led without some prior knowledge. This is particularly true in the E4 and above categories. The symbol † has been used after the adjectival grade to indicate routes where the grade is in doubt either because the first ascent has not been authenticated or the climb has had insufficient ascents to arrive at a consensus grade.

Route Quality
A starring system is used to indicate the quality of the routes, the very best routes being given three stars.

Artificial Grades
Three artificial grades are used. A1 indicates in situ aid or good placements. A2 will involve some long reaches, dubious rock and poor placements. A3 is the most serious category.

## TECHNICAL NOTES

New Routes
Descriptions of all new routes should be sent direct to Geoff Milburn, 25 Cliffe Road, Whitfield, Glossop, Derbyshire, SK13 8NY. Second-hand information from the magazines is often insufficient.

### BRITISH MOUNTAINEERING COUNCIL
The B.M.C., Crawford House, Precinct Centre, Booth Street East, Manchester, M13 9RZ is the official body representing the interests of climbers. Clubs and individuals may, on application, become members.

### COUNCIL FOR THE PRESERVATION OF RURAL ENGLAND
The Sheffield and Peak District branch has a fine record of defending the Peak District from the various threats to it. Contact Lt. Col. G. Haythornthwaite, 22 Endcliffe Crescent, Sheffield 10.

### MOUNTAIN RESCUE AND FIRST AID
Dial 999 and ASK FOR THE POLICE OPERATIONS ROOM. Rescue Equipment is kept at White Hall Centre for Open Country Pursuits, Long Hill, Buxton. Telephone: Buxton 3260. There is also a Mountain Rescue Post at The Mill, Upper Hulme and in the near future it is intended to set up a post at Ilam Hall. Yet another source of rescue equipment is the Ranger Briefing Centre at Stoney Middleton. Telephone: Hope Valley 30541.

### IN CASE OF ACCIDENT
1. If SPINAL INJURIES or HEAD INJURIES are suspected DO NOT MOVE THE PATIENT without skilled help, except to maintain breathing.
2. If BREATHING HAS STOPPED, clear airways and commence artificial respiration. Do not stop until expert opinion diagnoses death.
3. STOP BLEEDING by applying direct pressure.
4. SUMMON HELP.

Reports of accidents should be sent to the Secretary of the Mountain Rescue Committee, R. J. Davies, 18 Tarnside Fold, Simmondley, Glossop, Derbyshire.

# LIMESTONE AREA

## DOVEDALE
by Chris Calow and Mike Browell

---

O.S. Ref. SK 139547 to 151513

SITUATION
The climbing is concentrated into the section of the valley of the River Dove between Milldale and Thorpe Cloud, the river itself forming part of the county boundary between Derbyshire and Staffordshire.

APPROACHES
Dovedale can be approached from either Thorpe village in the south or Milldale in the north. Both ends are easily accessible from the main Buxton-Ashbourne road, the A515. There is ample, but paying, car parking at the southern entrance and restricted parking at the roadside in Milldale. The main footpath through the dale follows the Derbyshire and true left bank of the river. It is joined from the south by crossing the river at either a footbridge near the car park or the Stepping Stones further upstream; and from Milldale by crossing at the packhorse bridge. It is worth noting that when the river is very full the Stepping Stones are impassable and wading may be necessary. In wet weather the path becomes excessively muddy and wellingtons will be useful. The only bridge in the dale is located under Ilam Rock and by using this, all the crags and pinnacles, with the exception of Dovedale Church and Dovedale Castle, are accessible from the main path, regardless of which end of the dale is used as the starting point. There is no right of way from the Stepping Stones up the Staffordshire side of the river and some crags must be reached by wading the river.

ACCESS
This section of Dovedale is owned by the National Trust and their byelaws apply. They are prepared to allow climbing to take place, but are concerned about the possibility of injury to the general public caused by rock dislodged by climbers. Concern is also expressed regarding illegal access to Dovedale Church via the right bank and climbers are asked to observe these requirements.

CHARACTER
Dovedale has become a justly popular climbing ground. Most of the climbing is steep and exhilarating and with good holds,

16 LIMESTONE AREA

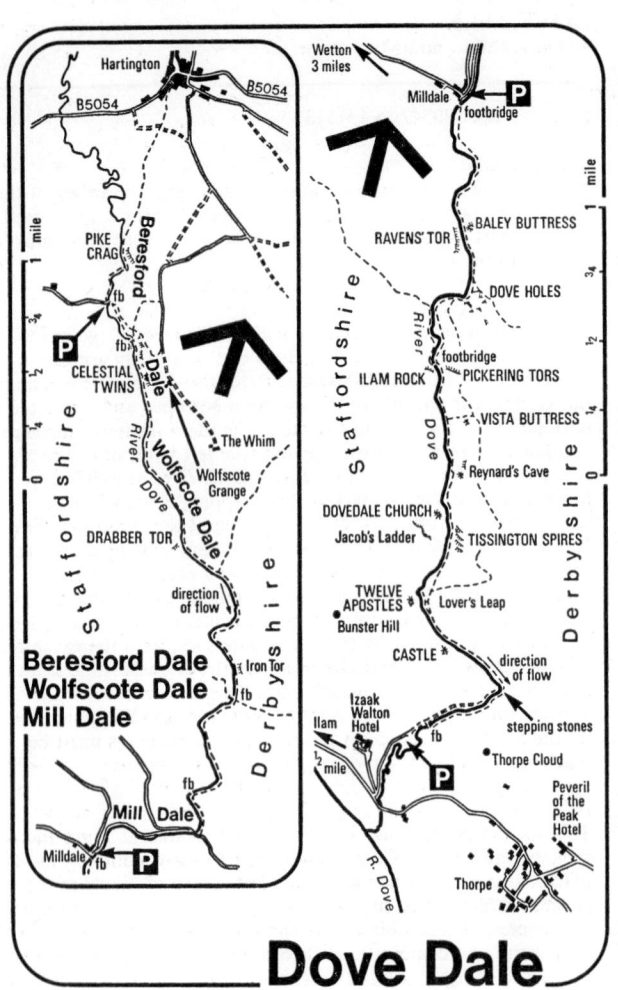

though the harder climbs tend to be very fingery. Most of the crags are isolated tors or pinnacles, which are often superbly positioned and add character to the climbs. On the other hand, whilst the harder face and crack climbs are generally on sound rock, the easier-angled slabs and ridges can be very loose. Furthermore, the summits of the pinnacles usually have loose blocks. Great care must be exercised in these cases because the dale attracts many tourists and the simian antics of climbers guarantee an audience. Descent is often by abseil and many of the in situ pegs are in poor condition.

## HISTORY (Giles Barker)

Before 1950 the rock climbing history of the dale is sparse and despite the many pinnacles there were few ascents. Apart from legendary endeavours, the first significant ascent appears to have been made by Samuel Turner who, in 1903, climbed up a rope he had manoeuvred over Ilam Rock and stood on his head on top —quite a feat! E. A. Baker recorded this in 'Moors, Crags and Caves of the High Peak'. However, it was not until 1914 that Siegfried Herford, A. R. Thompson and a Mr. Peacock made the first clean ascent of Original Route. It saw few repeats in the succeeding three decades; Henry Bishop and J. W. Puttrell, and Eric Byne and Clifford Moyer were possibly the only successful parties. The only other climbers who operated here between the wars appear to have been Frank Elliot and the Nottingham Mountaineering Club. Elliot led them up two routes on Pickering Tor; one was Original Route. He also made an ascent of Ilam Rock, though the line he took is unknown.

The first intensive development began in the 1950s, when the Rock and Ice club made several new routes. As usual, Joe Brown was to the fore, free-climbing the classic Venery, Brown's Blunder (with some aid on pitch two) and the Ridge on Pickering Tor. Slim Sorrell and Nat Allen aided The Groove, which was later climbed with only one peg by Brown and Don Whillans. Brown also climbed Pickering's Overhang and Wong Edge with Whillans, Southern Rib with George Band, using varying amounts of aid, and the classic aid route of White Edge (which was covered in ivy) with Ron Moseley. Also at this time John Sumner climbed Left-Hand Route and Roy Leeming did Lewd Wall, both as predominantly artificial climbs.

Although a good deal of aid was used on these climbs it was often mainly because of the condition of the rock. Most climbs were in an appalling state, with loose overhangs, collapsing ledges and copious vegetation. Hence pegs were often used to enable climbing to take place; top-roping and abseil inspections were not widely used. Usually only a few pegs were carried and many climbs involved large sections of free-climbing; they were serious expeditions of a nature difficult to comprehend today. Most aid pitches were done for practice. Whillans recalls, "Limestone was not regarded as proper climbing so it was permissible to put pegs in anywhere . . . we used stacks of pegs; we knocked pegs in just for the sake of knocking them in". However, details were not recorded and when Graham West's limestone guide appeared in 1961 they were mostly recorded as artificial climbs.

Leeming returned in the mid-50s along with Steve Read, Derek Carnell, Phil Brown and Steve Hunt. They produced Phil's Route, The Arete, Right Route, Whacko, Pickering Flake and George as essentially aid routes. However, Campanile and Silicon indicated the potential for free-climbing.

This potential was realised by the next developments, although these occurred only after the 1961 guide had been published. They took the form, initially, of two classic climbs, Snakes Alive and John Peel, which have maintained their place amongst the best in the dale. Pete 'Trog' Williams and John Amies made the first ascents, along with those of Beginner's Luck, Raven Girdle and Brown's Blunder free. Tony Howard, Tony Nicholls and Bill Tweedale explored Dr. Livingstone and Stanley Wall in the jungled Tissington Spires and added Cat's Eye Corner. In the latter half of the 60s work progressed towards a new guide; as usual the pace of exploration quickened. Leeming discovered Thunderball (with four aid points), Anaconda (with one peg), the Church Girdle (which had an aid pitch) and created a magnificent free climb out of Southern Rib. Nat Allen climbed Watchblock Direct with one aid peg and, with Carnell, Hortus and Simeon. Bob Hassall and John Critchlow opened up Baley Buttress with Bill Baley and the excellent Claw, using a point or two of aid on each, and The Beak was led by Trog Williams. Also about this time Phil's Route was converted into a spectacular free route with one point of aid; Harry Smith and Roy Leeming were both successful, though it is uncertain who was the first.

Standards were rising, a fact emphasised by a series of routes which fell to Jack Street. With various partners he succeeded in establishing Dovedale as a high standard climbing area. Many notable climbers arrived only to fail on his routes and few people recognised the remaining potential. In 1966 he discovered Parrot Face and the ferocious Claw Left-Hand. Along with Geoff Birtles he was involved in eliminating the aid from Left-Hand Route in 1967. He climbed Aquarius in 1968 with Tom Proctor. In 1969 he found Groovy Baby with Chris Jackson, reduced the aid on Pickering Flake to one peg and made free ascents of the Church Girdle and The Groove. All these were eclipsed however, by his magnificent Adjudicator Wall, which in 1969 was thought to be the hardest climb in Derbyshire; it repulsed attempts at a second ascent for some years. His final contribution was Harold Wilson which he climbed in 1970 with Alan McHardy.

Others joined in just as the guide was about to be published.
In 1969 Tom Proctor climbed most of the Lewd Wall with only one sling for aid, calling his route Central Wall. Terry Bolger added Vex four months later. Paul Nunn and Jeff Morgan shared leads on the excellent Yew Tree Wall (one aid sling), Black Flip (five points of aid) and the superb George (two aid pegs). Nunn also climbed Mandarin in the following year. John Carey and Mick Guillard made the aid route Blockhole Wall redundant with Tormentor, climbed Deflector and engineered the Flying Circus. Al Evans and Rod Haslam bolted their way out of the darkness to complete The Bat, one of the most popular artificial climbs in the Peak District.

After the guide appeared in 1970 in volume 8 of Rock Climbs In The Peak, developments of new climbs inevitably slowed a little, but many of the harder climbs were repeated and gradually aid points on routes such as Adjudicator Wall, George and Central Wall were eliminated.

The indefatigables, Allen, Carnell and Derrick Burgess supplied the first new routes in 1971, these being most of the Chelsea and Keep Buttress routes, Hell Peel and Nutcracker. Ken Jones climbed the latter route free at about the same time, calling it Amoeba. Keith Myhill followed with a more powerful contribution, Raven, which superseded the aid climb Middle Route. The single resting nut was soon dispensed with. Myhill also added Hecate at this time.

In 1972 Ed Drummond ascended Easter Island and provoked a controversial issue by claiming that his route replaced White Edge and that renaming was necessary, 'to discourage anyone from looking upon this ascent merely as an alternative way of doing White Edge'. Many were disturbed by this attitude; Rocksport summed up their reactions, 'Fame does not give him the right to dictate to another climber how he should climb'. Ironically it was an alternative way up 'The White Edge', and Drummond was correct to name the climb since most of it covered completely new ground, only using the 'artificial line' for the top fifteen feet. On a more conventional note 1972 also saw the ascents of Tennessee Waltz and Rock and Roll by A. Hill, and Gordon 'Speedy' Smith's interesting Filtration.

In 1973 Terry Bolger climbed Desolation Row and Victoria Falls. Bob Whittaker converted the aided variation to Watchblock Direct, Paxadin Wall, into the fine Nancy Whisky.

Then came the lull before a deluge of new climbs which began in 1976. In that year Whittaker rediscovered Harold Wilson, thinking it to be unclimbed and called it Judgement. Pete O'Donovan free-climbed the formerly aided Brutus and Martin Taylor dispensed with the pegs on Whacko. The most impressive ascent was made by a raiding Yorkshire team when Ron Fawcett climbed The Gladiator. The crack on this had previously formed the substance of the aid route The Girdle. He also climbed The Wong Edge free.

With talk of a new guide, the task of rechecking all the existing routes proved to be the catalyst to a spate of new climbs which surpassed any previous period of development. By 1977 aid climbs had become few and far between; attention became focused on the free-climbing potential of the gaps in between them. Chris Calow and John Codling were the most active contributors. Calow threw down the gauntlet in 1977 with Quiet Life. It was taken up by Codling the next year starting a fine series of routes with Calamity Jane, Wild Bill and solving the long-standing problem of the Dove Holes' Wall with The Umpire. To these he added Chunky Punky, Uncle Sam (solo), Final Witness and, with his brother Jerry, Crosscourt. At the same time Boardwalk, Crisis, Redeye and the extraordinary Ten Craters of Wisdom were climbed by Calow.

Codling later returned with Calow to complete the superb line of Caesar and surpassed himself with an outstanding number of falls before succeeding to solo Suspended Sentence. Fittingly they both share honours on their finest route, the intricate and compelling Orange Peel.

There were other contributors. John Fleming added What Crisis? and besieged The Arete on Dovedale Church with Calow, finally succeeding, using a sling for resting, with Tales of the Riverbank. Ron Fawcett returned and climbed past this indiscretion to establish this route as the hardest in the dale. He also climbed free the remaining aided section of The White Edge which over the years had gradually been whittled down to twenty feet. Phil Burke nearly solved another long-standing problem with his direct finish to Central Wall using a peg for aid. It has since been climbed free by Chris Hamper.

As the guide reached its final stages Codling made further developments with Judge Jeffries, Rosebowl, Simeon Direct and the impressive Wild Country. Meanwhile, Dave Jones added Swallow Tales and joined Codling for the much fancied Deltoid Shuffle, and Dave Wiggin found Ultravox. In the spring of 1980, Codling and Jones teamed up again and switched leads on The Temptress, so named because of the beckoning ring peg on the second pitch. Presumably this is not the last route to fall. The last eight years have nevertheless made the gaps narrower, though we may look to the future with anticipation and the gaps with amazement.

## BALEY BUTTRESS
The crag is situated opposite Ravens Tor and half a mile downstream from the packhorse bridge at Milldale. The major routes are to be found on the steep south face, however, some short climbs exist on the walls up the screes on the north side, the best of these being:

**1  Supertramp**   25 feet   Very Severe †
5a. The prominent undercut arete situated just up the hillside.

**2  Farnz Barnz**   25 feet   Very Severe †
5b. The face right of the arete.

**3  Flying Blackberry**   145 feet   Hard Very Severe/A1
The first climb on the south face.
1. 75ft.5b.Reach the groove on the left and climb it to a small roof. Follow a crack right to a good foothold. A possible finish to the top here. Continue along the crack with 3 aid pegs to The Claw. Traverse right to a small ledge.
2. 70ft.4c.Climb the corner to a ledge then finish up the diagonal fault.

**4  Claw Left-Hand**   80 feet   Hard Very Severe   ★★
5b. The daunting and overhanging groove 6 feet left of The Claw, gives a strenuous pitch. Where the angle eases at a chockstone, traverse right to finish up The Claw.

**5  The Claw**   135 feet   Hard Very Severe   ★★
A splendid climb of varied character.
1. 70ft.5a.Climb the central thin crack to an overhanging chimney and ascend this with difficulty to a stance on the left.
2. 65ft.4c.Traverse right along a break and climb a diagonal fault to the ridge.
   It is also possible to reach the chimney by a rising traverse under the overhang from the start of Bill Baley.

**6  Swallow Tales**   80 feet   E2
6a. Start below the righthand side of the black overhang at a thin crack. Up this and cross the overhangs on their right. Gain the groove and up this to the traverse of The Claw. Finish direct.
There are two variation starts:
i) 5c.Climb the wall 5 feet right of The Claw.
ii) 5b.The crack parallel to and just left of Bill Baley.

## 22 LIMESTONE AREA

**7  Bill Baley   100 feet   Very Severe**
Start 35 feet right of The Claw, below two parallel cracks.
1. 30ft.4b.Gain the righthand crack from below and climb it to a tree belay.
2. 70ft.4b.Take the groove and shattered wall on the left to a niche and finish up the pleasant crack on the right.

**8  The Beak   40 feet   Hard Severe**
4b.Higher up the hillside to the right is a corner. Climb this and move awkwardly left round the overhang at the top.

50 ft right of The Beak is a scree gully and right again some secluded slabs bounded on the right by a chimney.

**9  The Filter   70 feet   Very Severe**
4c.Start at a tree and climb the slabs direct to the left end of a leftward-curving scar. Move left and up to finish.

**10  Filtration   75 feet   Hard Very Severe**
5b.From the foot of Baley Chimney, traverse diagonally left across the slab until it is possible to break through the overlap. Move back right under a second overlap and surmount this via a wide crack.

**11  Baley Chimney   75 feet   Very Difficult**
The chimney on the right.


## RAVENS TOR
A steep imposing cliff opposite Baley Buttress, with some of the best climbs in the dale, mainly in the higher grades. It is best approached from Milldale, either by walking down the Staffordshire side of the valley or by following the main path and wading the river. If approaching from the south, cross the bridge at Ilam Rock. The climbs are described from Left to Right.

**1  Jackdaw   45 feet   Very Severe**
The crack which ends 15 feet from the ground is gained from the main corner on the left and is followed to the top.

**2  Short Wall   45 feet   Very Severe**
4c.Start up a crack below a tree and after 15 feet move diagonally left up a flake to a niche then go back right and up to a tree.

**3  The Doddle   45 feet   Hard Severe**
Start 25 feet left of Southern Gully and climb the right side of a pillar and crack above to a niche. Move left to finish.

DOVEDALE 23

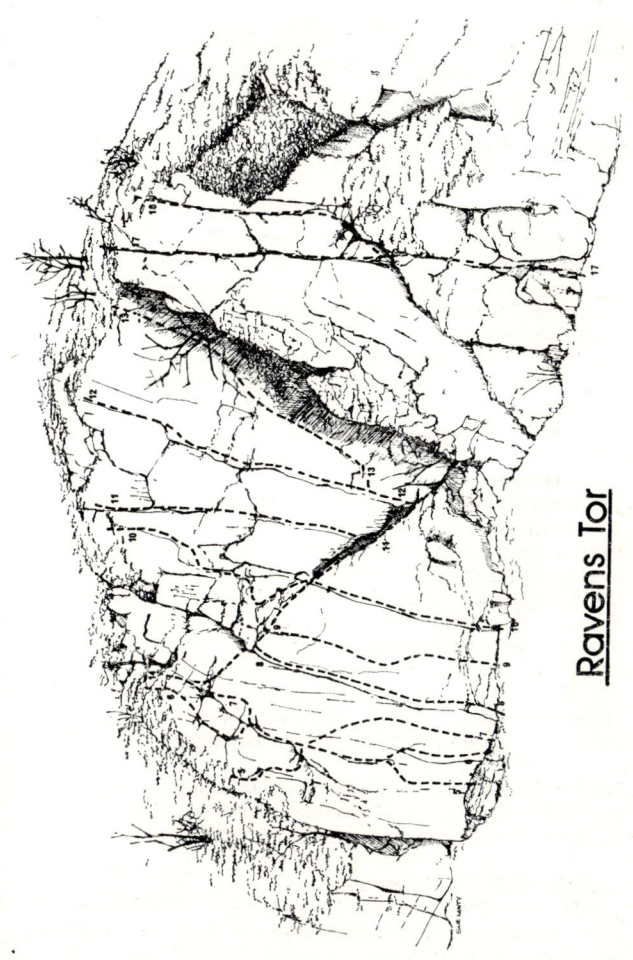

Ravens Tor

## 24 LIMESTONE AREA

**4 Southern Gully**  55 feet  Hard Very Difficult
The scruffy corner crack leads past a tree into a grassy basin.

**5 Tennessee Waltz**  120 feet  Hard Very Severe
1. 60ft.5a.Climb a thin crack 20 feet right of Southern Gully and move across right to the unstable flake which is followed to a leftward finish. Belay on slab to the right.
2. 60ft.5b.Climb over the bulge slightly left of the belay, peg runner in a groove and step left to a crack which is followed to a loose finish.

**6 Southern Rib**  165 feet  Hard Very Severe  ★★
Good climbing to suit a catholicity of tastes. Start 15 feet left of Left-Hand Route.
1. 55ft.5a.Climb the bulging crack until forced across left to a rather unstable flake, which is followed to a move left onto a small slab stance.
2. 60ft.5a.Follow the slab and slanting groove above to a triangular roof. Pass this on the left and climb the exposed groove with a long exit right to a ledge.
3. 50ft.4a.Climb straight to a ramp and grassy finish.

**7 The Temptress**  155 feet  E4  †★
1. 65ft.6a.Start at the open scoop between Southern Rib and Left-Hand Route. Climb into the scoop and move steeply up right on layaways past 2 peg runners to a flat hold. Move up then left to the ramp belay of Southern Rib.
2. 50ft.5c.Follow the slabs as for Southern Rib to a roof on the right. Traverse below this to a ring peg runner. Go straight over the small roof to a crack and climb this.
3. 40ft.4a.Climb straight to a ramp and grassy finish.

**8 Left-Hand Route**  130 feet  Hard Very Severe  ★★★
A strenuous pitch up the striking groove bounding the central face.
1. 80ft.5b.Climb the crack with increasing difficulty to a peg runner. Continue up the steep corner above to a ledge.
2. 50ft.4b.Follow a ramp on the left. Poor belay.

**9 Deltoid Shuffle**  130 feet  E4  †★
1. 80ft.5c.Start midway between Left-Hand Route and Raven. Climb a groove to a peg runner (missing?) at 15 feet. Continue up to a flake then right to a peg runner. Go up to a ledge, then follow the crack to the Left-Hand Route belay.
2. 50ft.5a.Ascend the wall above on widely spaced holds to a grassy scoop. Belay above and to the left.

## DOVEDALE 25

**10 Raven** 140 feet   Hard Very Severe ★★
A rather disjointed line, but with some excellent climbing. Start 25 feet right of Left-Hand Route.
1. 80ft.5b.Climb the steep thin crack to a difficult exit right onto the rake. Follow the rake up left then back right to a good thread.
2. 60ft.5a.Climb the groove on the right and make an exposed swing right onto a jutting block on the pillar face. Move up and right to easier ground.

**11 Aquarius** 100 feet   Hard Very Severe ★★
Start 20 feet up the rake of Brown's Blunder at a good thread belay below a steep pillar.
5b.Pull over the bulge to the right and follow the fierce crack to a ledge. Continue up the crack and over the inevitable grassy finish.

**12 Central Wall** 110 feet   E2 ★★
A fine route, especially when combined with the Direct Finish. It is an audacious line up the thin crack in the centre of the face. Start 20 feet left of Central Gully.
1. 70ft.5c.Climb to a ledge and follow the steep and strenuous crack mainly by finger-jamming, to its wider continuation which soon eases. Belay higher on the right.
2. 40ft.5a.Move up left and climb the exposed groove on the right side of the 'dome'. Belay well back.
2a.**Direct Finish**   30 feet   E3
   6a.Take the left parallel crack in the headwall.

**13 Hecate** 130 feet   Hard Very Severe
The wall right of Central Wall, then the top wall of Vex.
1. 70ft.5a.Climb to the pedestal of Central Wall. Move up and right, then straight to a loose finish on the traverse.
2. 60ft.5a.Move right steeply and go up the broken wall.

**14 Brown's Blunder** 110 feet   Hard Severe
1. 60ft.4b.Take the diagonal rake left of the dirty gully, with a hard move to escape to the belay ledge.
2. 50 ft.4a.A ramp on the left leads to a grassy finish.

**15 Central Gully** 100 feet   Difficult
The unattractive gully that splits the main face.

**16 Vex** 120 feet   Hard Very Severe
Start at the foot of the buttress right of Central Gully, at a large flake.

## 26 LIMESTONE AREA

1. 80ft.5a.Climb the flake and wall above, moving slightly right then go direct to an ash tree in the gully.
2. 40ft.5a.Step across the gully and climb the back wall for 20 feet. Traverse right to a ledge and finish direct.

**17  Venery**  150 feet  Hard Very Severe  ★★
The wall is characterised by two parallel cracks which run the height of the wall. The left one gives the route.
1. 70ft.4b.Climb a V-groove in the line of the upper crack, stepping right to belay.
2. 80ft.4c.Move up left to gain the excellent main crack which is followed all the way.

**18  Parrot Face**  135 feet  Hard Very Severe
The upper righthand crack.
1. 70ft.4b.Climb the groove as for Venery and belay below the righthand crack.
2. 65ft.5a.Follow the steep crack above to an overhang. Either climb over the bulge direct or escape neatly across the right wall to finish.

**19  Skewball**  80 feet  Very Severe
4c.Start 30 feet right of the fence. Climb a crack, pull out right and move across a short slab to a corner. Layback up the corner and climb right along the obvious rake to a ledge.

**20  The Girdle Traverse**  260 feet  Hard Very Severe  ★
1. 55ft.4b.Climb Southern Gully to the ash tree and traverse right across the slab under the overhang to a small slab stance.
2. 55ft.4c.Follow the slanting groove to a triangular roof, pass this on the right and break out rightwards round an exposed bulge to a ledge. Descend a short corner and belay.
3. 80ft.4c.Traverse right over a small nose and continue, in a fine position, across the central wall to a belay in the gully.
4. 70ft.5a.Descend the arete for 5 feet and follow a line of holds into the crack of Venery. Finish up Venery.


## DOVE HOLES
Situated just beyond a pump-house where Nabs Dale joins the valley from the left are the adjacent caves of the Dove Holes, a justifiably popular feature of the dale.

**1  The Ball**  80 feet  A2
The roof of the left and smaller cave gives the route. From a giant thread at the back of the cave climb out on bolts across the arching roof descending to reach the lip. Good tree belay.

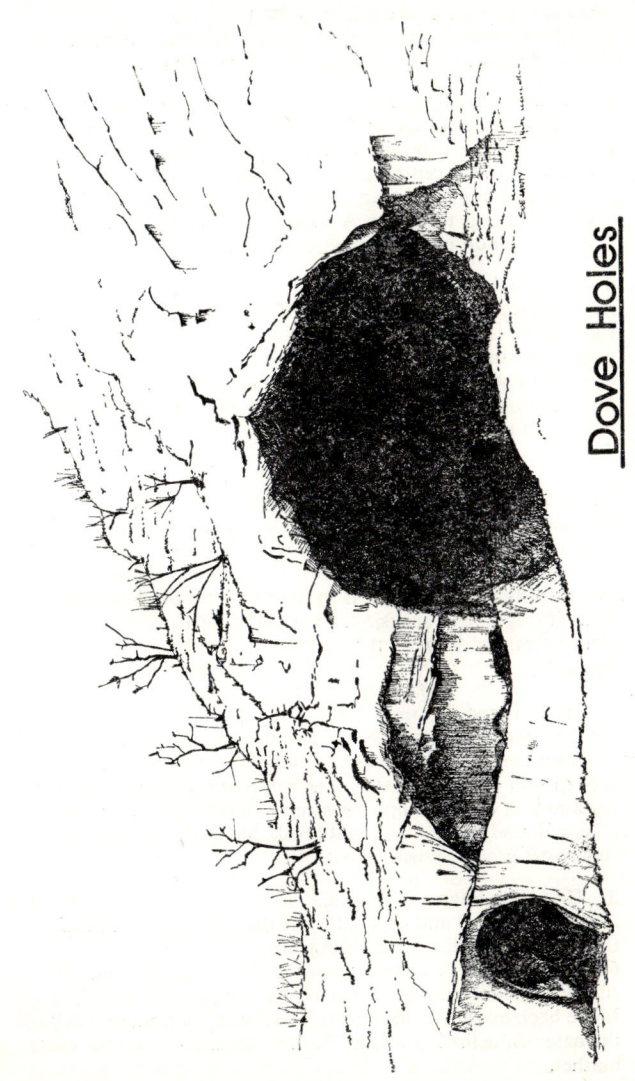

Dove Holes

28  LIMESTONE AREA

**2  Blacksmith**  80 feet  A2
Start in the centre of the wall between the caves. Free-climb to a ledge and peg up the wall to a bulge. Move right and surmount the two bulges to a stance on the left. Scramble off.

**3  The Bat**  120 feet  A2  ★★
The large cave gives one of the longest roof pitches in Derbyshire, though with little exposure until the lip. A popular wet weather route. Start at the central pillar at the back.
1. 80ft. Climb the pillar then go out across the roof on various bolts and pegs to the lip. A short wall leads to a good ledge.
2. 40ft. Abseil off or climb grass to the top.

**4  The Umpire**  60 feet  E2  ★
Airy and technically interesting climbing up the steep wall on the right of the larger cave.
5c. Start on the right and climb the wall and shallow groove to an exit right onto the left end of a grassy ledge. From the ledge, move up with difficulty to an undercut flake on the left. Continue directly to the tree.


## ILAM ROCK

A renowned feature of the dale, this great monolith with its impending and unbroken southern wall, makes an imposing sight. A bridge near its foot gives access. The climbing is generally very steep and solid and descent is by abseil from a block on the summit ridge. As a diversion, an exhilarating Tyrolean traverse can be arranged between the summits of Ilam Rock and Pickering Pinnacle.

**1  Easter Island**  95 feet  E1  ★★
This spectacular route takes the arete facing the river.
5b. From the ledge move right round the corner and climb the broken wall to a small ledge, then continue up the arete proper to good resting ledges. Climb the steep wall just right of the arete to a large thread in the horizontal break. Step left to climb the square-cut groove, finishing out left.

**2  The White Edge**  95 feet  E3  †★★
A more sustained and exposed route than Easter Island, taking the right edge of the overhanging face.
6a. Climb a series of finger pockets up the very steep wall, peg runner, until forced onto the arete. Follow this to a good ledge. Move back out left onto the face and climb a strenuous crack to the base of the final groove of Easter Island, up which the route finishes.

DOVEDALE 29

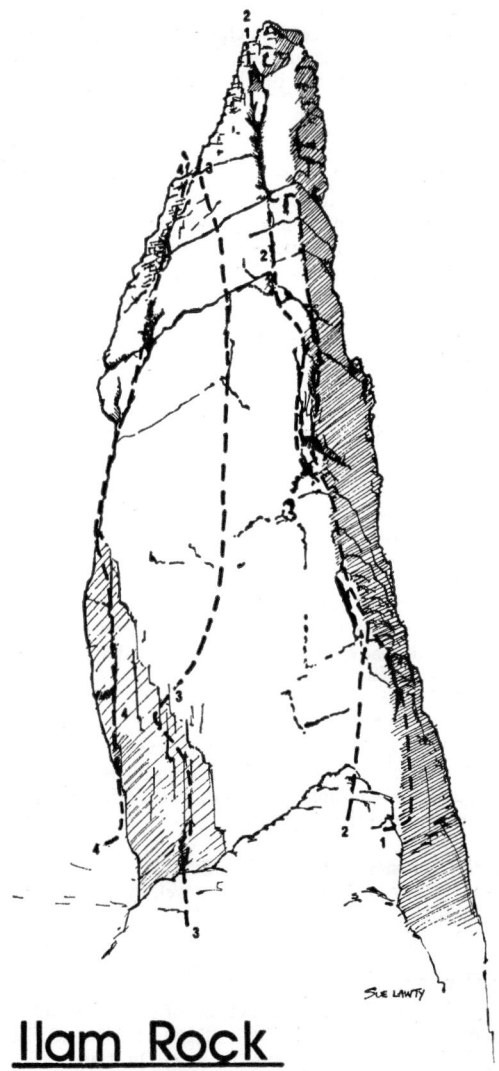

# Ilam Rock

## 30  LIMESTONE AREA

**3  Pleb's Delight**  85 feet  A3

Start at the left end of the ledge and climb up and right to a small niche. Follow a thin crack leading out right and go up the middle of the wall to a good horizontal break; finish direct up the smooth headwall.

**4  The Gladiator**  80 feet  E3  †★★

A powerful route.
5c. The crack on the blunt rib 15 feet right of The Groove is gained from below, peg runner, and followed strenuously to an exit left onto a small ledge. Move right round the arete and finish up the impending wall.

**5  The Groove**  70 feet  E1  ★

5c. The overhanging wide groove provides strenuous climbing to a dynamic heave onto a sloping ledge. Finish easily up the continuation corner.

**6  The Wong Edge**  70 feet  E2  ★

On the side of the pinnacle which faces the hillside is a steep thin crack.
5c. Follow this by sustained finger and hand-jamming passing the small roof on its right. Continue up the face to the summit.

**7  Original Route**  60 feet  Severe

From a tree near the top of the gully, climb the north wall keeping right of the crack near the summit. Rather vegetated. It is traditional, but inadvisable, to perform a head-stand on the summit.

### ILAM WALL

Above and to the left of Ilam Rock are two faces which look rather vegetated. The best approach is to scramble through the undergrowth directly opposite Lion Rock, to the left face. Walk under this and go up to the right face.

**1  Presidential Chimney**  60 feet  Very Severe

The obvious chimney at the left end. Keep well inside for most of its length and pull out left to finish.


### PICKERING TORS

Situated opposite Ilam Rock is a collection of pinnacles and ridges. The nearest to the path is PICKERING PINNACLE and it can easily be identified by a cave at its base. On it are:

DOVEDALE 31

**1 Pickering Ridge**   100 feet   Hard Severe
4b. Start left of the cave slightly up the hillside. Climb across right to a block and continue up the rotten ridge direct.

**2 What Crisis?**   100 feet   Hard Very Severe   †
5a. Climb the blunt left arete to a block. Step right and follow a series of deep cracks and grooves in the ridge to a small tree belay.

**3 Crisis**   70 feet   E3
Above the cave is a long open groove.
6a. Climb the wall right of the cave and cheat the overhang using an aid peg on the lip to enter the groove. Climb the elegant groove exiting right to block belays.

The remaining routes start from the saddle behind the pinnacle.

**4 Original Route**   80 feet   Severe
1. 50ft. Traverse right across the north wall, passing behind two trees to a stance on the ridge.
2. 30ft. Follow the summit ridge.

**5 Chunky Punky**   55 feet Hard Very Severe
5a. The sharp arete at the crest of the saddle is followed direct.

**6 The Flake**   65 feet   E1
5c. The fierce jamming crack on the left edge of the flake is strenuous. From the ledge climb the broken rib.

**7 Pickering's Overhang**   70 feet   E1   ★
5b. From the saddle move down and left to below an overhanging groove. Climb the groove and surmount the exposed and difficult overhang on the left. Continue up the broken upper wall, 2 peg runners, to the top.


PICKERING WALL
Follow the screes up the right side of Pickering Pinnacle to a face capped for most of its length by an overhang and with a hanging overlap bounding its right end.

**8 Wedgestone Groove**   70 feet   Severe
Start at two trees on a ledge at the left side of the face.
1. 50ft. Traverse 25 feet left to a groove, climb this and move diagonally right to a tree belay.
2. 20ft. Move up and left, over an unstable-looking block and climb the crack above.

## 32 LIMESTONE AREA

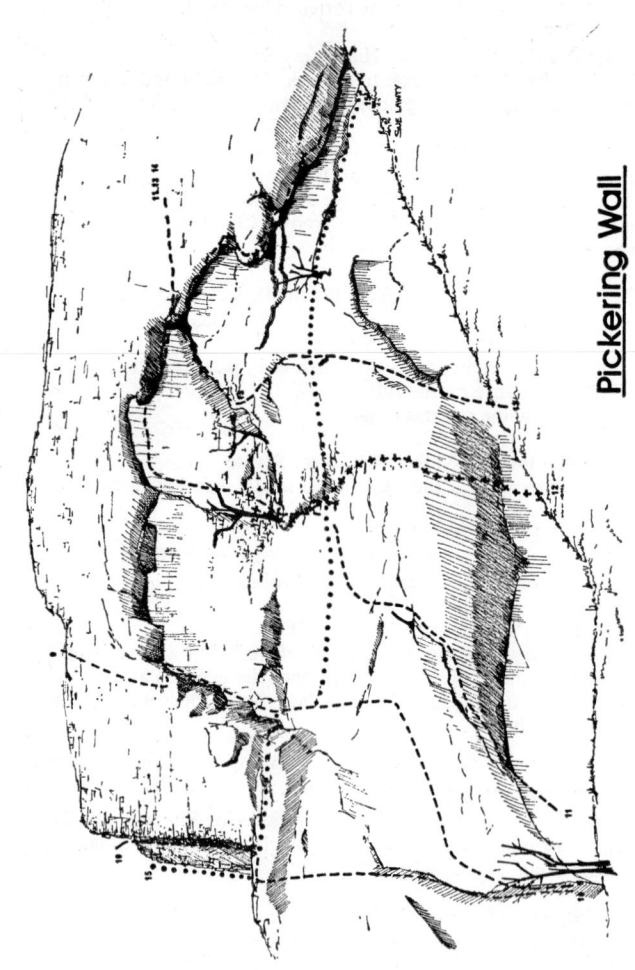

**9  Thunderball**  90 feet  Hard Very Severe  ★★
1. 50ft.5a.From the two trees, climb the wall behind for 10 feet and traverse delicately right to a good foothold, peg runner. With difficulty move straight up to a groove and belay above.
2. 40ft.4c.Struggle up the corner above, almost to the roof then swing out left to a ledge and climb to a tree. A more direct way is up the wall above the traverse on pitch 1, followed by the slab right of pitch 2 (E1, 5b).

**10  Final Witness**  60 feet  E1  ★
1. 45ft.5b.Start as for Thunderball but continue directly up a short groove and an improbable-looking steep wall on pockets to a ledge.
2. 15ft.The short chimney on the right to finish.

**11  Red Eye**  95 feet  Hard Very Severe
1. 55ft.5a.Pull onto the left end of the diagonal fault and follow it right to a tree stump. Climb the wall above then move right and go up to an ash tree belay.
2. 40ft.4c.Climb the groove behind and traverse right under the overlap to a loose finish.

**12  Suspended Sentence**  40 feet  E4  ★
6b.A short but technical problem requiring strong fingers and nerves. A series of finger pockets lead through the bulge to a flake and tree high on the right. Abseil off.

**13  Harold Wilson**  80 feet  E2
5b.Gain the prominent ragged black pocket from the steep ramp below and continue, past a flake, to a hidden finishing hold on the left. Peg belay on ledge above. Finish as for Palsy Wall.

**14  Palsy Wall**  75 feet  Hard Very Severe
5a.Follow the obvious wide crack formed by the leftward curving overlap to a good thread near the top, then traverse right, peg runner, to a loose and serious finish.

**15  Crosscourt**  95 feet  Hard Very Severe  †
1. 45ft.5b.Start up Palsy Wall and step down to a bush. Traverse with difficulty to Harold Wilson and continue left until under the tree of Red Eye.
2. 50ft.5a.Traverse left to the corner of Thunderball, go up this a few feet and move left, 2 peg runners, to a large ledge. Climb the arete to the left.

## 34 LIMESTONE AREA

**16 Dead Wood Gulch**  35 feet  Very Severe
Higher up the gully on the left is Upper Pickering Wall.
4c. Climb the left end of the wall and move right to finish.

**17 Pickering Buttress**  65 feet  Very Severe
4b. The buttress to the right of Pickering Wall. Start at the bottom righthand corner, climb up left and finish up the middle of the face.

### OVERHANG BUTTRESS
Between Pickering Buttress and Watchblock Tower is a buttress with a large overhang.

**1 Acquittal**  100 feet  Hard Severe
1. 50ft.4c. Start behind trees at the left end. Climb a slab and traverse right to a small ledge. Go over a bulge and up the slab to a large block.
2. 50ft. Escape left to easy ground.

**2 Deflection**  80 feet  Severe
4b. Start just left of Beginner's Luck. Climb a short wall until a step right gains a traverse line. Cross rightwards and go up to a cave. Move left across a cutaway and climb a short crack.

**3 Beginner's Luck**  70 feet  Hard Severe
1. 40ft.4a. Start at the toe of the buttress and climb a layback crack or a slab right to a ledge. Easily up the corner above until forced left by a roof. Go up to a ledge.
2. 30ft.4a. Traverse right under the overhang, then climb a short corner.

**4 The Jug**  80 feet  Very Severe
Start 15 feet right at two trees which form a cross.
4c. Traverse right to a tree below a shallow groove. Pull into this and up to a wide crack. Move left and up to the final groove of Beginner's Luck. Finish up this.

### WATCHBLOCK BUTTRESS
Downstream from Pickering Tors is a buttress with a conspicuous and precariously perched block on the top. Follow one of three scree paths to the buttress, which is indentified from below by a fine natural tunnel at the left end. Most routes start from the toe at the right end of the buttress.

**DOVEDALE** 35

**1 Ultravox** 120 feet  Hard Very Severe †
5b.Climb the lefthand outside edge of the cave up a short wall
and then ascend the groove above.

**2 Adjudicator Wall** 130 feet  E3  ★★★
A magnificent and sustained route of absorbing technicality and
with good protection.
5c.From the toe, climb up and diagonally left, several threads, to
a small ledge. With a long reach move left to the foot of a shallow
groove, climb this and step left into a crack, peg runner. Continue
up the steep crack direct.

**3 Nancy Whisky**  125 feet  E1  ★
Difficult climbing on compact rock.
1. 65ft.5b.Climb Adjudicator Wall to the start of the traverse left.
   Climb the groove above and exit right.
2. 60ft.4b.Traverse left through trees to a slab, left again to the
   rib and finish up this on huge holds.

**4 Watchblock Direct**  125 feet  Hard Very Severe
5a.Climb up direct from the toe to a bulge. Move right and pull
up with difficulty onto a broken wall. Up this to ledges and climb
the pleasant slabs finishing left of the Watchblock.

**4a Uncontrollable Urge**  125 feet  Very Severe †
4c.Climb the cleaned wall 15 feet right of Watchblock Direct,
to a tree. Step left and go easily up slabs.

LION ROCK
**1 St. Dunstan**  50 feet  A2
Ascend the front face to a large thread under the overhang.
Climb the first overhang moving left and the second direct.

Further downstream from Lion Rock the path follows a wooden
boardwalk and the river flows through a gorge whose walls are
heavily vegetated. At the upstream end of this wall, high up, is a
hanging groove.

**2 Boardwalk**  160 feet  Hard Very Severe
1. 55ft.4b.Climb the slab, moving first right under an overlap then
   back left to a ledge at the foot of the groove.
2. 65ft.5a.Struggle up the awkward groove and pass the roof on
   the right. Move across to a bay on the right and go up to a
   yew belay.
3. 40ft.Scramble through trees to the fields.

## 36 LIMESTONE AREA

### REYNARD'S CAVE
Where the valley walls fall back again, a path leads up left to Reynard's Cave, a popular feature with numerous non-climbing visitors. On the fine natural arch below Reynard's Cave is:

**1 Flying Circus** 90 feet A3
Start at a tree and take a line of cracks and pockets leading leftwards up the right wall and under the arch. Finish up a gangway leading left to a tree.

**2 Hell Peel** 120 feet Very Severe
Behind the archway and to the left is a broad buttress with a scar at half-height.
4b.Start at the left end, just right of a gully which runs up behind the buttress. Climb right and up to the scar at a semi-cave. Move right onto a steep rib and then climb direct to the ridge.

VISTA BUTTRESS is to the left of Reynard's Cave and higher up the hillside at the top of the ridge. It is a clean buttress with a perched block on its face.

**3 Vista Wall** 70 feet Severe
4a.Start left of a thorn tree and climb the wall and corner formed by the perched block. Finish up a crack and groove on the right.

**4 Rock and Roll** 70 feet Very Severe
4c.Take the large central corner and thin crack above, then step right to the arete and layback past a loose block to finish left of the overhang; sustained.

### TISSINGTON SPIRES
Tissington Spires are by far the largest collection of pinnacles and walls in the dale and offer some excellent climbs of quite unique character. Because of their complexity the routes are often difficult to locate, especially under summer foliage. A diagram is included to assist route finding. Approaching from Milldale and three quarters of a mile downstream from Ilam Rock, there is an old ruined pump-house on the left of the path. Downstream from this are the three approach gullies.
1. North Gully, 50 yards from the pump-house, for Campanile Pinnacle and the Col du Turd.
2. Central Gully, a large scree slope is 150 yards from the pump-house, for the Back Wall, Silicon etc.
3. South Gully, 200 yards from the pump-house, for the First Pinnacle and John Peel Wall.

# Dove Dale
## Tissington Spires

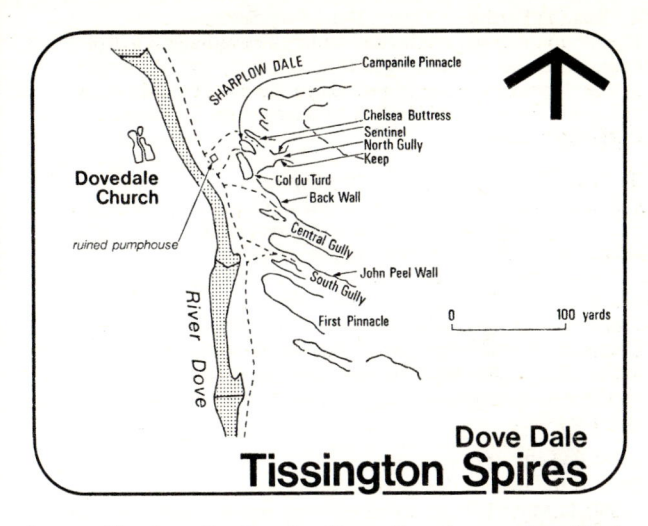

Approaching from the Stepping Stones there is a wooden stile at the end of the descent from Lover's Leap; the scree slope into South Gully leads off the river path a further 110 yards upstream.

## CHELSEA BUTTRESS
The buttress can be reached from a point slightly upstream from the pump-house. Follow the path that leads up a narrow valley (Sharplow Dale) and after 50 yards fork right up a scree slope. Alternatively from the back of the Campanile Pinnacle, move up leftwards over a grassy knoll and down the gully. The buttress is capped by a sickle-shaped overhang and split at its left end by a converging chimney which gives:

**1  Veterans' Chimney**   60 feet   Severe
4a. Climb the chimney then the ridge.

**2  Thunder Rib**   75 feet   Hard Severe
4b. Start at the large tree to the right of the buttress front. Climb a crack past a ledge. Finish left on good but dirty holds.

**3  Pensioner's Groove**   70 feet   Very Severe
4b. The filthy groove just right of Thunder Rib.

## 38  LIMESTONE AREA

**4  Roaring Forties**  45 feet  Hard Very Severe
Higher up the gully, on the wall under the overhang is a depression containing a swallet hole at 15 feet.
5a. Climb pockets in the depression to the hole, thread runners, and continue up the wide crack to the overlap. Surmount this exiting leftwards.

**5  Slime Traverse**  60 feet  Very Severe
4c. Start at the top of the gully at the right end of the overlap. Climb pleasantly to the overlap and traverse left to reach the overhang of Roaring Forties. Finish up this.

### NORTH and CENTRAL GULLY AREA
From the river path scramble up North Gully until the wall of Campanile Pinnacle appears on the left. A curving fault runs from left to right up this wall. Descent from the summit is by abseil or by descending from the ridge to a yew tree and traversing back into the gully.

**6  Campanile**  110 feet  Severe
Start at the base of the curving fault.
1. 50ft.4a. Move left and climb the right side of a large detached flake. From its top, step left to a corner and go up to a stance. Peg belay.
2. 60ft. Move right and up a short corner and right again across a large ramp to the nose. Over this to a tree belay.

**7  Whacko**  80 feet  E2  †
Start at the curving fault.
1. 60ft.5c. Climb the fault until it disappears and make a very trying reach for a good hold. Follow broken rock to a stance on the ramp of Campanile.
2. 20ft. Traverse right round the pinnacle to a yew tree.

**8  Fetish**  45 feet  Severe
The buttress that gives the route forms the division of the scree path that runs past the Pinnacle. From two trees at the right end, climb diagonally left and finish up the middle of the face.

### SENTINEL BUTTRESS
Scramble up North Gully past Campanile Pinnacle. Straight ahead the gully narrows and passes between the buttresses of The Keep on the right and The Sentinel on the left.

**9  Topsy Turvy**  80 feet  Hard Very Difficult
Climb the broken face supporting an old dead yew, starting 10 feet right of a large ash tree.

**10  Sentinel Crack**   50 feet   Severe
Start left of the ash tree and climb either a curving crack or the wall on the right to a final corner above.

KEEP BUTTRESS
**11  Keeper's Crack**   50 feet   Severe
The obvious groove and wide crack above in the angle of the buttress.

**12  Boomerang**   100 feet   Hard Severe
4c.Start as for Keeper's Crack. Climb the groove then traverse right across a slab to a corner and right again to finish up a wide corner crack.

Opposite and just below the start of Campanile, a gully leads off rightwards under the Back Wall and up to the Col du Turd. Near the gully foot and on the left is a large yew tree.

**13  Desolation Row**   100 feet   Hard Very Severe
4c.A repulsive route that starts left of the tree. Climb the grassy wall to below an overlap and follow this right to a pull out onto a ledge. Go over a bulge direct to the top.

**14  Victoria Falls**   110 feet   Very Severe
1. 80ft.4c.From the yew follow the rightward-slanting overlap until under a broken groove. Pull over onto a sloping ledge and continue diagonally left up the grooves before moving back right to a tree belay.
2. 30ft.Finish right across the slabs.

**14a  Model Worker**   100 feet   Hard Very Severe         †
5a.Start 20 feet right and climb the shallow groove over a bulge to a flaky crack. Climb this and the wall above.

**15  Hortus**   115 feet   Hard Severe
Halfway up the gully is an old upright ash tree near the wall.
1. 40ft.4a.Start at the tree and gain the ledge on the right. Move left and through an overlap before going up right to a stance below an overhang.
2. 75ft.4b.Move awkwardly left into a corner and climb it moving right to a yew tree. Traverse right across the slab and go up to a yew. Scrambling remains.

At the top of the gully is the Col du Turd. The main wall continues past the Col, eventually to become lost in the screes beyond.

## 40 LIMESTONE AREA

**16  Meander**   135 feet   Very Difficult
Just left of the Col is a large ash tree at 20 feet.
1. 55ft.Climb to the tree, step right and up slabs to a grassy break. Climb the steeper left wall to a rose bush.
2. 40ft.Traverse left and go up to a yew, then go right to a second yew.
3. 40ft.Climb the wall. Move right to a final short corner.

The following routes on the upper part of the back wall have a common first pitch that starts 40 feet right of the Col and takes the cleaned wall straight to a large ledge with an ash tree belay.

**17  Rose Bowl**   110 feet   Hard Very Severe                        †
2. 50ft.5b.From the left end of the ledge, climb the wall on huge holds direct to a large yew at 30 feet. Finish up the wall behind.

**18  The Ten Craters of Wisdom**   115 feet   Very Severe   ★★
A highly entertaining climb with some extraordinary holds.
2. 55ft.4c.Start 10 feet left of the belay below a short corner in the bulge. From the corner, climb straight up the steep wall and slab above then surmount the head-wall moving leftwards to finish.

**19  Simeon**   115 feet   Very Severe/Hard Very Severe   ★
A delightful route with good holds.
2. 55ft.Climb the bulging wall behind the belay, peg runner, to a line of good holds. From here there are 2 alternatives:
   i) 4c.Traverse right along these, then up to a ledge and finish up the steep wall on the left. The original way.
   ii) 5a.Continue straight up to a slab and the original finish. A better way.

The best descent is by traversing behind the upper yew trees and descending an easy 10-feet corner at the right end.

**20  Woodlouse Wall**   50 feet   Very Severe
Climb the short clean arete near the descent corner and traverse leftwards to tree belays.

The pinnacle, whose back forms the Col du Turd, has the following routes. Descent is by abseil.

**21  Rumble Ridge**   100 feet   Severe
Climb the tree adjacent to the left ridge and continue up the disintegrating ridge using all available trees. A poor route but a good starting tree.

**22 Tormentor** 140 feet   Hard Very Severe   †
Takes the front face, following a thin crack in the clean upper section.
1. 60ft.Climb cleaned rock to reach a grassy ledge away on the right.
2. 80ft.5b.Move back left along the ledge and climb straight up to and over a bulge. Follow the crack line above, peg runner, and traverse right by a horizontal crack into a groove leading to the shoulder.

**23 Deflector** 190 feet   Very Severe
1. 60ft.As for Tormentor.
2. 80ft.4c.Follow Tormentor for a few feet and continue the traverse left, below the bulge, to the far arete. Go up the arete to a belay on the saddle.
3. 50ft.Avoid the nose above on the left and go easily to the summit.

**24 Silicon** 80 feet   Very Severe   ★
4b.Start below two prominent cracks at the right end of the pinnacle. Climb the cleaned strip of rock to a peg runner and move left to the foot of the right crack. Climb this direct exiting right. Descend the back face.

SOUTH GULLY AREA
Further downstream a path leads off into South Gully. The first landmark is a cave at the foot of the First Pinnacle on the right. This is the start of Dr. Livingstone. Higher up the gully the path divides and the narrower left branch leads to a large wall supporting a prominent curving scar. This is John Peel Wall and here can be found several climbs of very high quality.

**25 Mandarin** 130 feet   Very Severe
1. 80ft.4c.Start left of Brutus and climb past trees to a line of rightward-slanting flakes. Follow these and move left to a ledge. Climb the face above to a hole and escape diagonally right to the grassy shoulder and tree belay.
2. 50ft.Follow the crumbling ridge.

**26 Brutus** 100 feet   E1   ★
5b.Climb the thin crack in the lower wall, stepping right below a bulge at two-thirds height into the continuation crack and so to the shoulder.

## 42 LIMESTONE AREA

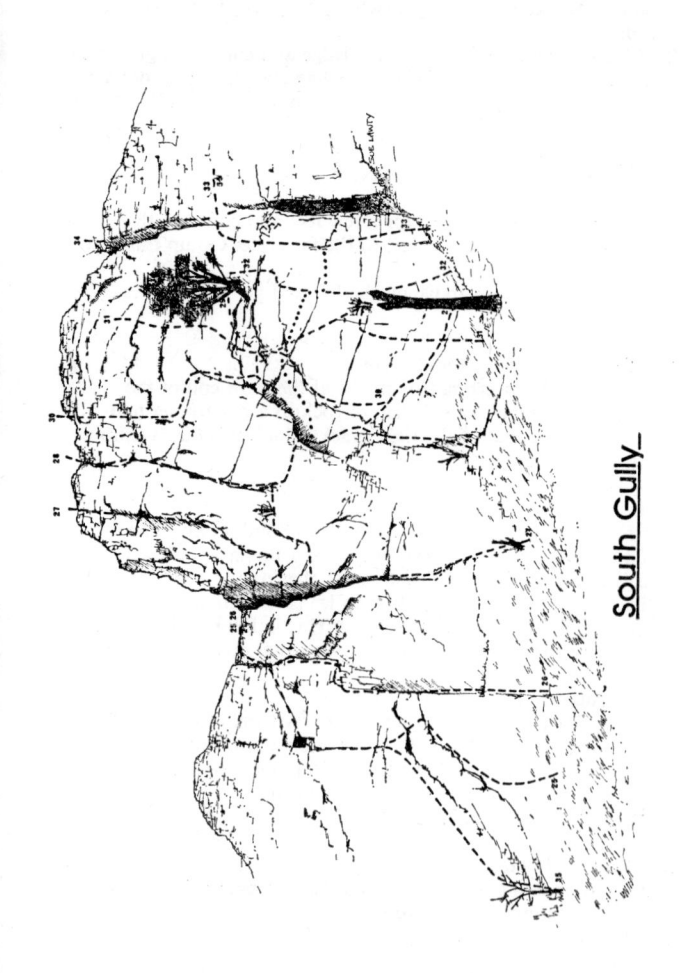

South Gully

**27 Caesar** 150 feet   E3                               †★★
A powerful route with contrasting pitches, taking the crack line
30 feet right of Brutus then the front of the bastion.
1. 70ft.5c.A fierce pitch. Follow the line of finger pockets with the
   occasional tiny foothold, peg runner, and continue up the
   groove above to a tree on the shoulder.
2. 80ft.5a.Descend the groove for 10 feet then move out right onto
   the face and climb two pleasant shallow grooves to the final
   airy bulge.

**28 George**   130 feet   Hard Very Severe                ★★★
Fine open climbing up the impressive crack left of John Peel.
5b.Start directly below the overlap of John Peel at a shallow
groove with a tree growing from its base. Climb the groove and
move up and left, peg runner, into the overlap. Step down the
groove and climb across the steep wall with difficulty, passing
below 2 peg runners, to the steep crack. Follow the crack and a
final awkward corner direct.

**29 John Peel**   180 feet   Hard Very Severe             ★★★
An excellent and exposed route of some delicacy despite its
steepness. It follows the large rightward-curving scar.
1. 100ft.5a.Start at a large ash tree growing close to the wall.
   Traverse left to a difficult move up and left, peg runner, into
   the main groove. Follow the corner and curving groove above
   to below the overhangs. Traverse right again and go up to a
   finely situated stance.
2. 30ft.5a.Using undercut holds, climb the ramp on the right and
   go across to the large yew tree.
3. 50ft.Climb up left over ledges, or abseil off the yew.

**30 Black Flip**   130 feet   Hard Very Severe
Takes a parallel but smaller overlap right of John Peel.
1. 70ft.5a.Climb the first 25 feet of John Peel and move up into
   the vertical overlap. Climb this, with some laybacking, to a
   steep exit left at its termination. Climb on to the stance of
   John Peel.
2. 60ft.5b.Above is a faint groove, which is taken to an aid peg.
   Traverse left with 3 aid threads. Finish up a broken groove.

**31 Wild Bill**   120 feet   E1                             ★
The wall between Black Flip and Yew Tree Wall.
1. 55ft.5c.Climb the first 15 feet of John Peel then go up to a
   horizontal break. Traverse right to a sturdy tree runner on
   Yew Tree Wall, then move back left slightly and climb direct
   to the stance of John Peel.

44  LIMESTONE AREA

2. 65ft.5b.Continue up the ramp on the right but only to gain an upper shelf on the left. Reach a further break above and finish up a crack.

**32  Yew Tree Wall**   130 feet   E1   ★★

A very fine pitch, steep and fingery, with the hardest move near the top. Start just right of the large ash tree and directly below the large yew at 65 feet.

1. 65ft.5c.Climb the steep pocketed wall to a sturdy small tree at 25 feet. Continue up the wall above and from a long thin flake move right and up, past an in situ thread, to the yew. Using the thread reduces the grade to Hard Very Severe 4c.
2. 65ft.4c.Traverse right along a break and climb the final easy rocks.

**33  Calamity Jane**   130 feet   Hard Very Severe

1. 75ft.5a.Climb directly up the wall 20 feet right of Yew Tree Wall to a difficult move onto a ledge level with the yew tree. Continue up the wall and move right across a ramp to a tree belay.
2. 45ft.Climb broken rocks to the ridge.

**34  Uncle Sam**   95 feet   Hard Very Severe

Higher up the gully is an obvious chimney ending at a bulge.
1. 50ft.5a.Climb the chimney and the crack in the wall above. Tree belay.
2. 45ft.Continue up easy broken rock.

**35  Orange Peel**   310 feet   E2   ★★★

A majestic expedition with technically sustained climbing in good positions. Start at a large twin-stemmed ash tree left of the flakes of Mandarin.

1. 130ft.5a.Climb the wall behind, then go diagonally right to reach the ledge on Mandarin and follow this to a tree belay on the saddle.
2. 60ft.5c.Descend the groove below for 15 feet and finger-traverse right along a thin crack to a good hole in an exciting position. Step up and move across to the base of the crack of George. Swing down and right, peg runner, into a belay on John Peel.
3. 120ft.5b.Climb a shallow groove just on the right to some hard moves across the overlap of Black Flip and a hand-traverse right along a horizontal crack leading into Yew Tree Wall. Descend this slightly and go across to Calamity Jane. Finish up this.

From the foot of the gully, the right branch of the path leads past a rock spur. At the top of the spur is:

**36 Faulty Towers** 60 feet Very Severe
4c. Start in the centre of the face, below a short broken corner high in the overlap. Climb the slab to the corner and traverse left below the overlap to the ridge. Descend the back face.

Returning to the cave at the foot of the First Pinnacle:
**37 Dr. Livingstone** 110 feet Very Severe ★
1. 70ft.4b. From the cave, climb the steep corner above by some enjoyable bridging and move right below the final roof.
2. 40ft.4b. Continue up the corner to the ridge. Either descend the back face or continue to the summit by a traverse across the back wall.

**38 The Mystery Tour** 70 feet Severe
4b. From the top of Dr. Livingstone, move down slightly and make a leftward-rising traverse across the back wall, passing under a small overhang, to the opposite ridge and so to the top.

**39 Stanley Wall** 110 feet Very Severe
Start round the corner right of the cave, at a wide crack.
1. 70ft.4c. Follow the wide crack to a further crack on the right. Exit from this to a stance on the left at the top of pitch 1 of Dr. Livingstone.
2. 40ft.4b. Finish up the corner behind.

**40 Amoeba** 110 feet Hard Very Severe
To the right of Stanley Wall is a broken wall with two caves. Start to the right of the caves.
1. 40ft.4c. Climb the crack past a small tree then move left across a slab into a cave belay.
2. 70ft.5a. Move back down, traverse left and climb the wall to a steep crack. Climb the crack and move right onto a grassy rake.

## DOVEDALE CHURCH
This uniquely structured crag is situated on the opposite bank to and just upstream from the pump-house. The crag is accessible only from the main path and involves wading the river. The approach from Ilam Rock is difficult and not recommended. Descent from the summit is by abseil. A prominent series of overhangs crosses the river face.

# Dove Dale
## Dovedale Church

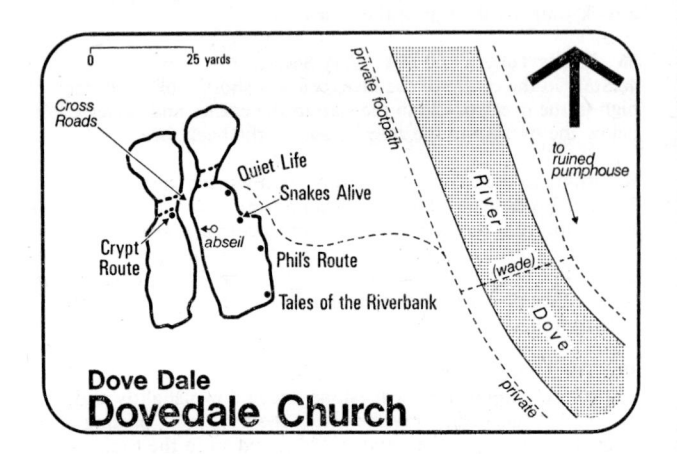

**1  Tales of the Riverbank**  100 feet  E4 ★★★
An exhausting route up the cracks on the impending left arete of the buttress.
6a.Climb the shattered wall and pull into the groove on the arete, follow this and step left to a crack. Climb up and left across the wall and then go back right to finish up the bulging wide crack. Very strenuous.

**2  Anaconda**  100 feet  Hard Very Severe ★★
Start below the broken open groove on the left of the long roof.
1. 60ft.5a.Climb the groove to the overhang and with some difficulty move up into the corner. Exit left to a stance.
2. 40ft.4b.Step down, traverse left across a slab and finish up the crack round the corner.

**3  Phil's Route**  100 feet  E2 ★★
An imposing pitch attacking the overhangs by the crack that splits them.
5c.Climb the wall and crack to the roof. Surmount the roof and continue strenuously, in the same line, over a bulge. Finish up the crack.

DOVEDALE 47

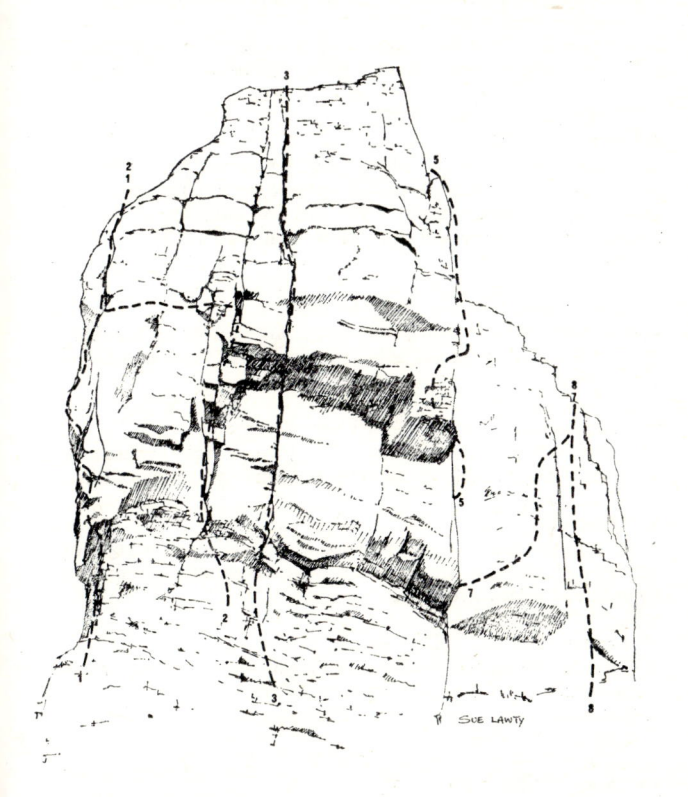

# Dovedale Church

## 48 LIMESTONE AREA

**4  The Right Route**   100 feet   A3
1. 60ft. Climb a thin crack over the bulge and main overhang above, to a slab stance.
2. 40ft. Continue over the bulge to a flake. Climb this and traverse right into the corner of Snakes Alive, just below the shoulder.

**5  Wild Country**   100 feet   E3   †★

An impressive route.
5c. Climb Snakes Alive for 10 feet, then go up to a peg on the left wall. Tension from this to reach a layback crack. Climb this and traverse left round the rib to a slab. Go up to join the Girdle. Move back round the arete and follow cracks to a ledge. Finish up the arete.

**6  Snakes Alive**   80 feet   Very Severe   ★★
4c. An excellent route which follows the large corner on the right of the roofs. Avoid the bulge by climbing the left wall and belay on the abseil peg.

**7  Judge Jeffries**   70 feet   Hard Very Severe
5b. Climb Snakes Alive for 10 feet then traverse right towards the arete until it is possible to climb up and finish as for Quiet Life.

**8  Quiet Life**   60 feet   E2   ★★
5c. Climb the audacious undercut scoop and crack to the right of Snakes Alive, with interesting crux moves to gain the scoop. Continue to a large tree.

**9  Horner**   100 feet   Hard Severe
1. 40ft. 4c. Pull over the overhang just right using a tree and climb the chimney/crack above to a good ledge.
2. 60ft. Ascend the chimney behind and step out left to finish. Belay on the ridge.

**10  Apse**   30 feet   A1
The thin crack on the back of the pinnacle is ascended using nuts.

**11  Bass**   45 feet   Hard Very Severe
Start by the 'cross roads' at the highest point of the gully which splits the pinnacles.
5a. Climb across the bulging wall of the back pinnacle to a peg runner on the left and, with some difficulty, pull onto the ledge above. Traverse right and scramble to the top.

DOVEDALE 49

**12  Cryptic Crack**  50 feet  Very Difficult
From the 'cross roads' move into the back archway and, starting on the left, traverse up right under the arch and finish up the wide crack.

**13  Crypt Route**  50 feet  Severe  ★
From the 'cross roads' the route is up the wall left of the archway. A short steep wall leads right into a chimney under another, smaller arch. The chimney is bridged exiting left.

**14  Watts Here**  50 feet  A1
The thin crack on the back pinnacle 25 feet down the hillside left of Crypt Route.

**14a  Bob Hope**  50 feet  E2  †
5b. Left of Watts Here, start in the centre of the river-facing face. Climb up and rightwards to an in situ thread runner on the arete. Step left and ascend direct to the top.

**15  Tonic Water**  65 feet  Severe
Walk through the archway in the back pinnacle. 20 feet up the hillside is a prominent groove.
1. 45ft.4b. Climb the groove and wide crack to a good tree belay on the left.
2. 20ft.4a. From the top of the block, climb the wall.

**16  Pussyfoot**  80 feet  Difficult
Walk through the archway and descend the hillside for 25 feet to the foot of a crack. Climb the crack past a tree low down.

**17  The Girdle Traverse**  250 feet  E1
Start in the gully that splits the two pinnacles, about 20 feet below the 'cross roads'.
1. 65ft.5a. Suspect rock. Climb into a niche and traverse right past two trees to a block belay on the ridge.
2. 40ft.4c. Descend the crack below to a slab and move right to a ledge.
3. 55ft.5b. Drop down the corner of Anaconda and traverse right with difficulty across the slab between the overhangs to a belay on Right Route.
4. 90ft.5c. Suspect rock. Continue to the arete and move up to the roof. Swing out right onto the steep wall and traverse the horizontal cracks into the corner, up which the route finishes.

THE TWELVE APOSTLES
About 500 yards downstream from Dovedale Church and just

## 50  LIMESTONE AREA

opposite Lover's Leap, is a large tower, close to the river but well-hidden amongst the trees.

**1  Senior Service**  90 feet  Severe
Climb the left side of the river face and short groove above, then traverse right before moving up and back left to finish.

**2  Grim Reaper**  90 feet  Hard Very Severe
Start as for Senior Service. Go up and right to gain a groove. Climb this moving left under the overhang. Finish up the wall.

### DOVEDALE CASTLE
Situated half a mile upstream from the Stepping Stones and recognisable by a cave at its left side. Approach on the main path and wade the river opposite.

**1  Castle Arete**  60 feet  Severe
4a.The broken left arete and steep wall direct.

**2  Cat's Eye Corner**  75 feet  Hard Very Severe
5b.From the left of the cave, traverse right above it and climb the obvious corner to a small ledge on the left, then go up to a large ledge. Climb the corner behind, step left and climb the wall. The corner can also be reached by pegging directly out of the cave at A3.

**2a  Quango**  75 feet  Hard Very Severe †
5a.Climb the faint crackline left of Cat's Eye Corner.

**3  Castle Groove**  80 feet  Hard Very Severe
5a.Start at a ledge right of the cave. Step up and right to a shallow rake then go left to the bottom of a wide crack. Step down, layback a short groove and move left into the main groove. Climb this.

**4  Castle Crack**  70 feet  Very Severe
5a.Follow Castle Groove to the wide crack. Climb this and a troublesome bulge above to easier ground.

**5  Castle Wall**  60 feet  Severe
4a.Climb the wall right of Castle Crack and traverse right along a horizontal fault to easier ground.

**6  Castle Slab**  45 feet  Severe
4a.From the gully on the right of the pinnacle, traverse left across the bottom of the slab for 15 feet then climb straight to the top.

# WOLFSCOTE DALE and BERESFORD DALE
by Mike Browell, Chris Calow and Dave Gregory

O.S. Ref. SK 122598 to 145551

SITUATION and APPROACHES
The dales are situated some 4 miles upstream from Dovedale and can be reached from either Alstonfield in the south or Hartington in the north. If approaching from the north, turn off the B5054 about 1½ miles west of Hartington and follow the signs for Beresford Dale which lead to the ford at the junction of the two Dales at Grid Ref. 128586. Limited car parking facilities here. Three separate crags give the climbing.
Pike Crag is on the east and true left bank of the river at Grid Ref. 129590, opposite a tower high on the other bank. From the ford, follow the path upstream on the true right bank, for a quarter of a mile and cross the river at an opportune footbridge just beyond a curious pinnacle which rises from Pike Pool. The crag lies up the grassy bank beyond.
The Celestial Twins are on the left bank at Grid Ref. 133582, about a quarter of a mile downstream from the ford. Cross the river at the footbridge by the ford and follow the path down the left bank.
Drabber Tor is on the Staffordshire, i.e. true right bank of the river about a mile downstream from the Celestial Twins, at Grid Ref. 139750. There is no right of way along the right bank so the best approach is to follow the path along the left bank either upstream from Milldale or downstream from the ford and wade across the river.

HISTORY (Giles Barker)
Although climbing has been recorded here since Graham West's 1961 Limestone guide, these dales have never enjoyed popularity, probably owing to their proximity to finer fare in Dovedale.
The first recorded climbs were credited to the Manchester Gritstone Club in 1961, by West. These were Roberts Roberts, Bender, Taddy Brown, Thom's Arete, Arrundale's Crack and Applause.
By 1970 a number of climbs had been done on Drabber Tor and were included in the Southern Limestone volume of Rock Climbs in the Peak. Jeff Morgan also added Castor to the Celestial Twins in 1969.
Development has been sporadic since 1970, but some excellent routes have emerged. In May 1973 Steve and Brian Dale with Barry Marsden discovered Pike Crag, climbing all of the routes

## 52 LIMESTONE AREA

there except for Dewdrop. Six months later they added this excellent and potentially classic climb.

Nothing seems to have been recorded since then until 1978 when guidebook work resulted in a large number of new climbs. Drabber Tor was attacked by Clive Jones resulting in War, Dutch Sunday, Flame and Peace; the latter being a particularly notable addition. Meanwhile Dave Gregory and Charles Darley climbed the pinnacle routes.

Bob Dearman and Mike Horlov joined in with Dog's Day, Pollux and Paraffle. Finally, as the guide was being assembled John Codling made some high standard additions with Strawberry Window, Bright Eyes, Fever Dream and A Man Possessed. Dave Jones then took over the lead to force Fingerdrive. History has it that Codling might well never have completed A Man Possessed had his bored and thirsty companions not threatened to mutiny and desert. His resulting surge of activity enabled them to make the pub before closing time with a fine ascent to celebrate, and a Codling legend to relate.


## PIKE CRAG

**1 Poet's Corner**   30 feet   Very Severe
4b. The corner on the left end of the face is reached by some difficult moves and followed to a tree. Abseil off or finish up poor rock.

**2 Dewdrop**   70 feet   E2   ★★★
An excellent route; the start is hard though the remainder is sustained and strenuous.
5c. Gain the prominent double-cracked groove from below and follow it almost to the roof. Step left, peg runner, and climb another steep crack line direct to a vegetated top.

**3 Gnome Sweet Gnome**   50 feet   Very Severe
4b. Climb the crack and chimney above to its closure. Move awkwardly right, peg runner, and up to a big tree.

**4 Fairy Flake**   60 feet   Very Severe
4b. Move up to the left of the obvious flake and climb it to a good ledge. Go up the small corner on the right to ledges which lead left to the big tree.

**5 Paradise Regained**   70 feet   Hard Very Severe
5a. Start at a thin crack 8 feet left of Central Crack and follow it over a slight bulge to a wider crack on the right. Climb this and traverse right, peg runner, to the large tree. Finish up the gully.

## WOLFSCOTE DALE and BERESFORD DALE

**6  Central Crack**   70 feet   Very Severe
4c.The obvious vertical fissure is climbed, with a hard move at half height, to the large tree. Finish up the gully.

**7  Paradise Lost**   70 feet   E1
5b.Some loose rock. Follow the shallow groove of Pixie Puzzle to a peg runner, step left and climb a strenuous crack to a ledge. Layback various flakes, roughly in the centre of the face and move left to the large tree on Central Crack. Finish as for below.

**8  Pixie Puzzle**   70 feet   Hard Very Severe                ★
1. 20ft.5a.Start at the shallow groove below and to the left of a huge gnarled tree. Climb the groove to a peg runner and move right to a good jug and so to the tree.
2. 50ft.4c.Move back left and climb the cracked corner and wall above.

**9  The Elf**   75 feet   Hard Very Severe
5b.Climb the very thin flake, peg runner, on the blunt arete to the right to gain a grass ramp and the tree. Climb past a smaller tree and finish up a crack.

**10  Hobgoblin Corner**   30 feet   Very Severe
4c.The corner at the right end is gained by a strenuous pull over the overhang below and is followed to a sycamore tree on its right.

### THE CELESTIAL TWINS

THE LEFT CELESTIAL TWIN
In the centre of the main face is a cave with a square entrance just off the ground, the Bivouac Cave.

**1  Pollux**   70 feet   Hard Very Severe
35 feet left of the cave at a pocketed barrel-shaped wall.
1. 40ft.4c.Climb the wall on various jagged pockets and friable flakes to a ledge and thread belay.
2. 30ft.5b.Attack the bulge above at a groove which leads to an awkward move onto a small ledge and a bad finish.

**2  A Man Possessed**   80 feet   E3                †★
5c.20 feet left of the cave is a crack and groove. Climb these, then move right and climb the impending wall with wild lunges.

**3  Castor**   80 feet   Hard Very Severe
5a.Some suspect rock. From just right of the cave climb to a break, traverse right and up to a second break, peg runner.

## 54 LIMESTONE AREA

Move up left to a rest in the large pothole. Escape on the right and climb to a ledge and final groove above.

**4  Fingerdrive**  80 feet  E3 †★
6a. As for Castor to the break. Gain two flakes on the left and go up to a bulge above the next horizontal break. Go over this and up to a hole in the top horizontal break (rest taken here). Finish direct via a thin crack and the odd lunge.

25 yards right is a large boulder and to its left a dividing terrace. The lower buttress contains some very scrappy lines but most will forego the invitation to horticulture and will start from the terrace.

**5  Hardly Heavenly**  20 feet  Very Severe
4b. Jam the crack beside a creaking flake at the left end of the terrace.

**6  Definitely Devilish**  20 feet  Very Severe
4c. The corner 10 feet right.

**7  Thom's Arete**  20 feet  Hard Very Difficult
The broken arete just right of the corner.

**8  Arrundale's Crack**  25 feet  Severe
The corner crack behind the hawthorn tree.

**9  Raquel Welch**  30 feet  Hard Very Severe
4c. Climb the steep wall just right of the corner, finishing over the obvious cracked nose.

**10  Applause**  40 feet  Hard Very Severe  ★
5a. Start 10 feet right of Arrundale's Crack. Climb the steep wall and move awkwardly right to some flakes leading up to a steep cracked groove to the top. A direct start is 5b.

**11  Bright Eyes**  50 feet  E1  ★
5c. Climb the steep wall to the right. Starting out left from the black corner.

**12  Fever Dream**  55 feet  E1  ★
5c. The finely positioned sharp arete is gained from the rightward-curving black corner in its left wall, and climbed direct.

**13  Roberts Roberts**  45 feet  Hard Severe
4a. The wide corner crack at the right end of the terrace is followed direct.

## WOLFSCOTE DALE and BERESFORD DALE

**14 Strawberry Window**  70 feet  E1
5c. Start from the cave right of Roberts Roberts. Climb its left wall and continue up the diagonal fault over the overhang moving left to a shallow groove to finish.

**15 Paraffle**  45 feet  Hard Very Severe
5b. Behind the boulder and to the right of a cave is a curving groove. Follow the groove with a hard exit right to some loose rock and a tree belay.

THE RIGHT CELESTIAL TWIN
**16 Taddy Brown**  90 feet  Severe
Start at the lowest point and follow a broken ridge to the righthand of two grooves, then on up the cracked rib.

**17 Bender**  90 feet  Severe
Start in the middle of the right half of the buttress and climb diagonally left under a line of overhangs to a steeper crack leading to a finish up loose rock and malicious dog roses.

**DRABBER TOR**
The climbs are described from left to right.
**1 Terminal Corner**  45 feet  Very Difficult
The chimney/corner left of a Y-forked ash tree. No belay.

**2 Vapid**  60 feet  Hard Severe
4a. Start 30 feet right of the ash tree and follow the leftward-slanting groove to the top.

**3 Gordian**  80 feet  Very Severe
4c. Climb direct to the vertical clean-cut corner in the upper part of the face and follow it, at first on its left wall.

**4 Dutch Sunday**  80 feet  Hard Very Severe
20 feet right again is a grey mark at the foot of the crag from which a line of flakes leads up right.
5a. Start just left of the grey mark and climb to a grassy ledge. Continue up a system of cracks and grooves above, stepping right to finish up a crack in the rib.

**5 Peace**  80 feet  E2                                        ★★
5c. Follow the line of flakes rightwards from the grey mark to a move left into a shallow corner. Climb up steeply to a good jug on the right and reach a horizontal break above. Move left and make a hard move to enter the easier groove.

## 56 LIMESTONE AREA

**6 Perlusive**  90 feet  Hard Very Severe
5b.Start as for Peace and climb the flakes rightwards into an indefinite groove. Climb this, peg runner, to a break and follow a rightward-facing groove to the top.

**7 War**  80 feet  Hard Very Severe
5b.Start 35 feet right of the grey mark at a depression in the base of the crag. Move up with difficulty to a large hold, peg runner, and continue on good holds, peg runner, up the groove left of a pinnacle.

**8 Flame**  60 feet  E1  ★
20 feet left of the wall and fence is a corner in the upper part of the face into which a layback crack runs rightwards.
5b.Follow the layback crack to its top and move left to a narrow cracked rib. Climb its left side to a horizontal break and finish up the left side of the arete above.

**9 Gourd**  35 feet  Hard Very Severe
5a.Climb directly to the groove and continue up it, peg runner, to the top.

**10 The Fault**  175 feet  Hard Very Severe
An unsatisfactory girdle which follows the lower horizontal fault. Start up Gordian and continue, with two aid pegs, along the fault past the thread on Peace, to finish up the groove of War.

### DRABBER PINNACLE
Situated 150 yards left of Drabber Tor. The rock is suspect but a stout block at the top gives a good belay.

**11 Fred Loads**  50 feet  Hard Severe
The broken corner and cracks at the left side of the buttress.

**12 Dog's Day**  70 feet  Very Severe
4c.Climb the wall 10 feet right of the corner to a crack in the upper section and finish up this.

**13 Bill Sowerbutts**  50 feet  Very Severe
4a.Follow the corner on the right, through an overhang, using a broken crack in the left wall.

**14 Professor Alan Gemmil**  30 feet  Very Severe
4b.The bulgy corner just right is followed direct.

57

# MANIFOLD VALLEY

by Giles Barker, Mike Browell and John Codling

O.S. Ref. SK 096561 to 107541

## SITUATION
The River Manifold rises as a spring on Axe Edge and flows southwards to join the River Dove near Ilam. A now disused railway has been converted into a tarmac footpath, and follows the river, winding southwards from Hulme End to Beeston Tor. All the crags are located along this section of the valley, and are easily accessible from this path.

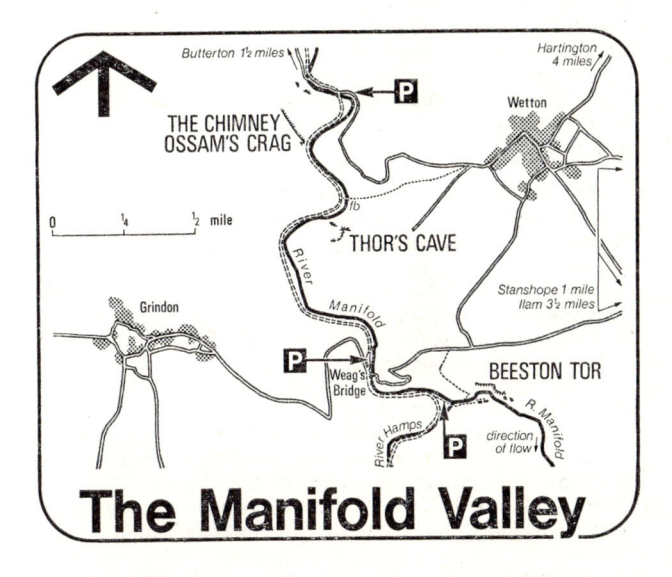

## The Manifold Valley

## APPROACHES
From the A515 Buxton-Ashbourne road, go through Alstonfield to Wetton. There are two approaches from Wetton:
For The Chimney, Ossam's Crag and Thor's Cave, follow the Butterton and Manifold Valley road, down into the valley. There is adequate car parking by the river. Thor's Cave can be reached more easily on foot by parking at Wetton. Follow the road until

## 58  LIMESTONE AREA

the crag is visible on the left, then take a narrow field lane and footpath to the crag. This route has the distinct advantage of being relatively level.

For Beeston Tor take the Grindon and Manifold road down hairpins to Weags Bridge. Sharp left along a farm road brings a field where cars may be parked (often at a cost). Stepping stones can be crossed, but at times of heavy flow this is not advised. Instead, walk along the opposite bank from Weags Bridge. A high level approach from the large open field before the first hairpin is possible.

### ACCESS

The Chimney and Ossam's Crag are owned by the National Trust, and managed by Mr. A. Coates of Grindon. Providing no damage is done, climbing is permitted.

Thor's Cave is situated on land farmed by Mr. Thompson of Carr Farm, Wetton. Providing no damage is done to walls and fences, he is willing to allow climbing. Beeston Tor is on the Duke of Devonshire's estate, which is farmed by Mr. Wint of Wetton. He is concerned about damage to walls and fences, but is willing to allow climbing.

### HISTORY (Giles Barker)

The Manifold Valley has, it seems, remained a hidden corner of Staffordshire for thousands of years. It is only in the past twenty years that the motor vehicle has penetrated its solitude, with tourist and rock climber alike being attracted to its gentle rolling hills and dramatic rock architecture. Even in this time one may be forgiven for thinking that the remoteness of the valley has restrained climbing development.

Recorded climbing began in the 1950s, and until the production of the Southern Limestone guidebook in 1970, the valley was almost the exclusive preserve of the Rock and Ice and Oread clubs. In 1954 Joe Brown, with Ron Moseley, in characteristic fashion climbed two of the classic routes of the area, West Window Groove and The Thorn. West Window Groove was climbed mainly with aid, but The Thorn succumbed with only two or three pegs, and has remained a superb free climb. As elsewhere on limestone, the climbs were quite bold because of the condition of the rock and the techniques employed. Brown conveys something of the seriousness in his autobiography, 'The Hard Years', in describing an epic attempt at a new route between Thunder and Lightning. Around this time Roy Leeming also visited the valley and pegged Tower Direct and the Curtain Variation start to West Window Groove. He returned in 1957 to add Slanting Crack (also on pegs).

These were isolated events, however, and the valley was overlooked while limestone crags elsewhere were undergoing thorough explorations. In fact the next significant event was in 1963 when Derrick Burgess and Nat Allen made the first tentative moves onto what was to become Beeston Eliminate; on this occasion they reached the top of The Thorn. For many years this pair untiringly explored the valley and inspired others to search for new rock. Many of the most enjoyable routes in the valley are products of their pioneering. In 1965 they unveiled the classic Cummerbund and opened up Chimney Crag with The Sweep. The following year they found the delectable Central Wall, and explored the wings of Beeston Tor with The Webb and West Wall Climb. To these they added over the years a whole host of easier and less important climbs.

The younger element of the Rock and Ice became interested in the valley, and often with Allen partnering them, began to discover some of the more serious problems. Gordon 'Speedy' Smith and Terry Burnell traversed out above the void to complete the Eliminate, finding two aid slings necessary. Then in 1966 Smith attacked Thor's Cave and departed with Thunder, Lightning and Starlight. Des Hadlum, who partnered Smith on these climbs, returned in 1967 to add Storm. That year also witnessed an 'outside' visit when Paul Nunn and J. Smith traversed Thor's Cave with Hagen.

'Speedy' Smith continued his assault in 1968 with The Fly (5 aid pegs), The Spider (3 aid points) and Ivy Gash (3 aid slings), while Hadlum climbed Patience with 3 aid slings.

Others began to make contributions. In 1969 Nunn continued his traversing with Perforation. Bob Dearman, unable to resist a roof, pegged Thor to reach the long groove above. He also visited Beeston in 1970 with B. Riley, climbing White Room (1 aid peg) and Buzz. The most important contribution of 1970 was Jeff Morgan's Beest, which, despite using eight aid points, brought an up to date concept to the Tor. When volume 8 of Rock Climbs in the Peak was published in 1970 forty-six climbs were included in the Manifold section.

Soon after the guide appeared, Tom Proctor and Keith Myhill made two major contributions to the area. Proctor free-climbed Tower Direct, applying his Stoney Middleton climbing techniques to the Manifold Valley. Myhill matched this effort with the sustained Twilight of the Tired Gods, which, though using 3 aid points, was based on free-climbing Curtain Variant.

Although the 70s have seen an upsurge in new developments and concepts in rock climbing, particularly since 1976, the Manifold has not witnessed any particular peak of activity. It is evident, however, that the valley has become established as a popular climbing area. As elsewhere on Derbyshire limestone, almost all the aid moves have gradually been eliminated; various people have been involved in this clean-up and it would probably be inaccurate to try to pinpoint each case. It is certain that many developments of this period compare favourably for quality with others in the Peak District; the new lines being no exception.

In 1972 Bob Dearman, tantalised by the vast expanse of roofs in Thor's Cave, returned with Bob Toogood and K. Bridgers to construct the epic Kyrie Eleison. With most of the aid in place, it has become easier, but at the time it was probably the most demanding roof pitch in the area. Steve and Brian Dale added another fine climb, Tempest, in the same year. In 1974 John Yates made a significant addition to Beeston Tor with his very bold ascent of The Black Grub. Yates placed the peg by hand and retreated for a rest. On returning, he hit it twice and climbed on. The peg fell out when the second reached it. It was not until four years later that this type of wall climbing was developed further, and Black Grub was repeated. Meanwhile, in 1976 Bob Dearman climbed the obvious roof line right of The Thorn (with some aid), Black Alice. Two years later Dave Jones and Bob Cope ventured onto the walls below Ivy Gash, finding some surprisingly reasonable and high-quality climbing in Evensong, Pocket Symphony and the fierce Catharsis. This pair also improved The Webb with a more direct pitch, though this had probably been done some years before by Steve Read. Gary Gibson also created a new pitch and borrowed the old variation pitch from the Eliminate to make an independent climb with Enough Time. In 1979 John Codling and Jones returned to examine the vast expanse of unclimbed rock above the traverse of Perforation. The resulting girdle, Beeston's third, was called Lord of the Dance. Codling had seen other possibilities, and with Tony Bristlin he forced the ridiculously steep Budgie out of Bertram's Chimney. Finally, in 1980, after tentative attempts by lesser parties, Phil Burke and Rab Carrington free-climbed Black Alice and pressed on and out over the top overhang of Beeston Eliminate to create Double Top.

There seems to be hardly any space left for new climbs, yet the gaps are there. One can be sure that some very high standard climbing will be done in the future. To most climbers, however, the valley will remain a delightful place to bask in the sunshine on superb limestone.

# MANIFOLD VALLEY 61

**THE CHIMNEY**
O.S. Ref. SK 096556

CHARACTER
Geologically intriguing, the chimney itself is the feature of the crag. Regrettably, the climbing is less fine and is mostly unfrequented; consequently vegetation runs amok. For approaches, see above. The crag is sheltered and east-facing, close to the road and easily accessible.

THE CLIMBS are described from Right to Left.

**1 The Chimney** 50 feet Moderate ★★★
The curious tube on the right of the crag. Reverse the route.

**2 The Chimney Direct** 65 feet A2
Follow the roof crack out of the left side of The Chimney. Continue up grooves to an oak tree.

25 feet left is a pothole entrance. 15 feet left again is a rising line of leftward-leading pockets.

**3 Inferno** 145 feet Hard Very Severe
4c.Move up left and then direct, moving right past a peg runner to a large block. Continue diagonally leftwards to a groove. Climb this. Continue direct to large trees.

**4 The Sweep** 175 feet Very Severe
1. 60ft.As for Inferno but continue past an elder to a grass ledge. Continue leftwards, then go right and up the wall before moving left to a stance.
2. 115ft.4c.Climb a rightward-slanting gangway. Trend left to the Hermit's Traverse. Move into Inferno. Finish up this.

**5 Hermit's Traverse** 150 feet Very Difficult
30 yards left of The Sweep, a path leads into a cave.
1. 30ft.To the right, a grassy rib leads to the traverse line, which is followed to a tree belay.
2. 60ft.Walk 25 feet into Hermit's Cave. Go right past Inferno to a bush-filled rake leading to a tree.
3. 60ft.Move over a rib, go right 30 feet then finish through trees.

## 62 LIMESTONE AREA

## The Chimney

MANIFOLD VALLEY 63

**OSSAM'S CRAG**
O.S. Ref. SK 096554

CHARACTER
Situated on the true right bank of the river, opposite Thor's Cave, the crag forms a spur on the hillside. An obvious overlap rises from left to right; this is Cummerbund; and below this, vegetated slabs yield some surprisingly clean and pleasant routes (some are not so pleasant though).

THE CLIMBS are described from Left to Right, starting on the left with a grassy ridge.

**1 Ossam's Ridge**   170 feet   Severe
20 feet left of the fence is a grassy weakness.
1. 110ft.Climb grass to a groove, and move up to a grassy ledge. Continue to a large tree.
2. 60ft.The chimney behind the tree; belay on the ridge.

15 yards right of the fence, a ledge with a tree on its right cuts across the base of the crag.

**2 Aperitif**   160 feet   Hard Very Severe
1. 90ft.5b.Step onto the ledge and traverse 15 feet left. Climb the wall to a sloping ledge, then cross the diagonal fault to a ledge on the left. Hard moves up the wall lead to a stance on Cummerbund.
2. 70ft.4c.Loose.Climb Cummerbund for a few feet until it is possible to traverse 30 feet left to a groove, which is exited on the right. Finish up broken cracks.

**3 Conventicle**   160 feet   Hard Very Severe
1. 100ft.5a.Follow Aperitif up the wall for 15 feet. Move right to a ledge. Climb the wall right of a small tree. Traverse right on pockets to ledges, then pass a small tree to belay on Cummerbund.
2. 60ft.5a.Ascend the groove right of the belay for a few feet, then go left onto the wall. Climb to a ledge and a loose finish.

15 yards right are some damp discontinuous cracks.

**4 Steerpike**   130 feet   E1   ★
1. 45ft.5a.Climb a short, left-leaning ramp to a crack and groove line. Ascend this to a sloping stance.
2. 60ft.5c.Move right across the slab to a tree. Climb the slab and gain the wall on the left. Go up to the third stance of Cummerbund; thread belays.
3. 25ft.The steep crack or Cummerbund.

# 64 LIMESTONE AREA

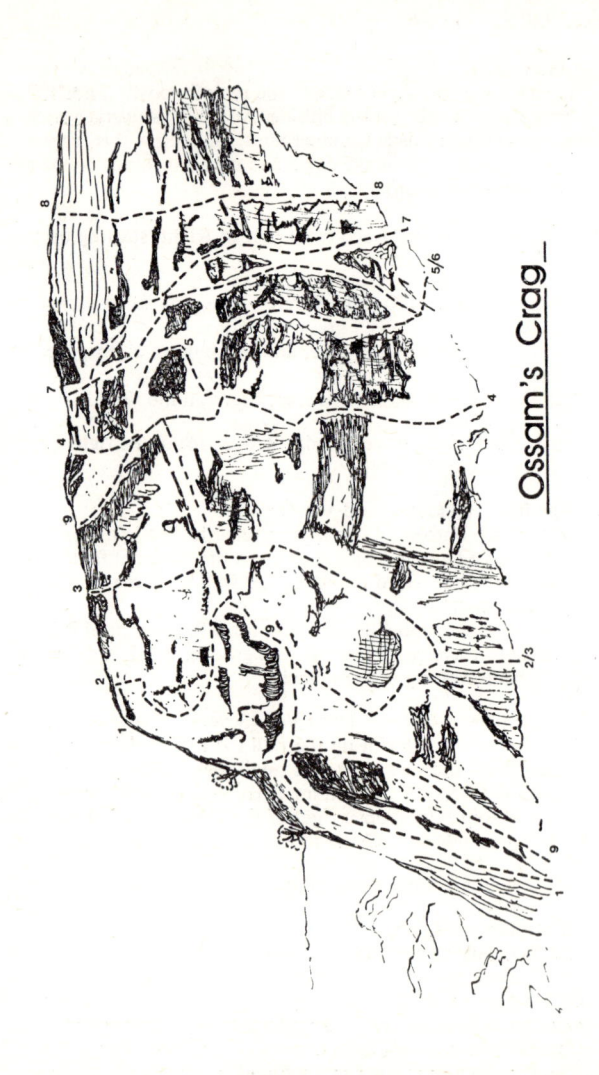

## Ossam's Crag

**5 Barquentine**  125 feet  Hard Very Severe †
A poor route. Start at a short slanting ramp 15 yards right of Steerpike.
1. 100ft. Go left across the slab and pull onto a ledge. Traverse 15 feet left, then climb the wall. Traverse left below the bulge to the peg runner on Steerpike. Climb the ramp on the right. Traverse left to the Steerpike belay.
2. 25ft. The steep crack or Cummerbund.

**6 The Ballad of Bilbo Baggins**  130 feet  Very Severe †
1. 100ft. Ascend Barquentine to a ledge. Climb the flake on the right over a loose block to a ledge. Climb a thin crack, go right to a small tree and up the slab to a bush. Peg.
2. 30ft. The wall and corner on the left.

**7 Mardi Gras**  100 feet  Very Severe
1. 60ft. Start behind a large tree. Traverse diagonally left to a small tree. Slabs lead up to a grassy bay.
2. 40ft. Climb a short groove to an overhang. Swing right to a grassy shelf and step left to the final corner of Bilbo, etc.

**8 Moss Slab**  140 feet  Severe
Start in a clump of bushes right of the large tree. Climb the slab past a tree at 80 feet to a tree stance. Scramble off.

**9 Cummerbund**  240 feet  Very Severe  ★★
The girdle is the most popular route on the crag. Start from the fence on the left.
1. 75ft. 4a. Climb direct to a groove and go over a bulge to a ledge and tree.
2. 65ft. 4b. Traverse right round the nose and follow the fault to a recess. Step right to a groove. Go back up to the flake. Continue right to a stance just left of blocks.
3. 60ft. 4b. Traverse under the line of blocks to a corner. Climb the wall on the right to a horizontal break and follow this right to a grassy bay.
4. 30ft. Go left easily to the ridge.


**THOR'S CAVE**
O.S. Ref. SK 098549

CHARACTER
Thor's Cave can be reached by a steep stepped path from the valley bottom. It is a popular tourist attraction, consisting of a steep limestone knoll capped by a huge cave with two entrances;

## 66  LIMESTONE AREA

the Main Entrance and West Window. In the winter it becomes a wind tunnel, often unhealthily cold. In summer it provides welcome shade. Some routes on the north (front) face are rarely ascended as they are loose and grassy. At least this protects the hordes of tourists.

THE CLIMBS are described from Left to Right, starting 20 feet left of the Main Entrance.

**1  Storm**   150 feet   Hard Very Severe †
1. 90ft. From behind the tree go up to a grassy ledge, past a large flake. Move right across the wall to holds in a groove and go up to a wide crack.
2. 60ft. Climb the crack, then the wall, moving left to a grassy finish.

**2  Thor**   140 feet   A3/Very Severe
Start 40 feet inside the cave below a bolt on the left wall.
1. 65ft. A3. Climb the faint weakness past the bolt to the roof. A line of bolts lead to the lip. Stance 10 feet up.
2. 75ft. Follow the shattered groove to the top.

**3  Kyrie Eleison**   205 feet   A3   ★★
The longest roof pitch in the Peak District, and one of the best. Most pegs are in place but some bolts are wearing thin. Start at the back of the cave.
1. 130ft. A3. Scramble up slabs to a dirty sentry-box. Peg out right to reach a fault leading inwards and upwards, until a descending crackline leads to the main entrance. After 70 feet, a hole (possible belay) is reached. Continue along bolts and threads. Pass the lip to a stance on Thor.
2. 75ft. As for Thor or abseil off.

**4  Starlight**   150 feet   Very Severe
A straightforward and direct route to the summit. Start just right of the Main Entrance.
1. 85ft. 4b. Go easily up to a large peg runner. Continue up the groove to a stance behind a tree.
2. 65ft. 4c. Climb the crack to the top.

**5  Lightning**   150 feet   Hard Very Severe   ★
1. 100ft. 5a. As for Starlight to the peg runner. Move right onto a ramp. Climb the wall leftwards, then direct to a spike. Move right along the break to a thread and go up the wall above to a groove. Belay at its top.
2. 50ft. 4c. Step left into the groove; climb it and a crack.

MANIFOLD VALLEY 67

## Thor's Cave

68  LIMESTONE AREA

**6 Thunder**  150 feet  Hard Very Severe  †
10 yards right is a small tree.
1. 55ft. Go diagonally right up a grassy slab for 30 feet to a short groove. Climb this for 10 feet, then traverse left to a crack which is followed to a ledge.
2. 60ft. Move right to a rib, then traverse left to a crack. Where it ends move left to another crack. Follow it to a ledge. A leftward traverse leads to the Lightning flake belay.
3. 35ft. Finish up the crack above.

**7 Tempest**  170 feet  E1
The loose arete left of Slanting Crack has good positions.
1. 30ft. Start as for Thunder to the short groove. Belay.
2. 110ft.5b. Climb the slabby groove for 25 feet. Move left onto the face and follow it past a thread. Climb the wall and cracks to ivy and continue past fields to a stance.
3. 30ft. Traverse right and finish up the corner.

The following climbs are all on the west face.

**8 Slanting Crack**  130 feet  Very Severe  ★
Scramble up vegetated rocks to a belay below the curving chimney, near the arete. A lefthand start (4b) from the small tree as for Thunder can be made.
4c. Climb the chimney to a groove. Ascend this to a grass terrace and climb the short corner above.

**9 Tower Direct**  120 feet  E3  ★★★
A fine strenuous pitch, starting from the ledge 15 feet up before the West Window (on the right facing out).
5c. Climb the steep wall following the righthand crack, peg runner, then make a difficult move left to a thin crack, peg runner. Climb the thin crack to a wider one. From ledges go up to a short corner and go slightly left to finish.

**10 Twilight of the Tired Gods**  120 feet  E3
Some exacting climbing up the hanging flake.
1. 50ft.5c. From the ledge of Tower Direct, gain the hanging flake from the left, and follow it to belay in West Window Groove.
2. 70ft.5b. Traverse left to a crack. Climb this then left again to a bush and ledges. Move up and climb the short corner to the top.

**11 West Window Groove**  110 feet  Hard Very Severe  ★★
The classic of the crag, taking the chimney above the window.
1. 50ft.5a. Climb cracks in the wall past a bulge until a step out

right to a ledge. Make a wide bridge across the window and move left into the cave.
2. 60ft.5a.Bridge up the chimney to easier ground.

**12  West Face Route**   200 feet   Very Severe †
1. 80ft.Climb the crack right of West Window Groove to a ledge below a flake in a steep wall.
2. 60ft.Climb the flake and gardened holds above to a break.
3. 60ft.Traverse right along the break to a pinnacle which is climbed up its righthand side.

**13  Hagen**   390 feet   Hard Very Severe †
A girdle of the cliff starting from Storm.
1. 90ft.As for Storm pitch 1.
2. 70ft.Continue up the groove for 20 feet. Traverse 15 feet right to a peg runner then move down diagonally to a small ledge. Continue up a short ramp to a ledge and tree.
3. 80ft.Climb the crack till it steepens, then go right to twin cracks on Lightning. Descend to the flake and climb a short crack to an elder. Traverse right to a large grassy ledge on Slanting Crack.
4. 50ft.More grassy ledges lead into West Window Groove. Belay above at some large blocks.
5. 100ft.Grassy rock until rock appears. Traverse a break to fields and finish up a prominent flake.

70  LIMESTONE AREA

## BEESTON TOR
O.S. Ref. SK 107541

---

CHARACTER
The River Manifold comes and goes, giving either easy access across a dry bed, precarious crossing of the stepping stones, or a longer walk down the opposite bank. The Tor is one of the most favourably situated in the Peak District, facing south and is sheltered from wind. Even in winter it is a sun trap. Views are superb, and not surprisingly it is very popular. Climbs are kept clean by traffic, many characterised by solution pockets which give surprising holds.
The large curving cave is Ivy Gash. Left of this are slabs, vegetated in their lower half. Below and right is a steep pocketed wall, and right again, bulging rock which gives way to towers, ridges and jungle.

THE CLIMBS are described from Left to Right. The first climb starts on the left of the slabs, 20 feet right of a small cave.

**1  Buzz   160 feet   Hard Severe**
1. 80ft. Climb the slabs rightwards to a tree belay.
2. 80ft. Go up to a big tree on the Eliminate. Ascend the wall on the right.

**2  White Room   140 feet   Hard Very Severe**            ★
Start on the right of a clump of trees, and scramble across gardened rock to a large tree.
1. 80ft.4c. Go left across the slab to a groove. Climb this and the wall above to a peg belay on the Eliminate pitch 1.
2. 60ft.5a. Follow the ramp rightwards to an overhang. Go round this to a grassy finish.

**3  West Wall Climb   170 feet   Very Severe**            ★
A good start to the Eliminate. Start as for White Room.
1. 50ft.4a. From the tree climb the slab via a curving flake to another tree.
2. 50ft.4c. Move right and up 15 feet, then move right into a small recess. Go down right onto the wall, and follow pockets to the bulge, which is taken direct to the cave stance of the Eliminate.
3. 70ft.4c. Move left and climb to the wide crack above. Climb this to ledges. Go left across a slab. Belay well back.

# MANIFOLD VALLEY - BEESTON TOR 71

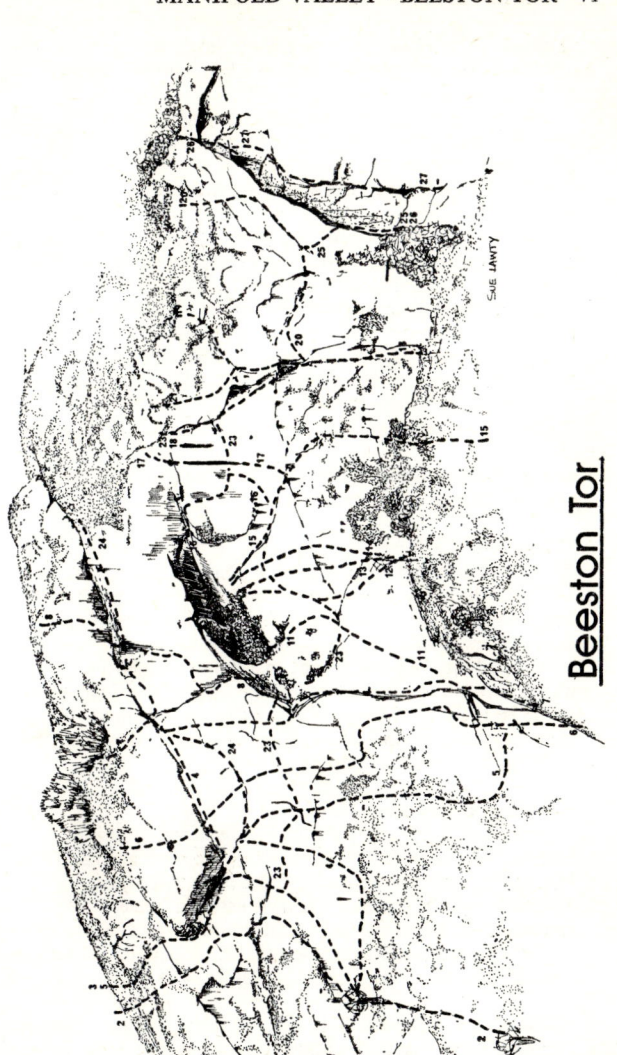

Beeston Tor

## 72  LIMESTONE AREA

**4  Enough Time**   200 feet   Hard Very Severe
1. 80ft.4a.As for West Wall Climb to the tree, then traverse 30 feet right to belay.
2. 50ft.5a.Climb the pocketed wall past a small recess to a thread, step right and gain the short groove. Exit leftwards and go up to the cave.
3. 70ft.5b.Traverse rightwards along the fault to the thorny rake.

**5  Patience**   220 feet   Hard Very Severe                    ★
Some good climbing, similar to The Beest, but easier. Start at the bottom of the vertical cleft of Ivy Gash.
1. 105ft.5b.Start below a groove, left of the vertical gash, and climb it, then traverse left across the slab under the bulges. Climb the arete and grass ledges to a thread belay.
2. 45ft.5a.Move left and go up to a niche. Climb the wall above past threads to a cave.
3. 70ft.4c.Finish up West Wall Climb pitch 3.

**Direct Start**
1.a) 100ft.5c.Climb the wall left of the groove to join the normal route on the traverse.

**6  The Beest**   230 feet   E3                                ★★★
One of the finest routes on limestone. Start as for Patience.
1. 120ft.6a.Climb the groove to the bulges. Go straight over the bulge and diagonally right. Continue up to a horizontal break, then traverse 30 feet left to a grass ledge and belay.
2. 110ft.5c.Move diagonally right to a bulge. Pull into a scoop and go up to the second pitch of the Eliminate. Move left and go up to the fault. Move right to a thread and climb straight over the overhang to a giant thread in a hole. Move right and go up to a holly tree belay.

**7  The Thorn**   160 feet   Hard Very Severe                  ★★★
A popular climb, the second pitch giving superb positions.
1. 90ft.4b.Climb the slab on the right of the vertical gash. Move left into the chimney and go up to a huge thread.
2. 70ft.5a.Move out left and up to an exposed bulge, 3 peg runners. Pull up on excellent holds into a groove. Move onto the left rib and climb to a thorny rake. (A peg for aid reduces the standard to an excellent Very Severe, 4c.)

**8  Double Top**   220 feet   E4                               †
1. 90ft.4b.As for The Thorn pitch 1.
2. 70ft.6a.Cross the roof by the crack line leading left and belay below the thorny rake.

## MANIFOLD VALLEY - BEESTON TOR

3. 60ft.5c.Move right onto the wall past an in situ thread above and move steeply right to finish up a prow.

The following routes all finish at the Ivy Gash, the usual descent being by abseil from a good thread at the lefthand end. It is possible to finish by the next route:

**9  Ivy Gash**   185 feet   Hard Very Severe   ★
1. 100ft.Take any route up to the cave.
2. 85ft.5a.Traverse out right onto the steep wall, past threads to a hole. Move up and right. Finish up a groove.

**10  Stagnation**   90 feet   Very Severe
1. 90ft.4b.Follow The Thorn for 40 feet. Go straight up on pockets, keeping left of Nocturne, to a hole. Move 5 feet up the diagonal crack. Finish up the diagonal break.

**11  Nocturne**   110 feet   Very Severe   ★
A pleasant pitch into the Ivy Gash.
4c.Follow The Thorn for 40 feet. Traverse right to a crack and go up diagonally leftwards, following the shallow weakness which leads into the Gash just left of the ivy.

**12  Pocket Symphony**   130 feet   E1   ★
1. 60ft.4c.Follow Nocturne, but continue to traverse along ledges to a dying elder. Devious thread belay.
2. 70ft.5b.Go diagonally left to threads below a horizontal break. Climb the pocketed wall direct over a bulging wall, past a hole, finishing right of the ivy.

**13  Deaf Dove**   120 feet   E1   ★†
1. 60ft.4c.As for Pocket Symphony.
2. 60ft.5c.Climb direct up to a steep wall five feet left of the scoop of Evensong. Continue direct up the wall finishing directly over the nose.

**14  Evensong**   125 feet   Hard Very Severe   ★
1. 60ft.4c.As for Pocket Symphony.
2. 65ft.5b.Climb direct to a scoop between ochre lichen patches. Climb directly over a bulge to finish as for Central Wall.

From the muddy slope, below Ivy Gash, a path leads rightwards below vegetated slabs to another smaller scar, which forms a prominent chimney. Before this is reached, a streak runs up from the path to the clean wall below Ivy Gash.

**15  Central Wall**   150 feet   Mild Very Severe   ★★
This climb finds an elegant way up a slab sandwiched between steep walls. The sustained quality gives it classic status.

1. 60ft. The gardened streak leads to peg belays.
2. 90ft. 4b. Go up the wall and diagonally left towards the slab. Gain it via a crack in a bulge, and follow it delicately leftwards to the Gash.

The main roof above Ivy Gash at this point was once breached by a bolt route.

**16  Catharsis**  140 feet  E3  ★★

A bold wall climb in a fine position.
1. 60ft. As for Central Wall pitch 1.
2. 80ft. 5c. Follow Central Wall pitch 2 to the short crack in the bulge. Traverse right across the wall and go up until a long reach gains a scoop. Step left then go up on pockets to a thread. Move left to belays.

**17  Black Grub**  140 feet  E3  ★★★

Brilliant climbing on pockets up the black streak which descends from the hole in Ivy Gash.
1. 60ft. As for Central Wall pitch 1.
2. 80ft. 5c. Follow Central Wall for a few feet, until a traverse right leads to a ring peg runner. Continue straight up the obvious black streak to a peg runner. Step up and left to the Catharsis scoop then move back right and up to the hole on Ivy Gash. Finish up Ivy Gash.

From the foot of the chimney above the path, scramble left to below the long groove line which bounds Central Wall on the right. Several climbs start here, using the peg belay of Central Wall.

**18  The Fly**  140 feet  E3  ★

6a. Gain the groove on the right and ascend until it steepens. Continue straight up the corner past several peg runners, stepping left to join the final grassy groove of Ivy Gash.

**19  The Webb**  130 feet  Hard Very Severe

5a. As for The Fly until the groove steepens. Swing out right onto a ramp, peg runner. Go rightwards up a crack to grass and follow this to trees.

**20  The Spider**  130 feet  Hard Very Severe  ★

5a. Climb the groove on The Fly for 30 feet. Traverse right across the blank-looking wall to a diagonal scar. Descend slightly across another wall to a ramp. Traverse along this into a groove and climb this moving left at the top.

## MANIFOLD VALLEY - BEESTON TOR

**21  Little Crow   130 feet   Hard Very Severe**
5a. Climb the groove of The Fly until a large hole on the right can be gained. Go diagonally right onto a ramp, and go up left to a bulge. Climb over this and continue up the groove above, passing The Webb.

The main crag has three independent girdles.

**22  Perforation   390 feet   Hard Very Severe   ★**
A low-level girdle of the central part of the crag; a few hard moves are separated by pleasant wall climbing.
1. 50ft.4a. As for West Wall Climb to the tree.
2. 100ft.4c. Traverse right past the stance on The Beest and go along a small slab onto the first pitch of The Thorn. Drop down and belay where a diagonal break goes out rightwards to Central Wall.
3. 100ft.4c. Follow this fault into Central Wall, and belay on the slab.
4. 50ft.5a. Continue past the ring peg runner on Black Grub to a constricted stance on The Fly.
5. 90ft.5a. Finish as for The Webb.

**23  Lord of the Dance   380 feet   E3   ★★**
A mid-height girdle taking the pocketed walls below the Eliminate and Ivy Gash, giving sustained and good climbing.
1. 50ft.4a. As for West Wall Climb to the tree.
2. 120ft.5b. Ascend diagonally right as for West Wall Climb, until a few feet below the overhang. Traverse to a rib and go round it to a short corner on Patience. Traverse into the scoop on The Beest using hidden footholds. Continue up and rightwards to handholds below the corner on the Eliminate. Step down and into The Thorn and go down it to belay in the chimney. A sustained pitch.
3. 90ft.5b. Climb down across a slab to a diagonal crack. Move right across a bulge on good footholds into the fault on Nocturne. Go right to a deep hole on Pocket Symphony, go up 6 feet, then right and across the bulge on Evensong to Central Wall slab.
4. 120ft.5c. Traverse right as for Catharsis and go up into the scoop. Continue right past a deep hole and some poor low holds to the final groove of The Fly. Climb this.

**24  Beeston Eliminate   255 feet   Hard Very Severe   ★★★**
A limestone classic. Scramble up the slope on the left of the crag to the start of the fault.
1. 90ft. Follow the fault to a cave. Or, better still, start up pitches 1 and 2 of West Wall Climb.

## 76  LIMESTONE AREA

2. 75ft.5a.Take a slightly descending line across the wall until below a groove. Climb the groove and wall above to belay in the thorny rake.
3. 90ft.5a.Move back down to the fault line, and follow it to a rose bush. The position here leaves little to be desired. Continue rightwards and up grass to finish.

The next climbs are on the towers and ridges to the right starting from the ledge on the right of Central Wall, reached by a steep scramble.

**25  Budgie**   120 feet   E4   †
Some very steep climbing up the bulging wall below The Spider. Start as for Bertram's Chimney.
6a.Climb Bertram's Chimney for 30 ft then traverse left along a break. At its end climb boldly up on hidden holds, past peg runners until a move left brings the relief of a footledge on The Spider; finish as for The Spider.

**26  Bertram's Chimney**   130 feet   Very Difficult   ★
The big chimney right of The Fly. Climb up past a chockstone then traverse right to easy ground. Beware of birds!

**27  Gary Gobstopper**   80 feet   Hard Very Severe
4c.Start 10 ft right of the chimney below a peg. Climb the loose groove to a ledge. Move 15 ft right and climb an overhanging groove. Go left above the peg runner and finish up Bertram's Chimney.

**28  Skylight Flake**   80 feet   Severe
To the right is a cave with a skylight. Crawl out of the skylight onto a grassy ledge. Gain the flake above and go diagonally along the slab above, climbing round a bulge. Scramble off left.

**29  Skylight Groove**   85 feet   Hard Severe
From the skylight traverse right along the grassy ledge to a corner. Climb this, go over a bulge and up a chimney.

The next feature is a large tree-filled gully, LYNX GULLY. At its top is a short wall, invisible from below.

**30  Twm**   75 feet   E2   †
5b.Climb the wall via the thin crackline, moving right at 30 ft. Very loose at the top.

## MANIFOLD VALLEY - BEESTON TOR

At the foot of the gully, a long ridge runs down into the river. Mid-way up the gully, the ridge throws down a large grassy face.

**31 Ocelot Groove** 140 feet Hard Very Difficult
On the left of the face is a clean groove.
1. 80ft. Climb the groove to an ash tree then ascend the wall to a grassy ledge.
2. 60ft. Go up the ridge to a ledge, then a slab and a corner.

**32 The Fox** 165 feet Very Severe
Start 20 feet right.
1. 120ft. Gain a ledge then go up a slab and across an overlap to a ledge. Go up slabs leftwards to a grassy break. Ascend a rib to bushes.
2. 45ft. Climb the crack to the top.

**33 Lynx Wall** 170 feet Severe
Start right of the centre of the face at a short groove below a tree.
1. 20ft. Go up to the tree.
2. 75ft. Climb the flake and go onto a slab. Go up and right to a grassy groove. Belay in a recess.
3. 75ft. Enter the groove, move left to a crack and up.

**34 Lynx Link** †
From the second belay on Lynx Wall, move right across the wall to Throwley Ridge Grooves.

**35 Oakover Grooves** 140 feet Hard Severe
A few yards left of Throwley Ridge Grooves is a prominent 40-foot corner with a large tree at its foot.
1. 65ft. Climb the corner moving right at the top to a tree. Climb easier rock to a stance below a corner in the bushes.
2. 75ft. 4a. The shallow groove, easy at first, leads to a ridge.

**36 Throwley Ridge Grooves** 300 feet Severe
At the foot of the ridge are some obvious grooves.
1. 60ft. Start from a sapling. Go up to the cracks and climb the lefthand one, into a groove and to a ledge.
2. 40ft. Move left into a shallow groove and up to a stance.
3. 200ft. Scramble up the ridge.

**37 Mollusc Wall** 145 feet Very Difficult
25 yards right of Throwley Ridge is a slabby weakness up a grassy buttress.
1. 55ft. Climb the slab to a stance.
2. 90ft. Go up to a tree and pinnacle. Climb the corner behind and continue up the ridge.

# CHURNET VALLEY AREA

## THE LOWER CHURNET VALLEY
by Stephen and Brian Dale

---

SITUATION
These crags are all within 2 miles of Alton, an ancient village with a picturesque castle, 5 miles from Cheadle and 9 miles from Ashbourne. It is one of the most beautiful areas in North Staffordshire.

As a climbing area the bad reputation of the Churnet Valley is well known. Anyone looking for poor rock, pebbles and 'Matto Grosso' will be well pleased with what they find here! However, a few climbs stand out as being worthy of a trip to the valley and are indicated with stars. These and the grades, owing to the nature of the rock cannot be compared realistically with the rest of the climbs in this book, although great efforts have been made to do this. Be warned, there are few easy climbs here and most remain out of condition. Almost without exception the crags are undercut and have considerably overhanging sections.

A narrow lane known locally as the Red Road runs between Alton and Oakmoor and gives a convenient approach to most crags but access is prohibited for 1 mile between the junction of the road running down Stony Dale and the lodge at the foot of Dimmings Dale.

HISTORY
Some of these crags were visited by David Penlington and members of the Oread M.C. in the spring of 1951 but he left no records of any routes. Ina's Chimney and Brad's Chimney on Park Bank Crags had most certainly been climbed prior to Penlington's visit.

Between 1959 and 1963 David Hudson and members of Denstone College C.C. did the majority of the routes on the righthand side of Park Banks Crags including Hollybush Hell, Defiance, Chilton's Superdirect, Left and Right Twin Cracks and the three easier routes to the left. During the same period they visited Wright's Rock and climbed Central Crack and Tunnel Chimney. In early 1969 Austin Plant and John Stubbs of the North Staffs M.C. climbed Spreadeagle on Rainroach. Plant returned later that year with Bob Hassall and climbed The Taxman, The Unveiling and The Fly.

Castle Crag was attacked in January 1970; Hassall, John Yates and Norman Hoskins climbed The Gallows and finished up the

## LOWER CHURNET 79

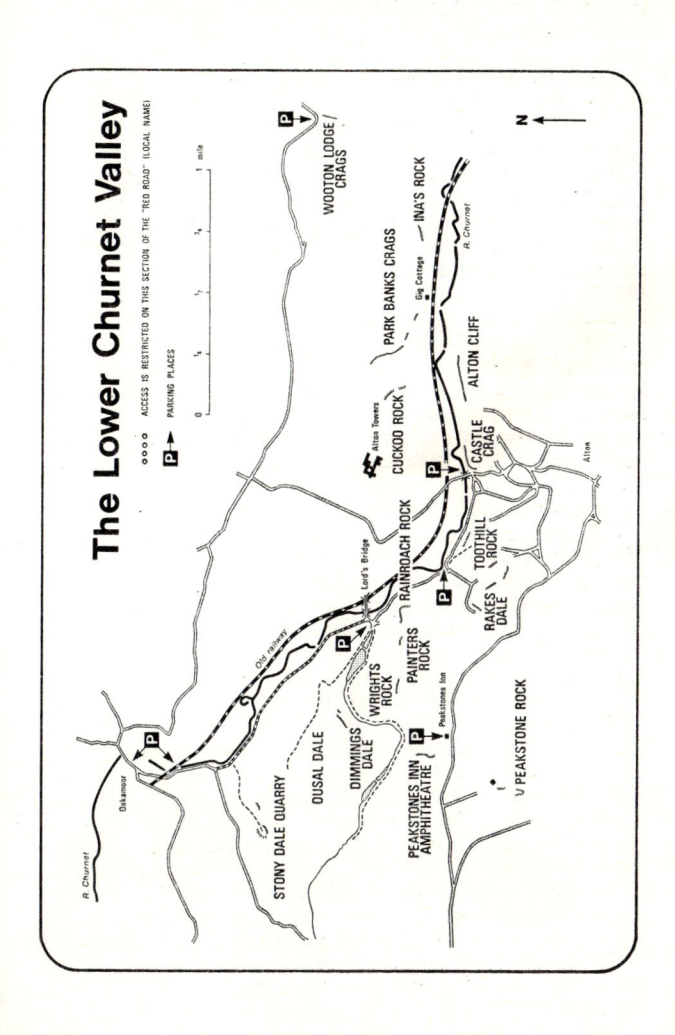

castle wall. Yates led the direct start to Pasiphae, Plant and Hassall did Minotaur and the excellent Labyrinth: Hoskins produced Daedalus and the exit to Theseus. The same group turned to the impressive Ina's Rock. Hoskins led Initiation Groove, Ground Support, Rawhide and Bloody Crack. Hassall led Tactical Weapon and Plant climbed Gladiator. They attacked Atlas which was climbed with a large wooden wedge in the final overhang. Hoskins then climbed Renaissance on Park Banks Crag. The end of spring found them on Wootton Lodge Crags where Hassall found the Long Traverse and Central Route. Hoskins led Ungodly Groove and the party then departed to trundle and dig elsewhere.

1970-71 was a mild winter and in January Yates visited Wright's Rock and led Sauron, The Hob and its variant finish on Tiger's Wall. On the same day he led The Highwayman and Hot Pants on Toothill Rock. Hoskins was back amongst the rhododendrons in February when he led Mark and Stephen on Park Banks Crag. Dave Salt stirred himself from writing up other people's routes and led The Prodigal and Per Rectum. Yates produced Extractum and Honest John on Park Banks and Barry Marsden found Tree Cima.

Yates now moved his attention to Peakstone Rock in April, when he led Peakstone Crack, Stumble Head, Plebble and Marajuander. Marsden was responsible for Afrodizzy Crack. These two spent some time in the undergrowth behind Peakstones Inn producing Scoop Wall, Right Wall, Scout Wall and B.J.M. Hassall put up two new routes on Ina's Rock in April. They were Donor and Amazing Grace.

Hoskins, Salt and Hassall climbed Icarus on Castle Crag. The following week the trio returned and Hoskins led the first pitch of Theseus in a thunderstorm. He then turned on Zeus (perhaps in retaliation) and in almost total darkness forced his way over the overhang using a sling on a large nut in the crack.

Yates, Marsden, Pete Ruddle and Chris Cartlidge visited Wootton Lodge where Yates led the first complete ascent of Ungodly Groove, the very thin Pull John, Quasimodo, Cripple's Corner and Wootton Wanderer. Marsden and Ruddle tried alternately to lead Hanging Crack until Ruddle used a big nut for aid and powered himself over.

Hoskins paid a visit to Alton Cliff and climbed The Brothers. Later with Salt and Ruddle he returned to show his find and Ruddle led (somewhat artificially) Rig a Dig Dig.

In March 1972 Hassall visited Lion Rock and climbed most of the routes. For 2 years following the publication of the old guide little or nothing was climbed in the valley!

In February 1975 Jonny Woodward and his brother Andy attacked Wootton Lodge Crags, removed the aid from Quasimodo and Hanging Crack and added A Phoenix Too Frequent. Later that year the same pair dispensed with the aid on Zeus on Castle Crag, The Fly on Rainroach and Tactical Weapon on Ina's Rock. They were also active on Park Banks at this time. For 2 years another lull in climbing followed until in 1977 when the Woodwards free-climbed Atlas making this and its neighbour Tactical Weapon two of the very best climbs in the valley.

In 1978 Stephen and Brian Dale took on the task of preparing a more detailed guide to the Churnet Valley. Steve Dale along with Barry Marsden found Northern Lights and Dancing Bear behind Peakstones Inn whilst lower down the valley Brian Dale and Ewan Murray climbed Christopher James. In the autumn of 1978 the Woodwards climbed Gentleman John without the aid and also the strenuous Jack The Traverse. They moved onto Alton Cliff and did several hard climbs including a free ascent of the excellent Rig a Dig Dig. Across the river on Park Banks they added the bold Patient Weaver and a few others. The Dales climbed Impacted Bowel on Ousal Crag and Murray was busy on Toothill Rocks producing the awkward Daddy Long Legs.

The winter of 1978-79 was a hard one and it was not until early summer that the area came under attack again. The Dales became obsessed with Dimmings Dale adding over 30 climbs including the excellent Top Brick, Slippery Caramel and Toast Rack. Murray, during the first ascent of The Mexican had a spectacular fall from the lip of the overhang into the bushes below. On Wright's Rock the Woodwards were in action climbing Soar Off, Thorns and the difficult Alternative Three. On nearby Painter's Rock the Dales produced all the present routes whilst the Woodwards did Whispering Myth on Ina's Rock.

Towards the end of the summer the Dales climbed Desert Rat, Dust Storm and Sandbagger in Rakes Dale and then went on to find Stony Dale Quarry. Dance of the Flies was ascended and the quarry was left for the Woodwards to move in. They produced Doina Da J'al, Robin Hood and Friar Muck. On the same day they climbed the desperate Hand Jive on Lions Rock. Jonny Woodward escaped from the valley to climb 5,000 Volts, Dimetrodon and Times Arrow on the more open Peakstone Rock. At the end of a fine spell in May 1980 Steve Dale returned to Stony Dale Quarry and led Cave Crack, the greasy Long Lankin and Little Nick.

82  CHURNET VALLEY

## PARK BANKS CRAGS
O.S. Ref. SK 082429

SITUATION, APPROACH and ACCESS
The crags are on the south side of Alton Park just east of Slain Hollow, ¾ mile from the bridge at Alton. From the north side of the bridge an old railway track can be reached through a works yard and followed for ¾ mile to the old crossing gates. Through the left gate is the derelict Gig Cottage. Walk direct up the bank to a broad path, the Rock Walk, which runs below these crags and Ina's Rock. Park Bank Crags are to the left. No threats to climbing here have been encountered but it seems unlikely that free access on any of the crags in Alton Park would be allowed. The owners have not been approached—let sleeping dogs lie.

CHARACTER
The rock is Keuper Sandstone with bands of Bunter pebbles which tend to disappear when in use.

THE CLIMBS
50 yards right of a 20 foot roof, seen when approaching from Gig Cottage, is an overgrown crag.

**1  Coelred's Crack**   30 feet   Hard Very Severe
5a. The obvious crack is climbed direct.

The climbs are now described from Right to Left starting immediately left of the 20-foot roof.

**2  Holly Bush Hell**   30 feet   Severe
Climb the wide crack left of the roof past a holly bush to a pleasant slab.

**3  Defiance**   30 feet   Severe   ★★★
The narrow slab on the left is gained from the corner or from the left. An excellent introduction to the crag.

**4  Chilton's Superdirect**   30 feet   Very Severe
4b. Start at the 5-foot corner to the left. Go direct to a small ledge at 15 ft then go up the groove until a move right onto the arete of Defiance can be made. It is possible to move left from the groove to a ledge at 4c.

**5  Alien Wall**   30 feet   Hard Very Severe
5b. Climb from the depression 5 ft left with difficulty to a hard landing on the upper shelf. Finish up to the left.

## LOWER CHURNET

**6  Right Twin Crack**  30 feet  Severe  ★
The jamming crack to the left is interesting.

**7  Left Twin Crack**  30 feet  Severe
Not as easy as it looks! There are two possible exits.

**8  The Height Below**  30 feet  Hard Very Severe
5c. The arete 6 ft left is hard to start. Finish up a crack just right of Renaissance.

**9  The Renaissance**  30 feet  Very Severe  ★★
4c. The thin crack to the left. Delicate, strenuous and superb.

**10  Anthem for a Doomed Youth**  30 feet  E3
5c. Start 10 ft left and climb right to the arete then back left to a sandy ledge. Go up the wall above on poor holds.

**11  Easy Chimney**  25 feet  Moderate

**12  Blunder**  25 feet  Difficult
The tree root in the layback crack provides excellent holds.

**13  Uchimata**  25 feet  Difficult
Dirty but straightforward climbing up the crack to the left.

**14  Four Horsemen**  30 feet  E2
5c. The crack to the left is hard to start and leads to a break. Move up the nose on small holds.

50 yards left is a buttress with a superb chimney. Right of this is a steep wall with a broken arete.

**15  Honest John**  60 feet  Hard Very Severe
5a. Start on the right of the wall and traverse left strenuously then go up to a rhododendron runner. Above this go awkwardly right then straight up past a bush to a good slab and the top.

**16  Brad's Chimney**  60 feet  Very Difficult  ★★★
The obvious magnificent chimney.

**17  Patient Weaver**  65 feet  E5  ★
6a. Go up the small corner at the right end of the wall on the left for a few feet then out left to gain ledges; fingery. Go up these then left up a scooped wall to a good hold and a long reach to finish. A serious and unprotected lead.

## 84 CHURNET VALLEY

**18 The Overhang** 60 feet  E1
At the left end of the face is a block overhang with a ledge out on the right.
5b.Move up and swing onto the ledge on the right. Continue up the crumbling wall to a tree-bound ledge. Finish up the cracks on the right. Another poorly protected climb.

100 yards towards Alton Towers is a nose with a steep groove on the right side (not visible from the path).

**19 Tree Cima** 25 feet  Very Severe
4b.The groove is strenuous but at 10 ft go left using two stumps. Climb the nose and wall using a root to gain the top.

**20 Per Rectum** 30 feet  Very Severe
4b.The layback crack to the left using tree stumps is quite good.

**21 Extractum** 30 feet  Hard Very Severe
5b.The wet wall 5 ft left has some good holds and a hard move to gain a tree. Lasso a stump above the overhang. Use it with difficulty.

**22 Mark** 25 feet  Severe
The corner round to the left using trees on the overhang.

**23 Stark** 25 feet  Very Difficult
Climb Mark for 10 ft then left onto a ledge. Finish up the slab.

**24 Stephen** 25 feet  Very Severe
4a.The corner crack on the left. The final moves are awkward.

**25 Dark Star** 30 feet  E3
5c.The steep arete to the left is climbed with difficulty.

The crags continue towards Alton Towers though they have little to offer the climber. However, on the opposite side of Slain Hollow in Alton Towers' grounds is **CUCKOO ROCK**, O.S. Ref. SK 077429. It is well hidden from view except during winter. Approach from the bridge over the Churnet below the Castle. Walk through the works yard and down the railway for about 200 yards, then go over a fence on the left and up the steep hill going rightwards. A track runs below the Rock. This overhanging crag has **Rickshaw** an A2 with unsafe bolts.

## INA'S ROCK
O.S. Ref. SK 087429

SITUATION, APPROACH and ACCESS
The crag is 1 mile from the Churnet bridge in Alton on the eastern extremity of Alton Park. From Gig Cottage a good path runs north east for 300 yards to join Rock Walk which is followed east to the Rock. Care must be taken not to offend anyone.

CHARACTER
The rock is extremely steep and has a big chimney in its south-west face. The rock is Keuper Sandstone and is a little firmer than its westerly neighbour.

THE CLIMBS are described from Left to Right.

**1  Rawhide**  25 feet  Severe
The small chimney hidden in the trees left of the huge chimney.

**2  Gladiator**  30 feet  Very Severe
4b.The bulging crack to the right is quite hard.

**3  Donor**  40 feet  Severe
Climb the scoop on the right to a tree. Continue right to a corner finish.

**4  Amazing Grace**  80 feet  Very Severe
4c.Climb a shallow groove right of Donor until a traverse right to a stance. Climb the wall above past a peculiar hole then traverse right to Ina's Chimney finishing outside the chockstone.

**5  Ina's Chimney**  70 feet  Severe                           ★★
An excellent expedition into the bowels of the crag.

**6  Atlas**  80 feet  E2                                        ★★★
To the right is a stone pillar. Round the corner to the right a fierce crack splits the crag from top to bottom.
1. 5b.The crack is climbed out of the cave to a good ledge.
2. 5c.Climb over the roof with difficulty and up the easier crack above. Superb. One of the best climbs in the area.

**7  Ground Support**  75 feet  Hard Very Severe                 ★★
5b.Climb the thin crack just right of the cave to a bush. The wide crack above is not as hard as it looks. A good pitch.

86 CHURNET VALLEY

**8 Whispering Myth**  70 feet  E2 ★
1. 6a. Climb Ground Support for 10 ft. Traverse right to gain a faint line going left which is followed with difficulty to a bolt. Traverse right to a stance and belay.
2. 5a. Climb the thin crack left of the finish of Tactical Weapon.

**9 Tactical Weapon**  65 feet  Hard Very Severe ★★★
5b. From the ledge on the corner of the face climb cracks and rugosities to a small tree. The crack above is climbed to the top. Another magnificent piece of climbing.

**10 Initiation Groove**  35 feet  Very Severe
4b. Climb the groove round the corner to the right with help from a convenient tree.

**11 Bloody Crack**  20 feet  Very Severe
4b. The crack in the buttress 50 yards right is climbed direct to a ledge escaping right. The upper crack remains unclimbed.

**12 Crud On The Tracks,** Hard Very Severe is a girdle of the main crag.

# WOOTTON LODGE CRAGS
O.S. Ref. SK 095435

SITUATION, APPROACH and ACCESS
The crags are on a wooded hillside overlooking a farm track opposite the gates of Wootton Lodge. The entrance to the Lodge is 1½ miles along the lane from Farley to Ellastone. Farley is 1 mile north of Alton. Opposite the Lodge gates at an entrance to a cave is a small space for parking. Climb the hillside immediately right of the cave and then cross the ferny hill to the right of the crag. Although no problems have ever arisen, it is unlikely that climbing would be allowed.

CHARACTER
The crag is divided into two separate buttresses by a fern-clad slope. The left buttress is undercut in its centre and has steep walls on its extremes. The right buttress is undercut in its entirety and has a break running across at 20 feet.

THE CLIMBS on the main crag are described from Left to Right.

LEFT BUTTRESS
Up the hill above and left of the buttress is a small isolated rock with a tree. There are two Severes up the left and right of this.

## LOWER CHURNET 87

**1 Ungodly Groove** 30 feet E1
5b. The hanging groove on the left side is extremely strenuous.

**2 Central Route** 40 feet Very Severe ★★
4b. Climb the steep wall diagonally right to a ledge then traverse right to the foot of a crack. Climb this to the top. Good climbing.

**3 Pull John** 50 feet E4
6a. Climb the arete with difficulty moving right to a ledge. Go up the wall 15 ft right of the overhanging upper arete gradually moving left at the top. A serious undertaking with some poor rock.

**4 Quasimodo** 40 feet E2 ★
6a. Ascend the crack with difficulty over the overhang to the ledge and finish up the crack above.

**5 Cripple's Corner** 35 feet Very Severe
4b. From the extreme right of the crag traverse left up the bulging wall to a ledge. Finish up the crack on the right.

**6 Wootton Wanderer** 80 feet Very Severe
4c. Start on the left side of the crag and traverse right below the crux of Ungodly Groove to the large ledge on the corner. From the left end of the ledge go diagonally right finishing up Quasimodo.

Across the fern-covered bank 100 yards away is RIGHT BUTTRESS.

**7 The Long Traverse** 100 feet Very Difficult ★★★
Start at the left side and traverse right at 20 ft. A fine climb.

**8 A Phoenix Too Frequent** 40 feet E3 ★★
5c. From just left of Hanging Crack make a fingery traverse left to gain the upper wall which leads easily to the top. A good pitch.

**9 Hanging Crack** 30 feet Hard Very Severe ★★
5b. The overhanging crack is hard and strenuous but easier above the traverse line. A superb climb.

# CASTLE CRAG
O.S. Ref. SK 073425

SITUATION, APPROACH and ACCESS
The crag is directly below the Castle in Alton, overlooking the bridge over the River Churnet. On the south side of the bridge opposite the entrance to the Talbot Inn a track leads to Cliff Farm Cottage. Once inside the gateway turn right and head direct up the hill to the crag. The crag is on private land but small parties have met no opposition to climbing.

CHARACTER
Undercut for most of its length the crag has overhangs of various sizes topping the majority of the perpendicular walls. An obvious break crosses the crag at 35 feet.

THE CLIMBS are described from Right to Left. At the right end a metal pipe runs down a corner. Left of this is an arete, then a wall.

**1 Daedalus** 30 feet Very Severe
4a.Climb the arete direct to the top.

**2 Minos** 30 feet Very Severe
4c.Start 5 ft left of the arete and follow a crackline finishing just left of a tree.

**3 Minotaur** 45 feet Very Severe ★★
4c.The bent crack on the left is followed to a thread at 25 ft. From the top of the crack go right into a chimney. Climb this; finish left.

**4 Theseus** 55 feet Hard Very Severe ★
5c.Climb the wall 10 ft left of Minotaur then traverse right to below a sloping groove. Climb the crack in the sloping groove moving left at the top.

**5 Icarus** 50 feet Hard Very Severe ★★
5b.Layback the wide crack to the left to a difficult landing on the ledge on the right. Finish up the flake and wall above. Strenuous.

**6 Zeus** 50 feet E1
5b.Bridge up the cave on the left and swing right using a tree. Climb the overhanging crack with difficulty. Finish up a dirty gully.

## 7  Pasiphae   70 feet   Severe
From the tree on Zeus move up the groove to the right to the stomach-traverse ledge. Along this and through a slot to the junction with The Gallows. Left again 15 ft to a groove. Climb this to a belay. Abseil from the elder on the left. The climb can be done direct at 4b by moving left from the cave on Zeus and climbing a thin crack and wall on its left to reach the traverse.

## 8  The Gallows   50 feet   Hard Very Severe
5b. Climb vertical cracks above the opposite entrance to the keyhole cave with difficulty and pain. Finish up the steep upper crack by laybacking. Belay on the left. Abseil left off the stance.

## 9  The Labyrinth   250 feet   Very Severe   ★★★
It is possible to belay in various places on this tremendous climb and it is therefore described in one. 4c. Go up the corner by the pipe at the right end of the crag for 20 ft then go left past the arete and across with difficulty to Minotaur. Left again to Theseus. Descend 8 ft to a good foothold and go left for 6 ft then up to a wide horizontal crack. Traverse 20 ft left and gain a vertical position. Continue round to a good ledge. Step down and stomach traverse to the flake on Icarus. Climb this to the gully. 5a, descend the gully and swing left with difficulty to a shelf. Traverse this finishing at the abseil on The Gallows.

300 yards left of the Castle is a buttress which must be approached from the farm track below so as to cause no offence to the occupants of the Castle. Left of the block overhang on the right half of the crag is a ledge at 30 ft.

## 10  The Prodigal   50 feet   Hard Very Severe
5b. Start below the ledge with a hard move onto a small ledge on the right. Climb a crack to its top and traverse left with difficulty to the ledge. Finish up the dirty corner using a tree root.

## 11  The Graduate   45 feet   Hard Severe
Climb the slab with interest to a small ledge. Continue up the crack.

**ALTON CLIFF** is ¼ mile left. The climbs are described from Left to Right.

## 1  Rig A Dig Dig   35 feet   Hard Very Severe   ★★★
5c. Climb the short groove left of the large roof at the left end of the crag. Traverse strenuously right below the roof to an easier finish up the crack, grass and wall above. A superb pitch.

**2  The Brothers**  40 feet   Hard Very Severe
5a. Climb the pebbly arete 15 ft right to a horizontal crack. Make a hard move up left to a good hold and continue right of the tree finishing up the slab above.

**3  To Live Again**  30 feet   E3                                    ★
5c. Move left to the undercut arete left of the crack in the steep wall on the right and follow it until it eases.

**4  Transit Crack**  30 feet   Severe
Climb the crack to the top.

**5  Down To The Elbows**  30 feet   E3
6a. The ferocious overhanging off-width crack to the right of the gully right of Transit Crack.

**6  Pull Jonny**  30 feet   Hard Very Severe                    ★★
5b. The excellent crack 30 ft right of Down To The Elbows is climbed to its top. Step right and go up to the tree.

## TOOTHILL ROCK
O.S. Ref. SK 068425

SITUATION, APPROACH and ACCESS
The Rock occupies a position ½ mile west of Alton Castle. From The Talbot follow the Red Road for ½ mile to a sharp right bend in the road. It is possible to park here. A path climbs steeply through the wood on the left. This leads to the top of Toothill Rock. There are no access problems here.

CHARACTER
The crags are pebbly with a fair amount of vegetation in parts.

THE CLIMBS are described from Right to Left starting at Toothill Rock, which has a huge overhang at the right end.

**1  The Highwayman**  60 feet   Very Severe                    ★
1. 35ft.4b. The crack left of the roof is climbed to a large ledge.
2. 25ft.4a. Climb the wall past a small tree to the top.

**2  Hot Pants**  60 feet   Very Severe
4c. Start 6 ft right of the arete on the left and ascend the wall. Move left onto the arete, make some hard moves right and go left onto a ledge. Finish up the groove in the wall.

**3 Droopy Draws** 40 feet  Hard Severe
The jamming crack to the left.

**4 Tyre Pressure** 35 feet  Severe ★
To the left on the upper tier of the crag near the centre of the face is a short corner. Climb the corner, swing right, go up the wall and make an awkward move to gain the break. Traverse left to ledges.

**5 Parking Fine** 15 feet  Very Severe
4c.The wall left of the short corner, trend left and over a small bulge.

**6 Ants' Corner** 25 feet Very Severe
Further left is a huge pebbly roof with a corner crack on the left.
4a.The corner is most difficult near the top.

**7 Uncle's Arete** 25 feet  Very Severe
4b.Climb the arete on the left. The top gives the crux.

**8 Daddy Long Legs** 35 feet  Hard Very Severe ★
200 yards past several buttresses is an obvious crack.
5b.Ascend the crumbling wall to the crack. Make a hard move to gain good jams in the roof. The exit is awkward.

# RAKES DALE
O.S. Ref. SK 066424

SITUATION, APPROACH and ACCESS
A small dale ½ mile west of Alton Castle. From the sharp bend in the Red Road described in the approach to Toothill a sandy track runs into Rakes Dale. Follow this for 200 yards to a bend where another track goes off left. After 100 yards along this a gate is reached. For the crags on the left bank go along the track for 25 yards then break off left up the hill to the crag. For the crags on the right bank go discreetly over the fence on the right of the gate and climb straight up the hill to Rakes Dale Wall. The crags on the left bank are on land owned by Austin Plant (a climber who was actively involved in the early development of the Churnet). He is willing to allow climbing. Crags on the right bank are on land owned by a farmer in Rakes Dale who does not appear to mind climbers on his property, although he has not been approached.

THE CLIMBS are described from Left to Right starting on the left bank.

## AUSTIN'S CRAG

The crag is split into two buttresses by a fern-covered bank. The left one is very steep and has no climbs. On the left of the righthand buttress is a short dirty corner. 15 ft right is a flake at 10 feet.

**1  Dust Storm**  30 feet  Hard Very Severe  ★
5a. Climb direct to the flake then traverse left for 6 ft. Go over the bulge with difficulty past a tree. Finish up a short crack.

**2  Sandbagger**  40 feet  Hard Very Severe
5a. The tree-filled crack to the right is climbed for 15 ft. Traverse delicately left to a shallow corner and finish trending left to the top.

**3  Austin's Chimney**  30 feet  Moderate
The clean chimney/gully to the right.

**4  Desert Rat**  30 feet  Hard Very Severe  ★
5a. Climb the short hanging corner in the right wall of the chimney. Short but excellent.

**5  White Mouse**  30 feet  Very Difficult
Start at some chipped holds 20 ft right and climb to the break. Traverse left with an awkward step to gain the foot of the chimney.

The main buttress on the right bank is composed of a long, steep undercut wall—RAKES DALE WALL. This impressive wall does not sport any climbs but at the right end there is a good clean chimney.

**6  Rakes Dale Chimney**  30 feet  Hard Very Severe
5a. Ivy on the right is used to gain the chimney; hard to start.

The crags to the right are short and vegetated, but 400 yards right along the rim of the dale a steep and clean crag is worth mentioning. A slab on its right has several possibilities.

## RAINROACH ROCK
O.S. Ref. SK 063430

SITUATION, APPROACH and ACCESS
This impressive rock is ¾ mile west-north-west of Alton Castle. From the sharp bend in the Red Road previously described, walk a few yards along the road to a track that runs behind Holm

## LOWER CHURNET 93

Cottage and parallel to the road. The track goes below the crag.
After 400 yards along it fight dense undergrowth uphill to the
foot of the rock. No access difficulties here so far.

CHARACTER
The very steep rock is excellent but the crag is split by several
ledges each with an abundance of bushes.

THE CLIMBS: At the right end of the crag is an obvious
groove, which is the start of the first two climbs.

**1  Spreadeagle   60 feet   Severe**
Climb the groove to a good ledge. Go up the corner above to a
grassy ledge then walk 5 ft along this and climb the wall above,
finishing with a mantleshelf move.

**2  The Taxman   80 feet   Hard Very Severe**   ★
5a. As for Spreadeagle to the ledge. Climb the slab for 5 ft then
go 15 ft left to a bush. Swing across the corner and onto a ledge.
Climb up over another ledge and stomach-traverse right to an
overhanging corner. Finish up this with difficulty.

**3  The Unveiling   55 feet   Very Severe**
4b. Start 15 ft left and climb the steep wall to a ledge. Walk left
to an overhanging crack and climb it to its top. Go 5 ft right and
jam the final crack. The climb can be finished direct.

**4  Pebble Drop   60 feet   Hard Very Difficult**
Start at the base of the slab in the centre of the crag and climb
to a tree at 20 ft. Step right and climb a groove to a ledge. Climb
a crack at the back of the ledge.

**5  Climb To The Lost World   90 feet   Severe/A1**
Start just past the left edge of the central slab and climb a
vegetated crack to a ledge at 30 ft. Climb the overhanging crack
above using 3 aid pegs. Traverse 30 ft left and climb a crack.

**6  The Fly   35 feet   E1**   ★
5b. On the extreme left side of the crag is an overhanging wall
below a flake crack. Climb the wall and the flake.

94  CHURNET VALLEY

## PEAKSTONE INN AMPHITHEATRE
O.S. Ref. SK 055428

### SITUATION, APPROACH and ACCESS
A rectangular amphitheatre of crags behind the Peakstone Inn on the south side of Dimmings Dale. The best approach is from the Peakstone Inn on the Cheadle-Ashbourne road, B5032. The first crag on the left side is below the car park at the southern end of the amphitheatre. The car park has been used by climbers for many years without objection as have the other facilities of the inn. Perhaps the latter justifies the former. No access problems.

### CHARACTER
The rock is fairly firm but often green and damp.

**THE CLIMBS** are described from Left to Right on the LEFT side, and from Right to Left on the RIGHT side of the amphitheatre.

### LEFT-HAND SIDE OF THE AMPHITHEATRE
**1  Northern Lights**   45 feet   Severe ★★
The obvious line running left to right on the crag below the car park is followed to an awkward step onto a ledge. Finish up the arete.

100 yards right past a small buttress is THE BACK WALL.

**2  Dancing Bear**   55 feet   Hard Very Severe ★
1. 25ft.4b. Climb the slabby corner at the right end of the crag to a shelf. Go left to a huge thread belay.
2. 30ft.5a. Gain a standing position on the ledge, step left and climb the steep wall to a break. Mantleshelf out right onto a ledge and finish straight up. Airy.

The remaining climbs on this side are all situated across a slight gully and fern-clad bank to the right on the most northern point of the left side of the amphitheatre.

**3  Chockstone Crack**   25 feet   Severe ★★
The obvious crack at the left end of the crag is pleasant.

**4  Scoop Wall**   30 feet   Very Severe
4c. The centre of the concave wall on the left is climbed on small holds.

**5 Right Wall**  45 feet   Hard Very Severe  ★
5a.Start from a vegetated ledge 30 ft right. Climb the wall on good holds to a flake. Ascend this to a good ledge then go diagonally right and up the steep wall to the top.

**6 B.J.M.**  25 feet   Very Severe  ★
200 yards right is a small buttress with a steep crack.
4b.Direct up the crack and narrow chimney above.

**7 Scunt Wall**  20 feet   Very Severe
4b.Climb the wall just left of the crack.

## RIGHT-HAND SIDE OF THE AMPHITHEATRE
From below the car park cross the small stream and go diagonally across the bank to a small group of crags. The right end of the wall has several short problems and eventually becomes very overhanging at the left end terminating in an arete.

**8 Himac**  20 feet   A1
An aid route through the overhangs right of the arete.

**9 Onne Dunne**  20 feet   Very Difficult  ★
The pleasant arete to the left.
The excellent wall to the left is as yet unclimbed.

**10 Dead Tree Slab**  30 feet   Difficult  ★★
The pleasant slab at the left end with a dead tree stump at its base.

**11 Dead Tree Crack**  30 feet   Very Difficult
The crack to the left is awkward at first. Finish up the arete.

# WRIGHT'S ROCK
O.S. Ref. SK 058430

## SITUATION, APPROACH and ACCESS
The crag overlooks open fields high above Dimmings Dale. Follow the path past the crags on the right side of the amphitheatre round the corner. Wright's Rock can be seen overlooking the fields below. No objections have been made to climbing on this crag.

## CHARACTER
The rock is superior to most in the Churnet being sound and compact. It is generally steep and undercut.

**THE CLIMBS** are described from Left to Right starting at a cave.

**1 Stonemason's Route**  45 feet  Hard Very Difficult  ★★
From the cave go up and left to a good ledge. The wall above is quite hard. A good climb.

**2 Sauron**  30 feet  Hard Very Severe  ★★★
5a. The excellent corner to the right is climbed by bridging and laybacking to an awkward exit.

**3 Soar Off**  30 feet  Hard Very Severe  ★
5b. The green arete to the right.

**4 Sculptor's Wall**  40 feet  Very Severe
4a. The wall on the right to a large ledge. Finish up the wall above.

**5 Central Crack**  45 feet  Difficult
The obvious deep cleft to the right.

**6 Thorns**  40 feet  E2  ★★
5b. Start in a recess 15 ft right of the crack. Climb the overhanging corner to the ledge. Climb thin flakes just right of the tree and over the bulge into the wide crack to finish. A little friable.

**7 Alternative Three**  40 feet  E4  ★★
6a. Start 20 ft right of Thorns. Overcome the 15 ft undercut using a thin flake on the final horizontal section. Move left onto the overhanging wall just above the lip to a short layback flake. Finish more easily up this, and the wall above. A fine climb.

**8 Tunnel Chimney**  25 feet  Difficult
Start up either side of the slab on the right finishing up the dirty chimney above.

**9 The Hob**  25 feet  Very Severe
To the right of the chimney is an undercut sloping ledge.
4b. Go up the left side of the ledge to the right. Make a hard mantleshelf onto it. Traverse 6 ft right and finish up the bulging wall. It is possible to go left from the ledge and up a groove at HVS, 5a.

**10 Tiger's Wall**  20 feet  Very Severe
Further right is a fence. Above this is an upper tier.
4b. Start below the highest point on the face and climb direct to the top. The start is the most difficult.

**11  Ugly Puss**   20 feet   Very Severe
4b. Climb up to an obvious flake left of Tiger's Wall. Continue to the top using the flake.

300 yards east of Wright's Rock at the same level is **PAINTER'S ROCK**, O.S. Ref. SK 061430. The rock is not as firm as Wright's Rock being slightly sandier and a lot more pebbly. There are two buttresses, the first, as one approaches from Wright's Rock, is very overhanging with a pebbly base and although the upper wall is sound, only the climber with suicidal tendencies would attempt to gain it. This buttress falls back into a short corner dividing the two crags. The second buttress is fairly sound and is split by a large corner in the centre and left of this is a short upper tier. The climbs are described from right to left as one would normally approach them from Wright's Rock.

**1  Recess Corner**   20 feet   Very Difficult
The short corner left of the first buttress.

**2  Working Hunter**   50 feet   Hard Very Severe
5a. Go up the slab of the next buttress, climbing just right of the arete to a good ledge below the overhang. Climb cracks through this to a ledge. Traverse left to a tree and up a root-filled crack.

**3  Rabbit Stew**   55 feet   E2   ★
5b. Climb the groove 10 ft left delicately to a good hold at 15 ft. Go left to a flake and up this to a bulge. Make a hard move over this to a peg runner. Another difficult section follows until it is possible to go left to the top of Bright Eyes.

**4  Bright Eyes**   50 feet   E1
5b. Start 40 ft to the left and follow the faint crack into the final corner which is surprisingly hard.

**5  Glossy Finish**   30 feet   Very Severe   ★
Left of the next vegetated section is an upper tier. Start just left of the centre.
4c. Strenuously to a good ledge on the right. Climb the wall above with a long reach to finish.

**6  Undercoat**   35 feet   Hard Very Severe
6a. Go up to below the roof on the right. Traverse right round the corner finishing with a difficult mantleshelf just right of the arete. The nose has been climbed on a top rope.

## PEAKSTONE ROCK
O.S. Ref. SK 052422

SITUATION, APPROACH and ACCESS
The crag is on the side of a shallow hollow on Alton Common, 3 miles east of Cheadle. It is best approached from Cheadle on the B5032. 1 mile on the Alton side of the Highwayman Inn a farm track leads off right. This leads past a bungalow to an old farmhouse at the end. The crag is across the field on the right 400 yards away. Permission must be sought from the bungalow; so far this has always been granted.

CHARACTER
This peculiar group of rocks is in the form of a small ridge with crags on three sides. The east side is overhanging and loose, the south side is a steep face with an overhanging crack and the west face is a bulging wall with a pinnacle halfway along.

THE CLIMBS are described from Right to Left starting at the wall on the right of the south face.

**1  Stumblehead**   30 feet   Very Severe
4b. Step off the wall and climb the face bearing slightly left. A finish has been made going right at half-height climbing the hairline crack on poor holds. Hard Very Severe, 5a.

**2  Peakstone Crack**   30 feet   Very Severe
4c. The obvious crack with some hard moves over the bulge.

**3  Marajuander**   35 feet   Very Severe
4c. Up Peakstone Crack for 20 ft then traverse left with difficulty under the bulge to a thin crack. Continue round the arete and cross the wall to another crack. Finish up this.

**4  Dimetrodon**   30 feet   E3
5c. Climb the shallow groove to the left of the crack to the break. Go left 30 ft and climb the final wall on small holds. Unprotected.

**5  Plebble**   30 feet   Hard Very Severe
5b. Climb the wall with difficulty to the thin crack on Marajuander. Follow this to the top.

**6  Five Thousand Volts**   25 feet   Hard Very Severe   ★★
5a. The excellent wall round the corner is climbed direct starting 10 ft right of Afrodizzy Crack.

**7 Afrodizzy Crack**  25 feet  Very Severe  ★★
4c. Climb the crack laybacking round the final bulge.

**8 Times Arrow**  30 feet  E1  ★★
5b. Climb the slight scoop 10 ft left of the crack. Go left to a break below the roof. Move 5 ft left and pull over using a jug. Finish up the slab. A good pitch.

**9 Back Side**  15 feet  Hard Severe
The pinnacle above the crack to the left is climbed up its short side on large holds to an awkward finish. The pinnacle has been girdled in both directions at Severe.

# DIMMINGS DALE
O.S. Ref. SK 062432 to 045436

SITUATION, APPROACH and ACCESS
A fine wooded dale running down to the south side of the River Churnet at Lord's Bridge, 1 mile upstream from Alton. It is best approached from the Red Road. 1 mile from Alton Castle is a Lodge at the foot of the dale opposite Lord's Bridge. Cars can be parked here. The Serpentine Drive follows a stream up the south side of the dale passing several ponds. There are crags scattered all over the dale so the approaches are included in the description of the individual crags. Most of the buttresses are hard to find on the first visit. No access problems have been encountered.

CHARACTER
The rock varies considerably from crag to crag; pebbly and sandy rock is prominent although some buttresses are quite sound such as Lord's Buttress.

THE CLIMBS: at the lowest of the ponds is a gate. A small valley runs down from the left and at the top of the right bank of this valley, obscured by trees is a vegetated buttress. Right of this is FISHERMAN'S CRAG.

**1 Fisherman's Crack**  25 feet  Severe
The crack in the centre of the wall on the left of the buttress.

**2 Basket**  35 feet  Very Severe
4c. The front face is steeper. Go up the short wall then right below the block and up the right side to gain its top. Reach the top using roots. The crack has been climbed direct at 5a.

Near the top end of the pool, about 200 yards from the gate, take a direct line through the trees and bushes. SMELTING MILL BUTTRESS can be seen through the undergrowth. At the left end of the crag is a short dirty corner with a large tree to its right.

**3  Slip Knot**   70 feet   Hard Very Severe
5b. Climb the corner for 10 ft then follow the break delicately right to the arete. Climb this to a horizontal crack which is traversed right across the overhanging wall in a fine position.

**4  Dimmingsdale Crack**   55 feet   E1   ★★
5b. The fine chimney crack to the right is climbed direct with two very hard sections.

**5  Iron Ore**   70 feet   Hard Very Severe
30 ft right in the centre of the wall is a flake at 10 ft.
5b. Gain the flake and pull onto a good foot ledge. Traverse left for 10 ft then up with difficulty to good ledges. Go right across the ledge to a good pocket, reach the break using this and step left below the bulge. Climb direct over this and finish with an awkward mantleshelf.

**6  Green Slab**   70 feet   Hard Very Severe
20 ft right is the Moac Block. Up the bank right of this is a good slab.
5a. Climb easily up the slab to below twin cracks. Traverse left and onto the ledge below the bulge on Iron Ore. Finish up this.

**7  The Mexican**   35 feet   Hard Very Severe   ★★
To the right a short corner leads to the upper section of the crag. A superb crack splits the overhang.
5b. Ascend to the roof and follow the crack to the lip using good flakes. Make a hard move over this and finish up the wide crack.

**8  Chocolate Orange**   20 feet   Very Severe
4c. The corner just right of The Mexican is delicate and mossy.

**9  Twiggy**   20 feet   Severe
4a. The steep crack up the right wall of the gully is awkward.

**10  Fagen**   25 feet   Severe   ★
Climb the steep crack on the front face by laybacking.

From the top of Fagen looking down on the left a big fir tree can be seen. A crag near this gives a good climb. Hard to find.

**11 Christmas Tree Crack**   25 feet   Very Severe

4b. Start just left of the tree and step left into the steep crack.

On the right side of the drive 250 yards from the gate is a short section of fence. A direct line taken from the fence up through the trees and bushes leads to LORD'S BUTTRESS, a fine crag clear of undergrowth, with excellent rock and several classic routes. From the drive it is totally obscured by trees. The routes are described from left to right. At the far left end is a 10 foot wall with some hard problems. Above and right is an overhanging buttress with a hole at half height. Right of this is a steep cracked gully.

**12 Slippery Caramel**   55 feet   E2   ★★

1. 25ft. Climb the gully to a belay at a bush.
2. 30ft.5b. Climb the short overhanging crack to a ledge. Using a pocket in the wall left of the corner climb the arete of the corner. Move right at its top to a ledge. Wide crack finish.

**13 Christopher James**   60 feet   Very Severe

1. 25ft.4b. The steep crack 10 ft right of the gully to a ledge.
2. 35ft.4a. From the right end of the ledge traverse right to the foot of the chimney.

**14 Lord's Arete**   60 feet   E3   ★

5c. 15 ft right is an arete; just round this is a shallow groove. Climb this to a sandy ledge. Move up the arete and make a hard move up the wall to a sling. Use this to gain the break. Swing left onto the hanging arete. Continue with difficulty to the top.

**15 Top Brick**   45 feet   Hard Very Severe   ★★★

5a. Reverse the last few feet of Christopher James to below two obvious pockets. Use these and make a long reach to the right end of a shallow cave. Trend left to a good thread then go diagonally right to finish over a pocketed bulge. A fine route on good rock.

**16 Lord's Chimney**   30 feet   Very Difficult

Climb the chimney on the outside by good bridging.

**17 Reverse Charge**   40 feet   Very Severe

4b. 30 ft right of the chimney is a green corner. Traverse left along the break from the corner to the arete. Pull up using a flake, step left and continue direct to the top.

## 102 CHURNET VALLEY

**18 Toast Rack** 100 feet Very Severe ★★★
1. 40ft.4b.Climb the green corner right of the last route for 10 ft. Go left to the arete. Continue round to a belay in the chimney.
2. 60ft.4b.Follow the break across the steep wall and onto the front face. Traverse delicately left and onto a large ledge. Walk off left. An excellent climb with a well-positioned crux.

**19 Rhody Crack** 25 feet Very Difficult
Further right is a small buttress. Start under the prow at the right side. Climb swinging left onto the lower prow. Mantleshelf to finish.

150 yards up the drive from the fence below Lord's Buttress, direct through the bushes is PEBBLE BUTTRESS, a very sandy crag with an abundance of pebbles. On the right of the crag is a slab with a crack.

**20 Grott** 25 feet Difficult
The slab and crack to the trees. Interesting.

170 yards further up the drive at a large boulder on the left directly through the trees is LONG CRAG which consists of four buttresses each split by a gully. The left crag is loose and has no climbs. The central part of the crag has an easy break at 15 feet with an excellent slab on its left.

**21 Root Slab** 30 feet Severe
Climb the tree roots in the gully for a few feet and follow the break right to the arete up which the climb finishes.

To the right is a long wall 15 feet high, steep and clean. Right of the wall at a lower level the small buttress has one route.

**22 Drop Leaf** 20 feet Hard Severe
4a.Climb the groove in the roof left of the obvious boulder and gain the break. Traverse left and finish up trees in the arete.

GENTLEMAN'S ROCK can be seen up in the trees on the left of the first of the upper ponds when walking the Serpentine Drive.

**23 Gentleman John** 45 feet E3 ★★
6a.The overhanging crack is difficult to huge jugs. Climb the slabby crack above avoiding the final overhang on the right.

**24 Jack the Traverse** 100 feet E3
5b. A girdle from left to right along the bottom breaks at 15 ft.
Start from a boulder on the left and traverse ascending gradually
as far as Gentleman John. Finish up this.

The next climbs will require extensive cleaning before an ascent.

**25 Lady Jane** 45 feet Very Severe
5a. Start below the large birch tree above the slab on the right.
Traverse left 15 ft and continue direct up sandy ledges.

**26 Bill the Bandit** 30 feet E1
5b. Start as for Lady Jane but go direct to the birch tree.

A broad track follows the right bank of the lowest pond. Follow
this keeping to the lower track where the path forks. Continue
past the old smelting mill cottages to a small brick outhouse on
the left. Just beyond this a path cuts up through the trees; take
this and after 50 yards go right up the hill. EARL'S ROCK
appears in the trees just past the second of two large pine trees.
It is covered in ivy at the right end with a large 'hermit's' cave on
the left. A wide crack gives:

**27 Maloof** 20 feet Hard Very Severe
5b. Gain the ledge and climb the awkward crack above.

Follow the path from Earl's Rock up through the wood to a
fence. Go back from the fence along the same path to another on
the left. This leads to the left bank of OUSAL DALE. 150 yards
along the path is a pleasant little crag.

**1 Bubble** 25 feet Very Severe
4b. Start in the middle of the pebbly wall and go diagonally right
to the recess in the overhang. Finish over this.

**2 Squeak** 40 feet Very Severe
4b. Round the corner to the right is a low wall. From the top of
this traverse the obvious line left round the buttress.

OUSAL DALE is best approached from the lower pool by taking
the right track at the point where the path by the pool forks.
After a few hundred yards it bears sharp right. On this bend are
COTTAGE ROCKS. The climbs are described from right to left
starting on the small crag 30 feet back from the path.

**3 Pine Tree Wall** 25 feet Difficult
The obvious weakness in the wall to the pine tree.

**4  Footpath Climb**  20 feet  Difficult
The flake in the centre of the buttress by the path.

**5  Strenuosity**  35 feet  Very Severe
4b. On the right of the main crag is a wide corner crack. Climb this to the top, traverse left and finish up the wide crack.

**6  Pocket Wall**  25 feet  Very Severe
4b. Start 10 ft left of the corner and climb steeply to the break. Finish as for Strenuosity.

**7  Crusty**  35 feet  Very Difficult
Climb cracks in the slab on the left starting from behind a small birch tree in the centre. Continue more easily to the top via a prominent boulder.

Follow the track for 100 yards to a bend. 100 yards round the bend is LONE BUTTRESS. The front face consists of a series of bulges; on the left side is a steep wall.

**8  Lone Wall**  30 feet  Hard Very Severe
5a. Start on the right side of the wall at the base of the crag. Go direct up the wall using a thin crack near the top.

**9  Even Lonelier**  35 feet  Hard Very Severe
5b. From the ledge 5 ft left of Lone Wall traverse right to a ledge below the overhang. Climb over this near the arete using a ripple.

300 yards along the path is OUSAL CRAG. The lower half of the crag is a steep pebbly wall. There is an excellent break across the entire buttress which gives a good girdle traverse.

**10  Thum**  25 feet  Very Difficult
From the boulder at the left end of the crag climb the short wall to a crack running through the overhang. Climb this to the top.

**11  Solo Chimney**  30 feet  Very Difficult
The chimney right of Thum past a good chockstone at half height.

**12  Moto Perpetuo**  35 feet  E1  ★
5b. Climb the scoop at the right end of the main face moving left to gain the break. Move left and up the obvious diagonal crack.

**13  Impacted Bowel**  120 feet  Very Severe  ★★
1. 65ft. 4c. Start left of Thum and follow the break to the chimney. Move round the arete and across steep rock to a stance below the final crack on Moto Perpetuo.

2. 55ft.4b.Continue along the break to the final corner at the right end of the buttress. Finish up this.

## STONY DALE QUARRY
O.S. Ref. SK 048483

SITUATION, APPROACH and ACCESS
The quarry is high on the south side of Stony Dale, a small dale that runs down to the Red Road ½ mile from Oakmoor. There is plenty of parking space at the car park by the Red Road in Oakmoor or at the old station 400 yards further down the road on the left. A short section of wall runs along the south side of the Red Road 200 yards beyond the junction with the road down Stony Dale on the Alton side. A path goes steeply up from the right end of the wall. 30 yards along the path another leads off right and this is followed into the Quarry. No access problems have been encountered here or at Lion's Rock.

CHARACTER
The crag is an impressive array of vertical corners and aretes. The rock often remains damp but when dry the routes are good. Allow two warm dry days.

THE CLIMBS are described from Right to Left. The most obvious features as one approaches are two huge unclimbed corners.

**1 Peggers' Original**  60 feet  A2
The thin crack 15 ft right of the left corner with some poor rock.

**2 Dance Of The Flies**  60 feet  E1  ★★★
5a.The arete of the left corner is usually dry and gives some very fine climbing. It will get easier with use.

**3 Little Nick**  45 feet  Hard Very Severe
5b.The crack 30 ft left is climbed strenuously to its top where 1 peg runner enables a sandy shelf to be gained. Finish up left.

**4 Doina Da J'al**  30 feet  E3  ★★★
5c.The superb clean dry arete left of the corner is climbed on the left wall above the break. Hard and unprotected.

**5 Cave Crack**  40 feet  Hard Very Severe
5b.Climb the delicate groove 10ft left to the cave. Finish up the difficult crack above to sandy ledges.

**6  Long Lankin**   65 feet   Hard Very Severe
5b. Go up the same groove to the traverse line. Go left 20 ft and climb a greasy crack to sandy ledges. Finish over a bulge with the aid of a tree. The crack can be reached direct but it is usually wet and slippery.

**7  Friar Muck**   30 feet   Hard Very Severe
5a. Go up the wall 40 ft left of the corner struggling through a tree to the break. Layback the final crack.

**8  Robin Hood**   30 feet   E1                                     ★
5c. Start below the bow-shaped crack above the break and climb the wall with a hard move to gain the break. Finish up the crack.

**9  Maid Marion**   25 feet   Very Severe
4a. The wall to the left is taken diagonally to the top.

At a point some 40 yards back down the path from the quarry another path goes right into a small quarry with an excellent bivvy cave on its right side.

**10  Short Ride**   20 feet   Very Severe
4b. The clean arete to the left of the cave.

Continuing through the quarry after 30 yards some stone steps are reached. These lead down to LION ROCK. The rock here is excellent. The right end is in the form of an upper and lower tier split by a grassy path. The climbs are described from Right to Left starting at some obvious twin cracks on the lower tier.

**1  Evensong**   30 feet   Very Difficult
Direct to the ledge finishing up the wider crack above.

**2  Psalm**   30 feet   Severe
Go diagonally left from the start of Evensong to a ledge at 10 ft then up the slabby scoop. Finish up the wall above. Variations are possible.

**3  Magnificat**   40 feet   Severe                                 ★★★
The overhanging corner crack to the left is taken direct finishing more easily up the slabby corner above. An excellent climb.

**4  Hand Jive**   60 feet   E4                                      ★
6b. Climb the overhanging wall left of the corner to a flake that crosses the roof rightwards. Follow this to the lip on the right side of the nose. Pull over with difficulty and bionic fingers then go left to a final short groove above a small tree. Strenuous.

**5  Rocking Stone Crack**   25 feet   Hard Severe ★★
The obvious fine layback crack to the left of the roof. Steep.

**6  Descant**   20 feet   Hard Severe
20 ft left is a short corner. Climb to its top, step left and go up to a dead tree.

**7  Canticle**   25 feet   Very Severe ★
4b. 35 ft left is a steep arete. Climb this for 10 ft then step right up to a short diagonal crack. Finish up this awkwardly.

# THE UPPER CHURNET VALLEY
by Gary Gibson, John Codling and Stephen Dale

---

HISTORY

The early days of Sharpcliffe Rocks are somewhat obscure, but it seems likely that when the nearby hall was a youth hostel many of the hostellers passed away pleasant hours scrambling on them.

In 1973 John Yates, Barry Marsden and Brian and Stephen Dale climbed most of the problems described. Notably Yates soloed Puffed Wheat, Blu-Tac, Stickfast, Special K and the superb Kaleidoscope. The rocks were then neglected again.

In early 1979, Gary Gibson visited the crag adding Killjoy; he repeated others and then disappeared impressed. Gibson returned and along with Ian Johnson added more routes checking those already there. Another visit was made to climb the rest of the slab routes and in July, Gibson produced the thin and serious Kobold and the technical Krakatoa. The plum line Knossos was top roped and ascended in the same month.

The first description of any climbs on Belmont Hall Crags was in the M.A.M. Journal of 1962. Such routes as Cave Crack, The Flake Traverse and Cave Rib were done during this period. Later that year, Bob Hassall and Dave Sales added the superb Kneewrecker Chimney and Sales' Bulge. Accompanied by G. Martin and J. Wilding they climbed Deadwood Crack, Twisting Crack, Hassall's Crack and Wiglette. Norman Hoskins produced The Joker and The Clown in 1971 needing a point of aid on each climb.

Immediately following the guide in 1974, the Woodward brothers, Jon and Andy visited and removed the aid from the crag. During work for this guide, Gibson added The Jester and Life in the Wrong Lane.

Harston Rocks were first stumbled upon in 1951 by the Oread M.C. whose members set to work cleaning and climbing with a vengeance. The driving force was provided by David Penlington who was responsible for The Helix, Fandango and the very bold Titan's Wall amongst a host of others. Virtually all the obvious climbs on the edge were products of the Oread during this period. Ernie Marshall climbed Glyph and Martin Ridges Via Trita. These were included in 'Climbs on Gritstone' Volume 4 in 1957. At this time the overhanging left wall of Harston Rock was pegged, later to be named Impending Doom and subsequently climbed free. Apart from a solo ascent of The Nose in 1961 by Nick Longland little was done until 1970. Austin Plant, whilst checking the Staffs. Gritstone Guide added The Cheek and

UPPER CHURNET 109

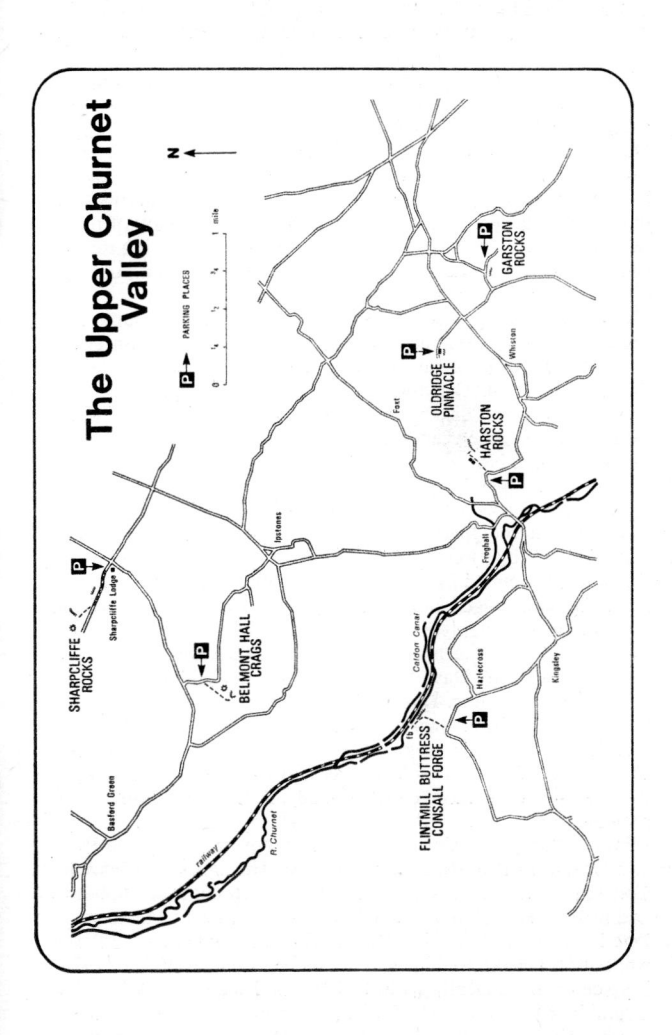

Ostentation. Martin Boysen went overseas to train in jungle penetration. He returned to climb Black Widow on the vegetation-ringed Gib Buttress. He also climbed the backbreaking Palsy Wall and The Slug. Steve Bancroft scooped the biggest recent prize with his ascent of D.N.A. on Harston Rock, setting a new standard in technical climbing.

During the build-up to this guide in 1978, the enfants-terribles from Staffordshire got to work. Gary Gibson and the Woodward brothers, unknown and unbelieved made their contributions at a time when independence was being sacrificed for the joy of the technical move. The brothers' Much Ado About Nothing turned back many before their first ascent. Gary replied with a number of short interesting problems, the best being the girdle, Megalomania. John Codling cleaned up, producing a couple of problematic walls, Melancholy Man and Taming of the Shrew. One big challenge remains, the undercut and bulging arete left of D.N.A. It is hoped that there will be a clean contest.

Garston Rock was discovered in 1952. All the major faults were climbed in the same year by Alan Simpson of the J.M.C.S. and Martin Ridges. Nothing was done until John Codling and Gary Gibson started playing about in 1979. All the slabs and aretes between the cracks fell quickly, the most significant being J.C.'s problematic Don Quixote, the airy Technocrat and Tricky Woo. Mick Hernon interjected with a characteristically bold lead of Runaway, so named because of a spectacular tumble from the crux. The knife-edged arete to its right, named Tequila Sunrise in absentia, was probably first done by Ewan Murray.

Oldridge Pinnacle has a similar history; all the cracks were climbed in 1952 by Dave Penlington. The faces and aretes went in 1979 to John Codling. He started by a roped solo of the then unled Tour de Force then turned on the South Face naively described in the previous guide as unclimbable. The central wall, The Gateless Gate, was soloed after many attempts. Qui Vive to the right was done more conventionally. A futuristic girdle remains to be done.

Flintmill Buttress in Consallforge was discovered by Austin Plant and Hassall in 1970. In June of that year Hoskins led the excellent Constant Rumble. Hassall and Ralph Fawcett climbed Manifesto and in 1971 Hassall did The Missus. Fawcett, Barry Marsden, Pete Harrop and Jeff Wincott cleaned and ascended Nosey Parker whilst Bob Hassall and Dave Salt climbed Full Frontal. In 1974 Marsden pegged Death Wish. In 1977 the Dale brothers found Grumbling Wall and Indecent Exposure and in 1978 this trio climbed the superb Peeping Tom and the easy but airy finish to The Missus.

# SHARPCLIFFE ROCKS
by Gary Gibson

---

O.S. Ref. SK 015520

SITUATION, APPROACHES and ACCESS
The rocks lie in the grounds of Sharpcliffe Hall. From Ipstones take the B5053 northwards, turn left at a crossroads after ½ mile. Park at a sharp bend ½ mile further. Continue down the unmade road leading to Sharpcliffe Hall. After 400 yards go across the field on the right to the first group of boulders. These are STRAW BOULDERS. The rocks belong to Sharpcliffe Hall and if carried out discreetly, climbing does not appear to be prohibited.

CHARACTER
The rock is Triassic conglomerate. Large sized pebbles are in abundance and frequently snap when used, thus making the climbs occasionally harder. The cracks are very painful to climb and seem only to suit the masochist.

THE CLIMBS are described from Left to Right. The first climbs are on a large arched boulder in the middle of a mass of boulders known as STRAW BOULDERS.

**1 Peep Show   Very Severe**
4a. The wide left flake on the front of the boulder.

**2 Cabana   Very Severe**
4b. Pleasantly up the black slanting flakes to the right.

100 yards further is a more continuous stretch of rock. This is BLURRED BUTTRESS. On its left is a wide crack:

**3 Pebblesville   Hard Very Severe**
5a. The small bulging wall left of the crack.

**4 Hush Puppy   Very Difficult**
Climb the wide crack.

**5 Hot Dog   20 feet   Very Severe**
4b. The sloping groove just to the right.

**6 Johnson'sville   20 feet   Hard Very Severe**
5a. Go up the steep wall using hidden holds.

**7  Bowcock's Chimney**  20 feet  Very Difficult
The pleasant twin-cracked chimney just to the right.

**8  Puffed Wheat**  20 feet  Hard Very Severe  ★
5b.The fine wall on the right is climbed up its centre.

50 yards in front and slightly right is GROGAN BUTTRESS which has a fine wall on its left side.

**9  Gorgonzola**  20 feet  Hard Very Severe
5a.Climb the smaller left side of the wall.

**10  Mr Grogan**  25 feet  Hard Very Severe
5a.Climb the centre of the wall on pockets and rugosities.

**11  Charlie Farley**  25 feet  Very Severe  ★
4b.The groove on the right on diminishing jugs. An excellent pitch.

**12  Rusks and Rye**  20 feet  Hard Very Severe
5b.The hanging crack on the front face provides a nasty climb.

**13  Comeback**  30 feet  Severe
Climb over the chockstone which leans against the face.

**14  Clinic Kid**  30 feet  Difficult
Climb the obvious boulder and slab above. Enjoyable.

To the right is TROUBLE AND STRIFE BUTTRESS.

**15  Vice**  25 feet  Severe
Climb the wide crack and chockstone.

**16  Veroa**  25 feet  Very Severe
4c.To the right is a thin crack. Climb it direct onto a ledge and easier ground.

**17  Genetix**  20 feet  Hard Very Severe  †
5b.The vague line left of the obvious arete in the small wall a few yards right.

**18  Blu-Tac**  20 feet  E1  ★
5c.An excellent route up the left side of the wall using the flake.

**19  Stickfast**  20 feet  Hard Very Severe
5b.The wall just right of Blu-Tac.

**20 Raven** 20 feet Very Severe
4a.The wall just left of the right arete.

**21 Spirella** 35 feet Very Severe
4a.A girdle of the wall from right to left along the obvious crack.

**22 Meninges** 20 feet Difficult
The separated slab to the right.

100 yards further is the largest crag, SHARPCLIFFE ROCK.

**23 Underhung Chimney** 35 feet Severe
4a.The shallow chimney left of the gully on the left of the crag.

**24 Konsolation Prize** 40 feet Severe
4a.The slabby left arete of Marsden's Eliminate.

**25 Marsden's Eliminate** 40 feet Moderate
The gully gives an easy ascent or descent.

**26 Knossos** 65 feet E4 ★†
5c.15 ft right of the chimney is a huge overhanging face. Start in the centre and climb right then back left to a good hand ledge. Traverse left to a diagonal crack and large runners. Climb the crack to a hole, swing right and up to finish. Strenuous. The pink curving line below the crack can be climbed at 5c.

**27 Krishna** 55 feet E3 ★†
5c.An excellent route with a hard finish. Climb the pink and black wall right of Knossos to a break. Step right and gain a crack from the right. Up this in a tremendous position to a small tree. Painful.

**28 Kenyatta** 50 feet E2 ★†
5b.The small bulging wall left of Kaleidoscope to a break. Climb the wall and go over the bulge to the break on Special K. Climb the flutings to the tree.

**29 Kaleidoscope** 55 feet Hard Very Severe ★★
5a.Start behind the large boulder below the slab. Follow the break from the right to an undercut. Go over this to a groove which leads to the upper wall. A Churnet Valley classic.

**30 Killjoy** 50 feet E1 ★†
5b.Climb the wall just left of the diagonal crack on the right to a break. Move up and left with difficulty into a green scoop. Climb the wall.

**31 Kobold** 50 feet E3 †
5c. Climb the diagonal crack to a bush. Pull over the bulge and continue direct up the slab on small pockets.

**32 Krakatoa** 25 feet E3 †
5c. From the left end of the grassy platform pull onto and up the thin upper slab, or climb 2 ft right at Very Severe, 4c.

**33 Kudos** 20 feet Very Severe
5a. Just right another bulge leads to a scoop and the top.

**34 Special K** 80 feet Very Severe ★
4c. From the left end of the platform step down onto the obvious break which leads left to a dead tree in a fine position. Finish above.
Right of Kudos is an easy way down. Below this is a fine blunt arete.

**35 Golden Sovereign** 15 feet Hard Severe
4a. The short enjoyable wall just left of the arete.

**36 Doubloon** 20 feet Hard Very Severe ★
5a. The superb undercut arete.

**37 Pieces of Eight** 25 feet Very Severe
4a. A wandering line up the slab just to the right.

Problems remain on the surrounding boulders but this is the end of the worthwhile climbs.

# BELMONT HALL CRAGS
by Gary Gibson

---

O.S. Ref. SK 007504

SITUATION, APPROACHES and ACCESS
The crags are 1 mile west of Ipstones overlooking a stream. The stream runs into Belmont Pools. The crags can be approached from either end of the valley but it is easier from the north. Take the road from Ipstones to Basford past the Marquis of Granby, through Stocks Green and Above Church. Follow this road down

a steep hill with a sharp bend and park at the bottom. Half way down the hill a path on the left leads to the first crag. The land which the crags are on appears to be quite public.

## CHARACTER
The rock on both the buttresses is good gritstone and is very clean giving excellent friction.

THE CLIMBS are described from Left to Right.

## LEFT-HAND BUTTRESS

**1 Vertigo** 45 feet Very Difficult
Either of the cracks at the left side finishing up a groove.

**2 Life in the Wrong Lane** 45 feet E1 †
5b.The wall 10 ft right past two bulges to a good ledge. The left groove is taken to finish on the left.

**3 The Clown** 50 feet E1 ★★
5c.Gain a small ledge just above an overhang 10 ft right of the last climb. Go up the wall left to a ledge, gain a small central groove and follow it to an easier finish. Good steep climbing.

**4 The Jester** 50 feet E4 ★★★†
6a.Attain a small ledge just left of the chimney. Go direct up the steep slab to a hard finish up the very steep face crack. Superb.

**5 Kneewrecker Chimney** 50 feet Very Severe ★★
4b.The obvious central climb is magnificent.

**6 The Joker** 50 feet E1
5c.The groove in the face left of Deadwood Groove is gained from halfway up that route. One peg runner.

**7 Deadwood Groove** 45 feet Hard Very Severe ★
5a.The slanting groove with an awkward finish.

**8 Deadwood Crack** 35 feet Very Severe
4c.The crack 15 ft right past a rotting tree to an equally rotten finish.

100 yards right is RIGHTHAND BUTTRESS which has a cave in its centre.

**9 Sale's Bulge**  20 feet   Very Severe
4c. The crack and bulge above the obvious shallow cave.

**10 Twisting Crack**  25 feet   Difficult
The crack to the right.

**11 Hassall's Crack**  30 feet   Very Difficult
The crack just left of the rib.

**12 Cave Rib**  40 feet   Hard Severe  ★
4a. The obvious rib. Avoid the small overhang finishing right.

**13 Cave Crack**  35 feet   Hard Severe  ★★
4a. Bridge out of the cave to the crack. Gain it from right or left.

**14 Flake Traverse**  50 feet   Severe  ★
Climb obvious flakes 15 ft right to a good ledge. Traverse 20 ft left to the tree and finish direct.

**15 Wigglette**  20 feet   Very Severe
4c. The face on the right on small holds.


# HARSTON ROCKS
by John Codling

---

O.S. Ref. SK 032477

SITUATION, APPROACH and ACCESS
This north-facing edge is hidden high on the side of a wooded valley a little north-east of Froghall village.
From the bridge over the River Churnet at Froghall take the A52 up the steep hill towards Ashbourne. Halfway up this there is a sharp righthand bend and a track leading left through a stone gateway. Park on the inside of the bend and walk the track to the farm. Continue in the same direction over two stiles. The first crag is about thirty yards up the hill. So far the farmer has not objected to climbers, only to any mechanical form of transport on his track. His dog objects to everyone.
With the exception of Harston Pinnacle, the rocks do not see much sun and are consequently green and slimy when wet. In the dry the soft sandy gritstone gives excellent friction.

## UPPER CHURNET

THE CLIMBS are described from Right to Left as one would normally approach them.

### DEVIL'S ROCK
The rock has an overhanging nose on its front face and a pleasant slab to the left.

**1  Introduction**  25 feet   Very Difficult
Start in the centre of the slabs on the right. Climb these and the wall above. **Variation:** Very Difficult. From the top of the slabs traverse left along a ledge.

**2  The Nose**  25 feet   Hard Very Severe ★
5b. Either start direct or approach the nose from the groove on the left. The final holds are hard to find.

**3  The Cheek**  25 feet   Very Severe
4c. Start as for The Nose. After 10 ft traverse left round the corner and go up the face above. **A Direct Start**, Very Severe, 5a is just left of the arete.

**4  Devil's Crack**  20 feet   Severe
The prominent crack 5 ft left of the arete.

**5  Rugosity**  20 feet   Severe
The wall 5 ft left of the crack.

**6  Footpath**  20 feet   Hard Difficult ★
Follow the line of cut steps to the top.

**7  Alternative Ulster**  15 feet  Hard Severe
The wall and crack to the left. Minute!

**8  The Saunter**  30 feet   Severe
A girdle of the left slabs. Start as for Alternative Ulster and finish as for The Cheek.

30 yards left is GIB BUTTRESS. It has a shelf on its left face.

**9  Wave**  35 feet   Difficult
Climb the right wall to a ledge. Take the bulge direct.

**10  Ripple**  40 feet   Very Difficult
The wall just right of the corner. Finish up the sloping groove.

**11  Crest**  40 feet   Very Difficult
Follow the crack to a shelf, then climb the slab above.

**12 Break** 45 feet Hard Very Difficult
Climb the corner 4 ft left of Crest. Traverse a few ft left and continue up the steep crack and wall above.

**13 Backwash** 40 feet Hard Difficult
Climb the corner, the crack and the wall, in that order!

The next buttress below and to the left is BISCAY BUTTRESS and it forms a sheltered bay. A prow on the left dominates the scene.

**14 As You Like It** 20 feet Moderate
The groove at the right end of the wall.

**15 Emerald Groove** 20 feet Very Difficult
The short green groove on the left. Finish either side of the overhang.

**16 Flake Wall** 30 feet Hard Severe
Difficult moves up the thin flake in the wall to the left lead to an escape up cracks above the ledge.

**17 Original Route** 35 feet Very Severe ★
4c. The corner of the bay has a very difficult exit. Scary.

**18 The Web** 50 feet Hard Severe
Climb the wall to the left of the corner. Traverse left below the prow and finish up the face to its left.

**19 Black Widow** 40 feet E2
5c. As for The Web to the break. Difficult and bold moves are needed to gain the prow on its right side. Finish left of the arete.

**20 Emerald Wall** 35 feet Very Difficult
Start on the frontal face of the lowest wall. Climb this and a corner on the right. Finish up the left wall of the prow.

**21 Corner Traverse** 75 feet Hard Difficult
Start below a birch tree on the left of the crag. Climb a short corner to the break. Cross the break into Original Route and a ledge. Continue in the same line, stepping down for a move, finishing up the groove.

The bottle-shaped buttress across the gully is PINNACLE BUTTRESS.

**22  Moore's Crack**  35 feet  Difficult
The wide crack and slabs near the top of the gully.

**23  The Sting**  30 feet  Hard Very Severe
5a. A mystifying route up the shallow groove to the left. Pockets on the right are of some use.

**24  Titan's Wall**  50 feet  E1  ★
5a. Climb the frontal headwall from pockets on the right. The crack at the top is poor and the falls will be long ones!

**25  Ostentation**  50 feet  E1  ★
5a. Start up the short chimney on the left. The wall above is hard and the overhang is harder still.

**26  Fandango**  50 feet  Hard Severe
Follow the chimney as for Ostentation but traverse left below the overhang to finish up a pocketed wall round the corner.

**27  Magenta Corner**  45 feet  Hard Severe
Climb a corner 12 ft left of the chimney. Continue up a slab to the base of a pinnacle. Ascend this.

**28  Glyph**  40 feet  Severe
Use a vague crack to reach the pinnacle as before.

**29  Rotondas**  30 feet  Severe
Start 6 ft left of the crack. Go up to a sloping shelf then left for a few feet up pockets. Finish in the centre.

The pinnacle can be ascended or descended from the col at its back by a route called **The Strid**, Difficult. There are four isolated buttresses to the left, each having a route.

**30  Oak Spur**  40 feet  Difficult
The right-hand buttress. Avoid the overhang on the right and finish up a wall.

**31  Moss Rose**  40 feet  Very Difficult
The narrow tower. A mossy wall leads to the crux. Hands on both aretes seem to be necessary for this.

**32  Frequency**  35 feet  Severe
The third buttress provides a fine crack, approached from a ledge above a difficult wall.

To the left a larger buttress can be picked out by its cave. This is CAVE BUTTRESS. The first route starts up a wall 20 ft right of the cave.

**33  Vereker's Venture**   30 feet   Very Severe
5a. A reach problem up the wall's right edge.

**34  Taming of the Shrew**   30 feet   Very Severe
5c. Start at Vereker's Venture but step left and tackle the bulge.

**35  Much Ado About Nothing**   30 feet   E2   ★
6a. The thin crack at the lefthand end of the wall. Mean!

**36  The Cave Crack**   30 feet   Severe
A very unhelpful chimney; strenuous.

**37  Palsy Wall**   30 feet   E1
5c. The undercut scoop and pocketed wall above the boulder.

**38  Palpitation**   30 feet   Hard Very Difficult
The awkward corner on the front face. Finish round to the right.

**39  Shelf Route**   25 feet   Hard Very Difficult
The lefthand wall of the buttress is climbed direct.

100 yards left is an isolated buttress; TECHNICIAN'S WALL.

**40  The Technician**   20 feet   Very Severe
5a. The dirty righthand wall. The last move is technical.

**41  Tiptoe**   20 feet   Hard Very Difficult
The short wall just right of the chimney.

**42  Diagonal Crack**   20 feet   Difficult
The prominent chimney crack.

**43  The Clam**   20 feet   Very Severe
5b. The rounded arete just left. Small holds only.

**44  Limpet**   20 feet   Hard Severe
The lefthand face direct.

**45  Megalomania**   30 feet   Very Severe
5b. A left to right girdle of the crag. Obvious.

100 yards left is the outstanding form of **HARSTON ROCK**.
It is a fine pinnacle with an undercut base.

**46 Via Trita** 45 feet Hard Very Severe ★
5a.Climb the crack in the lefthand face and step with difficulty
onto the shelf to the left. Finish up the rippled wall.

**47 The Helix** 80 feet Hard Very Severe ★★
5a.Start up Via Trita then step left after a few feet to an overlap.
The moves left to a small ledge are the crux. Continue up the slab
above to a horizontal break. Traverse left 30 ft then up the corner.

**48 Melancholy Man** 45 feet E1 ★
5c.An eliminate line on The Helix. Start at the base of Via Trita
crack but immediately traverse left along the small slab. Climb the
overhang then the slab above to the break. Step right and fight
the overhanging wall above.

**49 D.N.A.** 60 feet E3 ★★
6a.Gain the undercut scoop in the prow by some committing
moves. Leave it on the left using a horizontal break. The moves
to the next horizontal break are very technical. Finish up the easy
crack. The original finish has been incorporated into Melancholy
Man.

**50 Impending Doom** 60 feet E1 ★
5c.The steep lefthand face. Difficult moves lead to a ledge below a
rightwards slanting fault. Follow this, the last move being the
most difficult. Spectacular.

**51 Hatschek's Groove** 45 feet Very Severe ★
5a.Ascend the broken crack to a large ledge. The shallow groove
above takes some working out.

HARSTON QUARRY is down and to the left of Harston Rock.
Odd people have done routes there but none are worth recording.

## OLDRIDGE PINNACLE
by John Codling

---

O.S. Ref. SK 043480

SITUATION, APPROACH and ACCESS
This gritstone obelisk stands incongruously in a pleasant green field about half a mile eastwards of Harston Rock. An old railway track links them. If travelling on the A52 towards Ashbourne take a farm track to the left just beyond a righthand turning to Blakeley, half a mile north-east of Whiston village. Ask the farmer before climbing; he is friendly. The pinnacle has no easy routes up it. The climbs are described in a clockwise direction from a wide crack facing uphill and south-east.

**1  South-East Crack**  30 feet  Severe  ★
The awkward corner crack is the 'voie normale' here.

**2  Qui Vive**  30 feet  E1  ★
5c.The arete to the left. It can be approached from a crack to its left or from below. The last move is frustrating. Jockstrap vital!

**3  The Gateless Gate**  30 feet  E2  ★★
6a.This route accepts the main challenge of the overhanging wall. Start at the crack and finish over the bulge above on poor hidden holds. The finishing holds may require cleaning.

**4  The South-West Crack**  25 feet  Very Severe
4c.An awkward fissure just left of the stone wall.

**5  Battle Royal**  40 feet  E3  ★
5c.The arete facing the farm. Leaving a small groove at half height is the crux.

**6  Tour de Force**  45 feet  E1  ★
5b.The green face to the left. Move up then right to a hidden hole near the arete. Use this to gain a shelf. Finish up the wall above.

**7  The North Face**  55 feet  Very Severe  ★
4c.Start at the boulder below the face proper. Either climb it in the centre or by its right arete. The main face is ascended in the centre by a thin crack.

**8  Nom de Guerre**  30 feet  E1
5b.Climb the thin crack just right of the arete.

**9 Ivanhoe**   30 feet   Very Severe
5a. Climb the square-cut arete directly below the shelf.


# GARSTON ROCKS
by John Codling

---

O.S. Ref. SK 051476

SITUATION, APPROACH and ACCESS
The cliff can be seen from the A52. Turn left along Blakeley Lane half a mile from Whiston in the direction of Ashbourne. Turn left after about 600 yards. The cliff is in the first field on the right. Parked cars MUST NOT PREVENT ACCESS to the lane or field. Obtain permission to climb from the farm to the left of the crag. The sandy gritstone cliff is easy-angled but gets slippery in the wet. Its pleasant situation makes it an excellent place for a summer evening. The climbs are described from Right to Left.

**1 Tequila Sunrise**   25 feet   Very Severe ★
5a. The sharp short arete starting on the right.

**2 Runaway**   25 feet   E1
5c. The bulging wall just left of the gully.

**3 Feet of Strength**   20 feet   Hard Severe
The wide crack just left of the bulging wall.

**4 The Arete**   40 feet   Hard Very Difficult ★★
Start either side of the arete. Gain a scoop with difficulty then go straight up to a thread. Mantleshelf to finish.

**5 Technocrat**   35 feet   Very Severe
5a. The wall just left followed by a ribbed scoop. Use blinkers!

**6 Hole and Corner Crack**   30 feet   Severe ★
Climb the crack to a cave, step left and finish up the crack.

**7 Don Quixote**   35 feet   E1 ★★
6a. Gain a small groove from a weird hole. Continue up the wall.

**8 Skull Crack**   35 feet   Hard Severe ★★
Follow the wide crack direct; entertaining.

**9  Tricky Woo**   30 feet   Hard Very Severe
5a. Begin at an open corner but immediately step right to a wide horizontal crack. Make awkward moves up the blunt rib.

**10  The Chute**   25 feet   Hard Difficult
The open corner.

**11  Pillow of Winds**   25 feet   Hard Severe
The precarious arete to the left.

**12  One Knight Stand**   20 feet   Very Severe
5b. Straight up the middle of the wall on the left. Balancy.

**13  The Bishop's Move**   30 feet   Hard Severe   ★
Start 15 ft left of The Chute, gain the inclined crack and follow it to the arete, up which the route finishes.

**14  All The King's Horses**   60 feet   Hard Severe   ★
Start as for The Bishop's Move but continue in the same direction into the crack of Tricky Woo, eventually finishing just right of the Hole and Corner Crack.

There are a number of entertaining problems up the remaining rock to the left and on a boulder further left still. A larger buttress below provides more routes.

**15  Larva Wall**   25 feet   Very Difficult
The righthand slab of the lower buttress then through an overhang.

**16  The Stadium**   25 feet   Very Severe
5b. The delicate slab just right of the arete.

**17  Left Arete**   25 feet   Severe
The arete direct; the start is mystifying.

**18  Cave Wall**   25 feet   Very Difficult   ★
Go up into the cave right of the arete then steeply out onto the cracked wall above. Finish over the bulge.

**19  Rainbow Recess**   25 feet   Hard Difficult   ★★
Ascend the wall 8 ft left to the ledge. Step right and go up on small holds to the top.

**20  Triack**   20 feet   Hard Severe
The thin cracks lead to a bigger one.

## GARSTON BOULDERFIELD
A walk eastwards along a farm track until just past the farm leads to above a boulder field. There are many testing problems here.

## CONSALLFORGE, FLINTMILL BUTTRESS
by S. Dale and B. Dale

---

O.S. Ref. SK 004484

### SITUATION, APPROACHES and ACCESS
The crag lies on the south bank of the River Churnet, a mile to the south of Consall Station and $1\frac{1}{2}$ miles north-west of Froghall. The best approach is from the A52 Stoke-Ashbourne road. A lane runs through the villages of Hollins, Hazles and Hazles Cross between Kingsley Moor and Kingsley. Between Hazles and Hazles Cross a public footpath to Consallforge is well marked. This leads to the footbridge over the River Churnet immediately below and to the right of the crag. The foot of the crag is reached from the bridge by walking through the undergrowth. The crag is quite public and no access problems have been encountered.

### CHARACTER
The crag is a vast series of walls and overhangs from bottom to top. The walls appear less steep than they actually are. There are no climbs under VS and they can only be appreciated by competent connoisseurs well-armed with soft brushes. It is often damp but most routes go in the rain.

THE CLIMBS are described from Left to Right. At the left end of the crag is a broken groove with an overhanging chimney above. The first route takes the wall left of the chimney.

**1   Grumbling Wall**   65 feet   Very Severe
4b. The obvious rib leads to a wall. Move onto this and traverse right with difficulty to a smooth slab above the overhang. Climb across the slab and up the tower above.

**2   The Constant Rumble**   50 feet   Hard Very Severe   ★★★
5a. Climb the broken groove to the chimney. An awkward exit out of this leads to easier ground. An excellent route.

## 3  Miller's Melody   50 feet   Very Severe/A2
4b. 15 ft right a thin crack goes through the overhangs. This is gained awkwardly and followed using 5 or 6 pegs to reach the top.

## 4  Death Wish   70 feet   A3
1. Take the right parallel crack which crosses the big roof. Go up to a belay in a tree-filled bay.
2. Go 10 ft back down then traverse 15 ft right finishing straight up the obvious crack to an earthy finish.

## 5  Full Frontal   80 feet   Hard Very Severe   ★
5b. Climb the right of the two grooves 30 ft to the right of Death Wish to a roof. Swing right up the slab then left below the overhangs for 10 ft until a long reach enables an aid peg to be reached. Climb the crack above to a small ledge. Go up the overhanging groove with two peg runners to a hard finish.

## 6  Indecent Exposure   70 feet   Hard Very Severe   ★
5b. As for Full Frontal to the overhang. Go direct over the roof using an aid peg. Another aid peg is needed to gain the hard corner.

## 7  Manifesto   70 feet   Hard Very Severe
5a. 10 ft right a tree grows out of the crag. Climb the slab past the tree to the roof. Reach a peg runner on the left and pull up to the second roof. Go over this to a good ledge. Climb the crack.

## 8  Peeping Tom   70 feet   Hard Very Severe   ★★★
5a. Start 5 ft right and climb the crack and slab to below the roof. Traverse right using the break to a steep groove. Make a hard move up to gain good holds and continue to a large ledge. Finish up the wall.

## 9  Nosey Parker   70 feet   E1   ★
5b. 15 ft right is an indefinite crack up the slab. Climb this with difficulty to the overhanging groove. Use two aid pegs to start then follow the groove to the top.

## 10  The Missus   85 feet   Very Severe   ★★
4b. From the foot of the gully 15 ft right climb the slab to an awkward step right onto a ledge. Step up and left onto the steep cracked chimney and climb it to a slab on the left. Traverse left to the break and finish up Nosey Parker.

**11  The Spearhead**  35 feet   Very Severe
Right of the gully is a narrow pointed buttress.
4c. From the lowest point of the buttress climb the centre.

PRICE'S CAVE CRAG   O.S. Ref. SK 002493
This small crag overlooks the Black Lion Inn at Consallforge.
A few scrambles and climbs are possible on suspect rock.

WETLEY ROCKS   O.S. Ref. SJ 967495
These are on the north side of the Leek-Cellarhead road. They have been climbed on for years. The rocks left of the garage yield a good ridge climb at about Moderate to Difficult.

# GRITSTONE AREA

## THE ROACHES
by Dave Jones

---

*'The area has been for many years, a private zoo. Hen Cloud used to support a Yak, of which many tales can be told, and Emus once strutted around the Swythamley Estate. Unfortunately, these have now died off, leaving only herds of Red Deer and the occasional sight of Wallabies jumping along the foot of the crag...'*
North Staffs M.C. Guide 1968

O.S. Ref. SK 007621 to 002633

### SITUATION
The Roaches form a west-facing scarp on the south-western edge of the high gritstone moorland of the Peak District. They are $4\frac{1}{2}$ miles north of Leek and 10 miles south-west of Buxton.

### APPROACHES
From the south, take the A53 out of Leek (presuming your transport is still intact from the pothole barrage) towards Buxton. After about 3 miles the road dips (near the National Park boundary millstone) before climbing steeply up to the moors. Turn left 150 yards up the hill, along a lane leading to Upper Hulme. The lane curves to the right and divides, the righthand fork rejoining the A53 higher up the hill. Take the lefthand fork which descends through the hamlet and old dye works of Upper Hulme and rises again to open country. The castle-like ramparts of Hen Cloud appear on the right and the two tiers of The Roaches beyond. Park on the layby directly below the Lower Tier. From Buxton turn off the A53 halfway down the steepest part of the hill, about $\frac{1}{2}$ mile beyond Ramshaw Rocks. Continue past the Rock Inn and turn very sharply right down to the dye works. The P.M.T. Route 208 between Sheffield and Stoke-on-Trent goes along the A53 and there is a stop near the southerly lane leading to Upper Hulme. The Roaches are about a mile along the aforementioned route.
From the parking area, go through the gateway and follow the track leading right, then back left past Rockhall Cottage and go through a gap in the wall to the Lower Tier. A flight of stone steps leads to the Upper Tier.

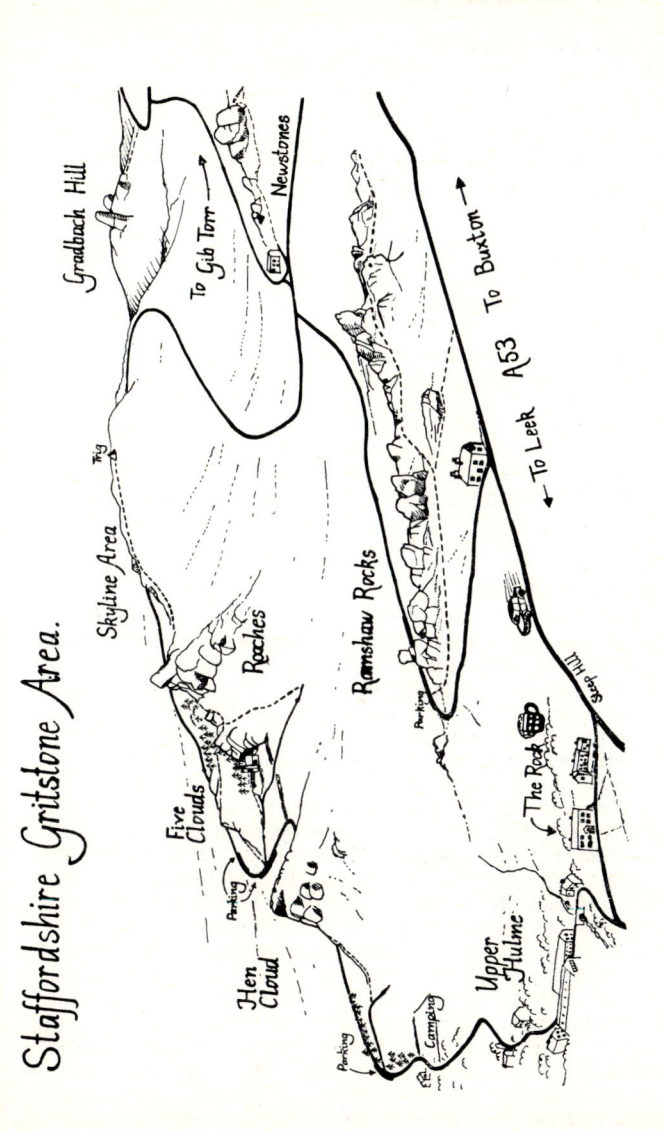

## THE ROACHES 129

## ACCOMMODATION

The nearest Youth Hostel is at Meerbrook (SJ 990609) at the north end of Tittesworth Reservoir, below The Roaches. There is a lightweight campsite (SK 008612) below Hen Cloud attached to the last farm on the right as one comes up the hill out of Upper Hulme, and one of the caravan/marquee variety (SK 012602) by the A53 half a mile south of Upper Hulme.

## ACCESS

Except for Rockhall Cottage, The Roaches is owned by the Peak National Park authority and is covered by local bye-laws. There are no access problems on the Upper Tier. However, Rockhall Cottage is built into the rocks just below the Lower Tier and agreement to restrict climbing on the Lower Tier to the hours between 9a.m. to 9p.m., and to respect the privacy of the cottage at all times, has been reached between the B.M.C. and the owners. It is hoped that climbers will adhere to these minimal conditions (whilst they are operative). The popularity of The Roaches area has had a direct detrimental effect on the ecology and climbers are further urged to respect the efforts of the Peak Park Planning Board to counteract the erosion of the paths and the general demise of the vegetation.

## CHARACTER

The Roaches form the finest and most impressive of all British gritstone crags. Rearing above the trees like a great wave about to break, they dominate the surrounding countryside. The view from the crest of the ridge is magnificent. To the north-east the open moor drops gently away to Black Brook and then up again to the gritstone plateau. Below the crag the decaying woodland gives way first to moorland and then meadows which carpet a wide valley floor rising again to Gun Hill. To the south Tittesworth Reservoir and Leek are close by whilst to the west beyond Mow Cop and Bosley Cloud, the view extends out across the Cheshire plain. The radio telescope of Jodrell Bank is often visible and in really clear conditions Cannock Chase, The Wrekin, the Welsh mountains, Helsby, the Wirral, Merseyside and even the Great Orme of Llandudno can be made out (if you have a good imagination). The crags themselves offer almost the complete spectrum of types and standards of climbing, much of it of the very highest quality. Indeed several routes would be contenders for the most outstanding climb on grit at their particular grade. The Lower Tier is a massive rounded gritstone. Blank walls and desperately thin slabs alternate with steep rough cracks. The lines are compelling and have a serious and single-minded air. The Upper Tier has a more complex structure. Its slabs and buttresses

are broken by a profusion of flaky roofs—occasionally of
sensational proportions—cracks and square-cut holds. Although
there are climbs of all standards here, the middle grade climber is
especially favoured with many top quality routes.
It is not surprisingly a popular crag, and the classics can become
congested on fine weekends. Solace may be found away from the
main areas or amongst the boulders under the Great Slab of the
Upper Tier, either polishing techniques on the numerous
exasperating problems or simply watching the spectacle from these
well-placed 'stalls'. The rock is sound apart from some roof
flakes which can be quite brittle. It is generally clean and dries
quickly though some ledges of natural drainage channels retain a
coating of sand after very wet weather. The harder climbs, being
ascended fairly infrequently, may develop their lichenous coats
once more and prospective leaders may feel it necessary to
re-clean. If this is the case please refrain from the vigorous wire
brushing that other gritstone crags have suffered from in the past.
New lichen can easily be removed by a bristle type brush. Whilst
on the subject of conservation many of the so called 'unclimbable'
slabs have in fact been ascended often using crucial pebbles.
Unfortunately these slabs are also abseiled down by 'heavily clad'
individuals and the risk of altering these 'test pieces' is great.
If you must abseil please use light footwear (e.g. pumps) or
practice on unused rock.

## HISTORY
The first report of any climbing on The Roaches was that of a
visit by the Kyndwr Club in 1901. They explored the Raven
Rock and showed interest in Rockhall. This cottage was formerly
occupied for nearly a century by Bess Bowyer, the daughter of a
Moss Trooper, who once terrorised the neighbourhood. It is
rumoured that Bess often sheltered smugglers, deserters and
thieves. She also possessed a handsome daughter of beautiful
voice and song who unfortunately was carried off one day by
strange men; old Bess, disconsolate, languished and died.
It was not until 1913 that further climbing activity was noted.
On this occasion a very tall, powerfully built youngster known as
Stanley Jeffcoat repeated Raven Rock Gully and added the
Chimney and Buttress to the left of the Great Slab. Also on the
Upper Tier A. S. Pigott led Bachelor's Buttress and the bold
Black and Tans. Morley Wood was active around this time with
leads of Left and Right-Hand Pedestal and Right Route to his
credit. Wood described his other test piece, Crack and Corner
thus: 'the top must some day become an easy day for a lady but
at present it is no place for a gentleman!' However, he did not
find the holds which were discovered later, possibly by an

unfortunate leader who pulled off the well-used clod of grass that used to hide the jug over the lip.

Via Dolorosa was climbed as a variation start to Raven Rock Gully and Kestrel Crack received an ascent during this period. Lindley Henshaw arrived on the scene after 1924 to master the Blushing Buttress via its Left-Hand and Right-Hand routes but the major climb was Ivan Waller's ascent of Bengal Buttress in 1930 which even today, with much more advanced protection techniques, still demands respect from the leader. The following year Inverted Staircase and Fern Crack were discovered before a period of inactivity, punctuated by war, followed.

Directly after the Second World War the Karabiner Mountaineering Club explored the Skyline Buttresses and were responsible for Slab and Arete, Mantleshelf Slab, Pinnacle Arete, Karabiner Chimney and Crack, these being described by R. D. Stevens in 1947.

Peter Harding was the next man to make his mark with his ascent of the fabulous Valkyrie in 1947. He was in fact just about to fail at the base of the flake when his groping foot finally landed on a hold which made it possible to continue left, albeit precariously, to make a major contribution to gritstone climbing. In the same year the Valkyrie Mountaineering Club was formed and before long they turned their attention on the crack cleaving through the overhangs to the left of Jeffcoat's Chimney. Joe Brown led the route and christened it Saul's Crack, a major addition coupled with a rise in standard for the crag. Brown's regular partner for these visits was of course Don Whillans and the next route to 'get the message' was the awesome overhang overlooking the pedestal of the Great Slab. Whillans, typically cool, crossed straight over this to produce another gritstone classic—Sloth. Meanwhile, Brown went on to climb Valkyrie Direct and Dorothy's Dilemma and together they added Aqua, the superb Matinee, the well-named Mincer and Bulger. All these ascents were described in Volume 4 of 'Climbs on Gritstone', 1957.

Shortly after this Brown and Whillans forced the dark and strenuous Crack of Gloom and stories were whispered of a couple of points of aid. Teck Crack also succumbed to forceful jamming by Brown and was promptly named after the Duchess of Teck who once visited the area. Brown continued his exploits with Choka and Rhodren whilst Whillans found the often greasy Slippery Jim and led Ackit by its Very Severe finish. Geoff Sutton, with partners from White Hall, put matters right by giving a climb to a misprinted line in the 1957 guide, hence the unusual name of Reset Portion of Galley 37.

In 1960 Alan Parker, Paul Nunn and Bob Brayshaw of the Alpha Club girdled the Lower Tier. Graham West was also active and

*Aquarius, Ravens Tor*

*Fingerdrive, Left Celestial Twin*

*Dance of the Flies, Stony Dale Quarry*

*Dust Storm, Rakesdale*

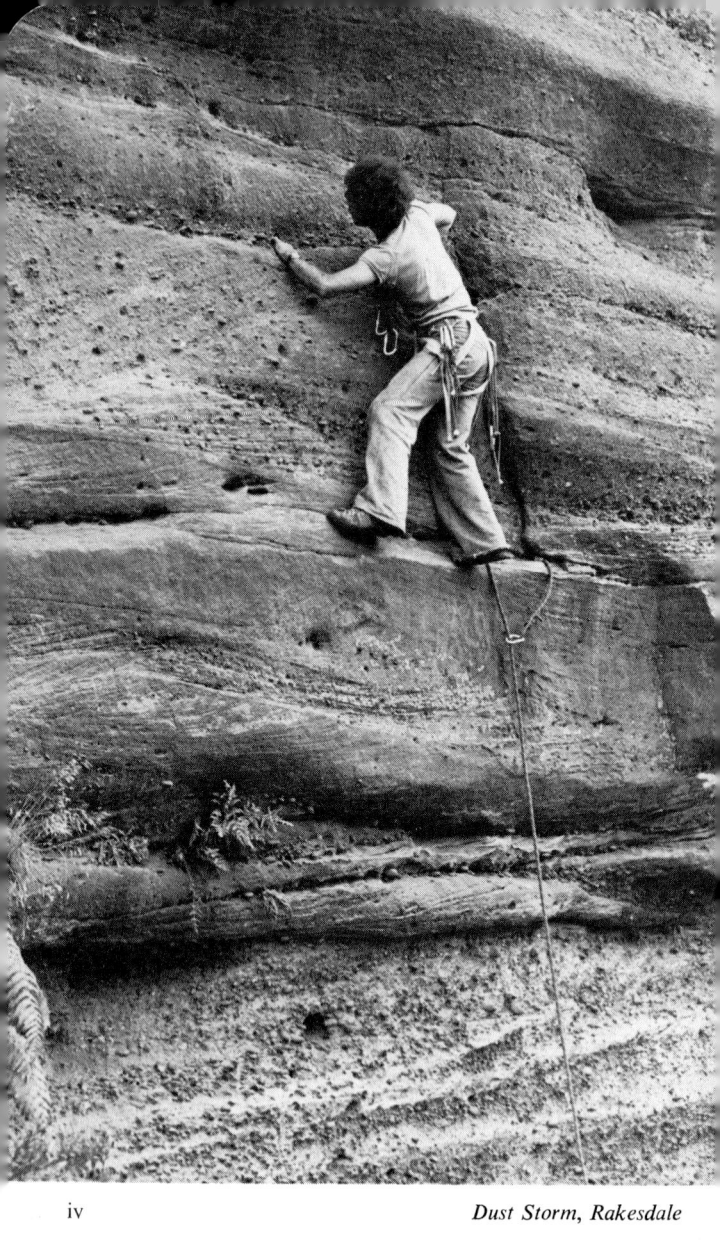

*Encouragement, Hen Cloud*

*Slowhand, Hen Cloud*

*Hunky Dory, Roaches Lower Tier*

*Appaloosa Sunset, Third Cloud*

produced the fierce Lightning Crack together with West's Wallaby on the Upper Tier. The latter ascent highlighted the possibility of routes over the stupendous overhang to its left. Mike Simpkins rose to the challenge and created three power climbs, all of them good, with Wombat, Walleroo, and Wallaby Direct, the former using a runner in the tree and the latter pre-placed protection. He later moved on to the Lower Tier to produce Elegy, one of the finest slab climbs on grit.

In September 1963 Dave Salt of the North Staffs M.C. fought his way up Hank's Horror on Skyline and during guide work led The Underpass on the Lower Tier. His partner on the latter, Colin Foord, went on to make magnificent leads of Tower Eliminate and the fine Hypothesis—directly after falling whilst top roping it! After the North Staffs paperback guide of August 1968 John Amies disproved Dave Salt's wager that everything possible had already been done. Amies promptly led Sifta's Quid but never managed to collect the pound. Early in 1969 it was Salt himself who added Pebbledash and on the same day John Yates managed to eliminate the sling move on Elegy. In July Mike Guilliard led Humdinger, a fine route, and in October of the same year John Gosling and Mike Simpkins hammered a peg in the wall right of Pebbledash and crossed it to give The Swan, an intimidating climb which is now done free. The next route to fall was not until September 1970 when John Yates bravely ascended Death Knell after surviving a spectacular tumble into the rhododendrons below. He also attempted The Swan but fell twice and so traversed higher, the variation being dubbed Up the Swanee—an extremely delicate undertaking. The last route of this era proved to be Ruby Tuesday on the Upper Tier by Guilliard and Yates, a very successful partnership.

After the production of the 1973 B.M.C. guide the North Staffs club directed their energy into fast cars, canal cruising and skiing. It was not until 1974 that any other important developments took place; on this occasion it was by the Woodward brothers, Andrew and Jon. Andrew claimed leads of Ascent of Man and Days of Future Passed. Amazingly they were barely teenagers. Their adolescent development was not to go unnoticed by the climbing press as they usually soloed routes after top rope rehearsals, graded them quite high for the time (interestingly they were quite accurate on the present day scales) and were outspoken. Andrew in particular was the main spokesman with radical statements such as "mountains are only training for boulders!" 1975 saw young men and established heroes visiting the area with the 'drive in and grab one approach'. John Allen and Steve Bancroft and Tom Proctor were responsible for picking off the plum of Trio Buttress with the very good Safety Net, but mysteriously left the crack just to the right. Remarkably this was to be solved by Gary Gibson in 1978. Allen also led the oft-fancied Commander Energy in 1975. Gabriel Regan visited the Lower Tier in the same year and succeeded in climbing the steep wall left of Prow Corner which had rejected many would-be leaders. The Woodwards began to explore the Skyline a year later, finding Nosepicker and the immaculate Mantis among others, some of which may have been done before.

1977 was to herald the beginning of an almost manic rush for first ascent glory with its attendant time warped dates and dubious route quality, making histories such as this a nightmare to sort out. Of the better quality Skyline routes Al Simpson did Happy Hooker, Fagash Lil and Tower Face whilst Dave Jones found that Bad Sneakers didn't give in easily. The Woodwards decided to start their slab campaign with Enigma Variation, San Melas and the fairly short but excellent Hard Very Far Skyline routes; Prelude to Space, Track of the Cat and Wings of Unreason, the latter being described as 'the hardest route in the World' basing this on the fact that they had never had to top rope a line so many times before leading it. Jerry Peel and Tony Barley paid a rare visit around this time to add Skytrain to Slab and Arete buttress.

The Lower Tier saw two important additions in 1977 with Gabriel Regan's ascent of the fine Smear Test which is now popular being possibly the most fallen off pitch on the Lower Tier and Jonny Woodward's Piece of Mind a formidably thin and serious test piece soloed after top rope inspections and at the time of writing still unrepeated. Ian 'Hots' Johnson of the Valkyrie Climbing Group showed his promise in a strong wind, with a lead of the technically superb Chalk Storm. He emerged from the top covered in the nasty white powder. 1977 was therefore a year of slab enlightenment with grades increasing accordingly. If 1977 saw an increase in pace then 1978 saw vast acceleration. Unfortunately some of the 'routes' offered were absolute rubbish. The main protagonists being hampered by a curious development of tunnel vision and myopia as 'lines' got closer and closer to existing routes. In some cases the difficulty being not in climbing the 'line' but in keeping ones hands and feet out of a neighbouring route.

Gary Gibson, finding a lot of spare time on his hands, explored the area thoroughly and produced such climbs as Graffiti, Poisonous Python, Crenation and War Wound together with two that almost certainly had been climbed before; Diamond Wednesday and Hanging Around.

The spring of 1978 also saw Phil Burke open up his impressive record with Schoolies which was to be climbed by a more direct

finish by John Codling a few weeks later. Punch was freed by
Jonny Woodward and Kicking Bird alternately strung together
by Al Simpson and Dave Jones. The short but hard Aspirant was
soloed by Gibson on one of many mid-week visits. He also reported
leads of Bed of Nails and the bold Valve in July. Jones found
Babbacombe Lee but this may have been done by Ken 'Mousey'
Poole at a time when things such as this were considered
'unjustifiable' to be recorded in a guide. In fact Ken Poole may
have been the first ascentionist of many of today's shorter 'new'
routes. Jones was also responsible for The Tower of Bizarre
Delights, a line snatched from under the noses of young men
who had left tell-tale chalk marks that stopped ten feet below the
top. Time was short and a cheeky top rope made the lead a
formality. Jonny Woodward finally rounded off activity with
Headless Horseman to the right of Kestrel Crack.

1979 dawned with a slowing down of the pace; Phil Gibson
however managed to get across the exciting Gypfast without the
shaky flakes rejecting him and Phil Burke excelled in the exposure
of Gillted and the first lead of Simpkin's Overhang; a stout lead
that many notables had shied from attempting. Not to be left out
Gary Gibson forced his way up Genetix. In 1979 the most serious
aspect of climbing, especially on the Lower Tier, was that of
belaying, for the resident of Rockhall took an exception to
climbers and expressed his views by wielding a rather sharp axe
(which earned him the nickname of Eugene, after a character in
a Pink Floyd song). Many an astonished leader looked down to
see his unfortunate second disappearing off into the undergrowth
out of harm's way. A fence was erected round the Lower Tier and
to their credit climbers kept away in order that negotiations
could take place. On the much quieter Skyline buttresses Jonny
Woodward top roped and led possibly Skyline's most serious
hard route, Acid Drop, whilst Gibson continued his exploration
with Topaz, 39th Step, Definitive Gaze, Split Personality and
Curvature.

Further access was not possible on the Lower Tier until the
spring of 1980 when members of the Valkyrie Climbing Group,
frustrated by ten months of seemingly fruitless debate, decided
to filter onto the crag. A brief encounter followed but they were
soon left to enjoy the climbing on this excellent length of cliff.
John Codling opened up proceedings with the extension of Smear
Test and the crossing of Elegy slab thus effectively creating a super-
girdle. Phil Burke continued his involvement by climbing the left side
of the Valkyrie overhang to give Sidewinder, a powerful route.
Meanwhile Gibson's eye for a line was maturing and he produced
three good routes with Circuit Breaker, Carrion and Licence to
Run. On the latter he unfortunately had to resort to a rest on a

136  GRITSTONE AREA

nut. Owing to close competition from rival teams he also rather greedily ascended the slab right of Piece of Mind using a hanging rope within reach in case he floundered. A few days later Thin Air was soloed by Phil Burke. Guidebook work uncovered a few overlooked inches of rock and Jones duly plugged this with Bareback Rider but one of the most impressive feats of the year was Jonny Woodward's, first time and on sight, lead of Antithesis, done in complete contrast to the style of his formative years.

New routes remain to be climbed on these escarpments but one can only hope that they will be of quality and not just quantity. Only time and ever developing attitudes will tell.

## ROACHES LOWER TIER
*'It has three desperate moves involving an unlikely toe jam move, a weird high sort of bridge and an all-out crystal move. There are no runners and a fall would land you painfully in the holly.*
*It will take me quite a time to pluck up the stupidity to lead it.'*
                                                         Jonny Woodward, 1979

LEFTHAND SECTION
The climbs are described in the order in which they are usually approached. The first listed are the climbs to the LEFT of the steps working from Right to Left.
15 yards to the left of the steps a hollybush grows out of an overhanging rock wall. 10 feet right of the holly is a slanting crack.

**1  Fred's Cafe**   20 feet   Very Severe
5a. Follow the crack and a short slab above a niche. Contrived.

**2  Lightning Crack**   60 feet   Hard Very Severe
10 feet left of the holly is an undercut layback crack.
1. 20ft.5b. Reach the crack with difficulty. Follow it.
2. 40ft.4c. From the tree step up then left onto a foothold at the base of the triangular wall. Up this to a sloping ledge. Finish direct or better, by a leftwards rising hand traverse, 5a.

**3  Teck Crack**   80 feet   Hard Very Severe                    ★★
1. 35ft. The boulder chimney for 15ft. Creep left to the crack.
2. 45ft.5b. The mean, unforgiving crack. Either finish left of the chimney or from its base, pull onto the right wall.

**4  Ackit**   50 feet   Hard Very Severe
Round the corner to the left is an obvious layback crack.
5b. Follow the crack to a bulge. Over this (crux) and up to the top. Escape left or right below the crux makes the route Very Severe.

## THE ROACHES 137

*Lower Tier*

Philip Gibson

The buttress left of the gully has short steep walls topped by a sloping slab. All the climbs involve mantleshelf encounters ranging from the straightforward to the diabolical.

**5 The Aspirant** 25 feet E2
5c. Start opposite Ackit. The flake and wall to a difficult exit.

**6 Days of Future Passed** 35 feet E3
6a. Follow a shallow crack in the arete to a nose-grinding finish. A must for the connoisseur of balance and mantleshelf.

**7 Ascent of Man** 40 feet E3 ★★
6a. From a shallow cave gain a flake above, runners. Traverse left across a sloping ramp and exit right. Superb climbing and very hard for a short person.

To the left is a steep arete; further left is a short corner crack.

**8 Bareback Rider** 30 feet E2
6a. Gain a small foothold on the arete. Make a difficult move up and hand-traverse steeply left to Slippery Jim.

**9 Slippery Jim** 25 feet Very Severe
4c. The corner crack direct to a tricky exit.

The wall to the left contains an entertaining hand-traverse.
10 yards further left is a recess overlooked by a jutting flake.

**10 National Hero** 45 feet E1
5b. Climb out of the cave by its right side. Gain the flake immediately and follow it. Continue up the small buttress behind. It is also possible to gain the flake from the right wall, Very Severe, 5a.

The opposite side of this narrow buttress forms a short steep slab with two problems: The small leaning corner, **Hot Burrito**, 4c and **Burrito Deluxe**, 5c, the right edge for quick thinkers! Landing undesirable.
Climbs have been done on isolated buttresses to the left of this area but, being in the trees, are often dirty and holds quickly become choked with pine needles. They have therefore been left for rediscovery by those with a horticultural bent.

RIGHTHAND SECTION
Returning to the steps, descriptions continue, working from Left to Right.

**11  Yong Arete**  20 feet   Hard Very Difficult
The steep arete beside the last flight of steps.

**12  Poisonous Python**  25 feet   Hard Very Severe
5b. The curving crack in the steep slab. Finish on right arete.

**13  Yong**  30 feet   Hard Very Difficult ★
The obvious corner crack with a slab to its right. Prickly jams.

**14  Something Better Change**  30 feet   E1
5b. The slab. Trend right towards the top. Unprotected.

**15  Wisecrack**  25 feet   Mild Very Severe ★
To the right at a slightly higher level is a buttress with a large block at its left corner.
4b. The slanting crack on the lefthand face.

**16  Hypothesis**  30 feet   Hard Very Severe ★★
5b. The left arete of the buttress is delicate and needs care.

The front face of the buttress has yet to be mastered direct. The closest approximation starts at the foot of the right arete.

**17  The Man Who Fell To Earth**  40 feet   E2 †
5b. Climb diagonally left to meet Hypothesis. Follow it for 15 ft then break out right.

Bengal Buttress lies to the right. It has a twisting crack on its left face and an undercut slab on its impressive front face.

**18  Cannonball Crack**  30 feet   Severe
Climb the twisting crack for 20 ft and make a precarious move left onto a boulder. Continue to the top.

**19  Graffiti**  45 feet   Hard Very Severe
5b. A rather contrived approach. Climb Dorothy's Dilemma until a move left is met, to reach a leaning corner. Follow this and the awkward crack above.

**20  Dorothy's Dilemma**  50 feet   Hard Very Severe ★
5b. Start level with the foot of Cannonball Crack below an arete. Delicately climb this via interesting and airy moves.

**21  Bengal Buttress**  90 feet   Very Severe ★★
4c. Start at the lowest point of the left arete. Straight up to a grass ledge, traverse right then up again to a break, runners.

Gain a standing position high up on the right arete where a trying move leads to the top of Raven Rock Gully. Step left onto the face and up a short crack. A classic product of its time being exposed, delicate and with disheartening protection.

**22  Schoolies   80 feet   E2 (direct)**                       ★★
5b. Start at the foot of the buttress below an improbable-looking overhang. Climb up to and over the roof on good holds to reach a ledge. Either climb steeply left to meet Dorothy's Dilemma (E1) or go direct up the centre.
It is possible to gain the ledge of Bengal Buttress from Raven Rock Gully by following Crack of Gloom for 10 ft then boldly hand-traversing left onto the front face. **The Direct Start**, Hard Very Severe, 5a.

**23  Crack of Gloom   70 feet   E1**
5b. Strenuously follow the crack into the gloom, exiting left round the chockstone. An exit right avoids the crux.

**24  Raven Rock Gully Lefthand   60 feet   Mild Very Severe**
4b. Follow cracks and grooves in the lefthand corner. Exit direct.

**25  Raven Rock Gully   90 feet   Difficult**                    ★
A popular climb. Follow the flakes in the back of the gully and squirm through the manhole.

**26  Swinger   60 feet   Very Severe**
4c. Follow the thin crack in the righthand wall of the gully. Continue by moving slightly left to meet Via Dolorosa.

**27  Sidewinder   95 feet   E4**
6a. From the foot of Swinger hand-traverse out right and climb a shallow groove in the blunt arete. Reach the protruding flake in the roof above then make strenuous moves left and up to gain a vertical flake. The arete finishes a bold, exposed route.

**28  Via Dolorosa   105 feet   Hard Severe**                   ★★★
Start at the foot of the buttress to the left of a cave.
1. 20ft. Ascend a narrow polished slab (hard). Move up and left through the much abused holly to a ledge. An easier start is to traverse diagonally right from Raven Rock Gully.
2. 35ft. Traverse left to the rib. Follow a short crack then a slab round to the left. Belay with care at a block.
3. 50ft. Traverse boldly up and right to reach a hidden flake. Climb this and a short corner then right to the arete. Continue just right of this.

**THE ROACHES 141**

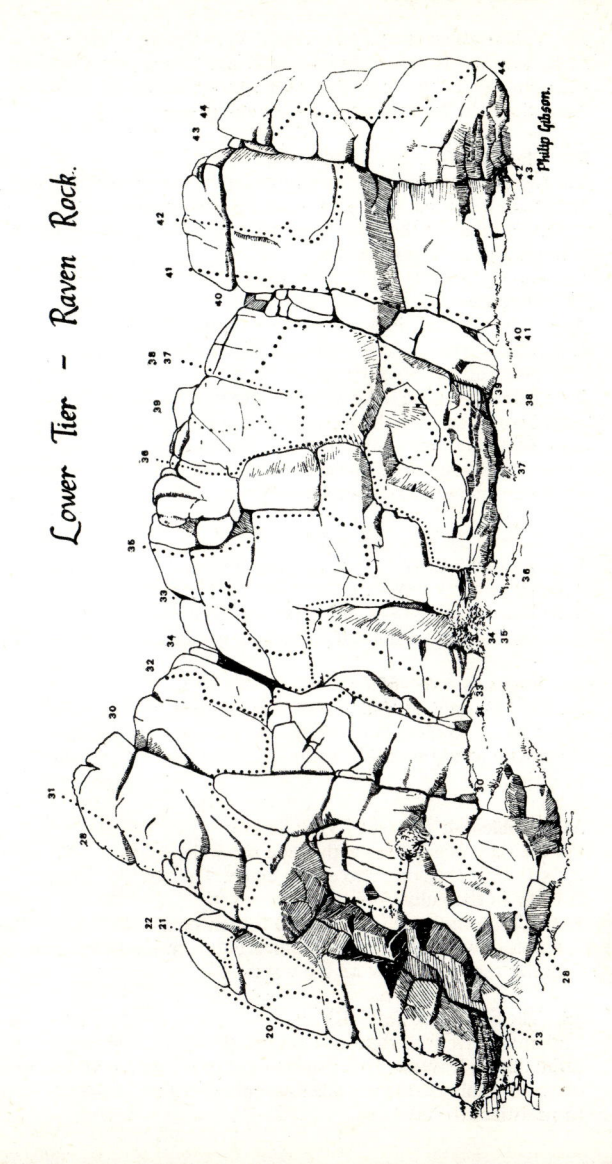

*Lower Tier – Raven Rock.*

Philip Gibson.

## 142   GRITSTONE AREA

**29   Valkyrie Direct**   95 feet   Hard Very Severe   ★
5a.Follow Via Dolorosa to its first belay. Climb cracks leading to the right side of the roof. Pull over to the foot of the Valkyrie flake. Step left then take the wide crack above.

**30   Matinee**   70 feet   Hard Very Severe   ★★★
The right wall of Raven Rock Gully is split by a compelling crack.
1. 5a.Climb the crack on glorious jams. Crevasse belay.
2. 5a.Continue up the wide crack to tackle the punishing final bulge and belly-flop finale.

**31   Valkyrie**   110 feet   Very Severe   ★★★
A grit classic. Start in a corner 20 ft right of Matinee.
1. 4a.Follow the corner to the foot of a wide crack. Traverse left to belay at the large triangular flake.
2. 4c.Climb over the flake and descend it. Step left with difficulty and continue onto the front face; exposed. A delicate and intimidating move gains a good ledge and easier climbing. An excellent expedition, however care should be taken to minimise rope drag and to protect a wobbly second.

**32   Licence To Run**   65 feet   E2   ★★
1. 4b.Follow Valkyrie pitch 1 to reach a black flake on the left. Belay as for Valkyrie.
2. 5c.Right to a layback flake. Up this then steeply right via hard moves to reach a good hidden flake on the right. Follow this.

**33   Eugene's Axe**   65 feet   E2
5c.The slab right of Valkyrie start is climbed moving right to its edge; go up to meet Pebbledash. Step left to a foothold, move steeply up (crux) to holds leading right to pockets and slightly left to finish.

**34   Pebbledash**   70 feet   Very Severe   ★
On the right is a corner with some rhododendrons.
1. 5a.Follow the corner to a thin crack. Traverse delicately left to belay in the gully.
2. 4b.Climb the wide crack for 10 ft then break out left to a flake and follow it. Climbers still quivering from the traverse may prefer the wide crack all the way.

**35   The Swan**   80 feet   E3   ★★★
The impressive wall right of Pebbledash is breached by an intimidating traverse. It is usual to use two seconds on this in order to minimise the monstrous pendulum should the leader fail to negotiate the crux.

5c. Start as for Pebbledash but follow the righthand crack; runner high up. Step right round a bulge and continue along the lip of a small overlap until the holds disappear. A fierce pull brings adequate holds on the next break. Finish up the widening crack above.

It is also possible to traverse higher up using the handholds of The Swan as footholds. This is **Up The Swanee**, E3, 5c.

### 36  The Mincer   60 feet   Hard Very Severe   ★★
12 yards right of Valkyrie is an obvious crack running rightwards below a series of overhangs.

5a. Climb a shallow groove, hard, and move right to start the crack or climb the bulging wall 6 ft right, 5b. Follow the crack round the nose. Finish up the wider fissure. A must for aspiring hard men.

### 37  Smear Test   60 feet   E2   ★★
6a. Start as for Pincer but climb the groove leftwards to meet Mincer. Follow it to below the wide crack. Step onto the slab to the right and cross it to a crack finish. Magnificent slab climbing needing concentration and a gentle touch.

### 38  Pincer   55 feet   Mild Very Severe   ★
4c. Start 5 yards right of Mincer below a short undercut crack. Climb left or right on layaways to a ledge below a groove. Traverse delicately right then go up to a horizontal crack. Follow this to the gully. Go up 15 ft then left to a crack and the top. Interesting climbing.

### 39  Kicking Bird   55 feet   E3   ★★
6a. Start 3 ft right of Pincer at the foot of a wide crack. Ascend the bulge leftwards then go over the small roof above. Step left into Mincer and follow it to below the wide crack. Step right onto the slab and make a difficult move to reach a small glacis to the right then continue direct.

### 40  Guano Gully   40 feet   Hard Severe
4b. The gully containing a jammed boulder. Move left to the crack to finish up the gully. The crack direct is awkward, 5a.

### 41  Mousey's Mistake   40 feet   Hard Very Severe
5a. Painfully overcome the right side of the boulder. Follow the gully for 15 ft, step right onto the left edge of Elegy slab and continue direct.

## 144 GRITSTONE AREA

**42 Elegy** 60 feet E2 ★★★
5c. Follow Bulger until above the roof. Improvise left and follow the flake. Continue to the top. Absorbing and elegant climbing.

**43 Bulger** 40 feet Very Severe
4c. The crack 5 yards right of Mousey's Mistake.

To the right of Bulger on the front of a narrow buttress is a 5a overhang problem. Further right is a large recess.

**44 Fledglings Climb** 40 feet Mild Severe
Make awkward moves up the left wall of the recess to gain a short crack. Continue up and left into Bulger.
Variation: Climb the shallow groove above the start, traverse right and finish up the deep groove, 4c.

**45 Little Chimney** 25 feet Moderate
The chimney in the left corner of the recess. A useful way down.

**46 Battery Crack** 30 feet Hard Severe
The wide crack out of the sentry box. Finish up Lucas Chimney.

**47 Lucas Chimney** 35 feet Severe
The evil slot in the right corner of the recess. Painfully ascend the chimney then swing desperately left to finish.

The buttress to the right, just behind the Cottage, has a crack splitting its upper half. Two diagonal breaks cross the top face.

**48 Hawkwing** 65 feet E1 ★
5b. Follow a curving crack line a few ft right of the chimney to a small ledge. Climb Kestrel Crack for 5 ft then left to the two breaks. Follow these with increasing respect and finish up the left arete. A harder variation is possible by hand-traversing the low horizontal break to the left arete; **Poison Gift,** 6a, †.

**49 Carrion** 60 feet E2 ★★
5c. Straight over the roof above the tree stump (a long reach and big arms an asset) to a ledge. Continue directly up the centre of the buttress to the top.

**50 Kestrel Cracks** 60 feet Hard Severe ★
4a. Either start up the slab to the right of a short crack and swing left below an overhang to the foot of the crack or climb the groove directly above the tree stump and move right to the crack. Follow the crack, past a chockstone to a gruelling chimney finish.

THE ROACHES 145

*Lower Tier (right)*

Philip Gibson.

## 146 GRITSTONE AREA

**51 Headless Horseman** 60 feet Hard Very Severe
5a. Follow Kestrel Crack to below the chockstone. Move right onto an arete and go up to an overhang. Go left round this then gain the exposed arete on the right and so to the top.

**52 Flimney** 55 feet Hard Very Difficult
Strenuously follow a short steep crack 5 ft left of rhododendron bushes. Continue right and finish up the corner.

**53 The Death Knell** 40 feet E4 ★★
5c. Follow the blunt arete just right of the rhododendrons with increasing difficulty until a long step right can be made to a crack. Go up this for 5 ft then use holds to the right. A runner, on a flake in the gully, considerably reduces the seriousness and grade. The upper cracks to the left have also been climbed.
**Amaranth**, E2, 5c is the slab 5 ft left of Death Knell (runner on flake).

**54 Rhodren** 35 feet Hard Very Severe
Right is a great perched flake. Above it is a Mincer style overhang.
5a. Climb the shallow corner behind the toe of the flake to the roof. Move right with difficulty to easier ground.

**55 Flake Chimney** 40 feet Moderate
Climb the edge of the flake. Finish up the chimney to the right. A direct start, Severe, goes out below the right side of the flake.

**56 Straight Crack** 30 feet Very Difficult
Bridge against the flake to start the crack behind it.

**57 Punch** 40 feet Hard Very Severe
Right of the great flake a small rhododendron grows above a groove and overhang.
5c. Vicious pulls gain the short groove. Move up then go right to climb two cracks and an arete above. A dirty climb.

**58 Choka** 35 feet Hard Very Severe
5a. Start 10 ft right of Punch below a crack in the roof. Surmount the roof gymnastically and continue up the widening crack.

**59 Circuit Breaker** 30 feet E2 †
5c. The arete to the right of Choka.

**60 Hunky Dory** 30 feet E3 ★
To the right is a steep wall and right again a slab.
6a. Follow the crack in the wall until it is possible to gain the

ledge on the right. Continue either direct to a step left or exit left straight away via an outrageous mantleshelf.

**61 Prow Corner** 30 feet Hard Difficult ★
The corner bounding the left side of the slab. Interesting.

**62 Chalkstorm** 30 feet E1 ★★
5c. Climb the centre of the slab on sloping holds. A technical masterpiece. A runner is usually placed just left of the overlap.

**63 Prow Cracks** 25 feet Difficult
The twin wide cracks on the right side of the slab.

**64 Commander Energy** 35 feet E2 ★★
To the right is a slim buttress with a flying arete.
5c. Ascend the narrow slab to the triangular roof; pull over this on its right side to gain a standing position (and wonder why you ever came). Ascend the sharp arete with conviction.

**65 Rocking Stone Gully** 25 feet Very Difficult
The chockstone-filled corner right of the last climb.

**66 Captain Lethargy** 25 feet Very Difficult
The crack 5 ft right. Finish to the left. A good jamming exercise.

**67 Sifta's Quid** 30 feet Severe
Two large bocks rest on a ledge halfway up the crag. Climb a crack to the righthand block. Continue with difficulty over the bulge.

**68 Piece of Mind** 30 feet E5 †★★
To the right is a blunt rib.
6b. Start on the left side of the rib. Follow it to moves on the right near the top. Holds imaginary, protection nil.

**69 Thin Air** 25 feet E4
6a. The slab to the right of Piece of Mind, the crux being to attain a standing position on the wrinkle.

The rocks further right are broken and form a ridge of boulders. The following expedition will be found extremely useful for introducing basic rock techniques to beginners.

**70 The Lower Tier Ridge** 500 feet Moderate and above ★
Start at the base of a triangular-shaped boulder beside the track that skirts round the righthand extremity of the Lower Tier.

Ascend this friction problem then move across 10 yards right to where the ridge proper begins. Follow any line along this.

**71  The Girdle Traverse**   260 feet   Hard Very Severe
Follow Bengal Buttress nearly to the top. Move right round the chockstone and continue until above Valkyrie's crux. Reverse Valkyrie to the crevasse stance and continue right to the corner. Follow the ramp right and a horizontal crack to descend a diagonal. Continue right to the top of The Mincer. One can traverse into Bulger taking a line close to the top of the crag.

**72  The Underpass**   170 feet   E1
From the foot of Dorothy's Dilemma traverse right to Bengal Buttress and follow it to the final crux moves, runner. Reverse the crux of Crack of Gloom. Traverse round the back then out of the gully onto the face below the large overhang. Continue below the overhang, cross Valkyrie Direct and swing down right to reach a big foothold on Matinee. Ascend a little then take the right fork of the Y-cracks to the corner. Traverse across Pebbledash to:

**73  The Super Girdle**   150 feet   E3                    ★★★
6a. Follow The Swan past its crux then continue right to The Mincer below its wide crack. Cross Smear Test to its crack then continue slightly down right to the gully. Traverse Elegy slab level with the top of the flake to finish up Bulger. A very intense experience involving a fair proportion of the thinnest slab climbing in the area.

## ROACHES UPPER TIER
*'. . . and The Sloth in particular has been the subject of heated argument as to its standard. Hard Severe has been mentioned by some but more expert opinions seem to consider Very Severe appropriate.'*
Staffordshire Guide 1968

THE CLIMBS are described from RIGHT to LEFT as the usual approach is from the stone steps splitting the Lower Tier.
The first climbs are on a small overhung buttress situated some 70 yards down the hillside when viewed from the top of the steps.

**74  Pepper**   25 feet   Very Severe
5a. Climb the overhanging front face to gain a ledge. Trend leftwards to finish up the crack.

## THE ROACHES  149

**75  Garlic**   25 feet   Hard Very Severe
5a. Start in a short corner to the left. Swing right onto the ledge of Pepper and finish over the final overhang on its right side.

**76  Genetix**   35 feet   E2
The next buttress contains an impressive overhanging prow. The first climb starts just right of a sharp undercut rib below the overhanging arete.
5c. Gain the roof flakes with some difficulty. Pull over onto the right side of the arete and finish direct on green sloping holds.

**77  Calcutta Buttress**   25 feet   Very Severe   ★
4c. Start left of the sharp rib. Pull up to the small roof and move left to a balancy mantleshelf. Continue up right then back left at the break. (The first roof taken direct is strenuous.)

**78  Calcutta Crack**   20 feet   Severe
The obvious crack to an awkward and tiring finish.

**79  Sign of the Times**   20 feet   Hard Very Severe
5b. The undercut rib to the left. By using holds on the rib gain the wall to the left. Finish direct via a short flake.
The undercut nose 10 ft left provides a 5b problem and can be used as a start to the Girdle.

**80  Between the Tiles**   80 feet   Hard Very Severe
4c. This takes the buttress, at half height. Passing below the prow is awkward and the finish, up a scoop, proves tricky.

The next buttress to the left is Blushing Buttress which is split by a gully. The smaller buttress has flakes on its right face.
**81  Sparkle**   25 feet   Mild Very Severe
4b. Climb the flakes until a traverse left is possible. The direct finish is Hard Very Severe, 5a.

**82  Rib Wall**   25 feet   Difficult
The wall 5 ft left to a big ledge. Continue straight up.

**83  The Rib**   25 feet   Moderate
The right rib of the gully is difficult to start.

**84  Grilled Fingers**   30 feet   Very Severe
4c. The left wall of the gully. Steeply up the wall right of the large flakes to finish direct with difficulty. Long reach desirable.

150 GRITSTONE AREA

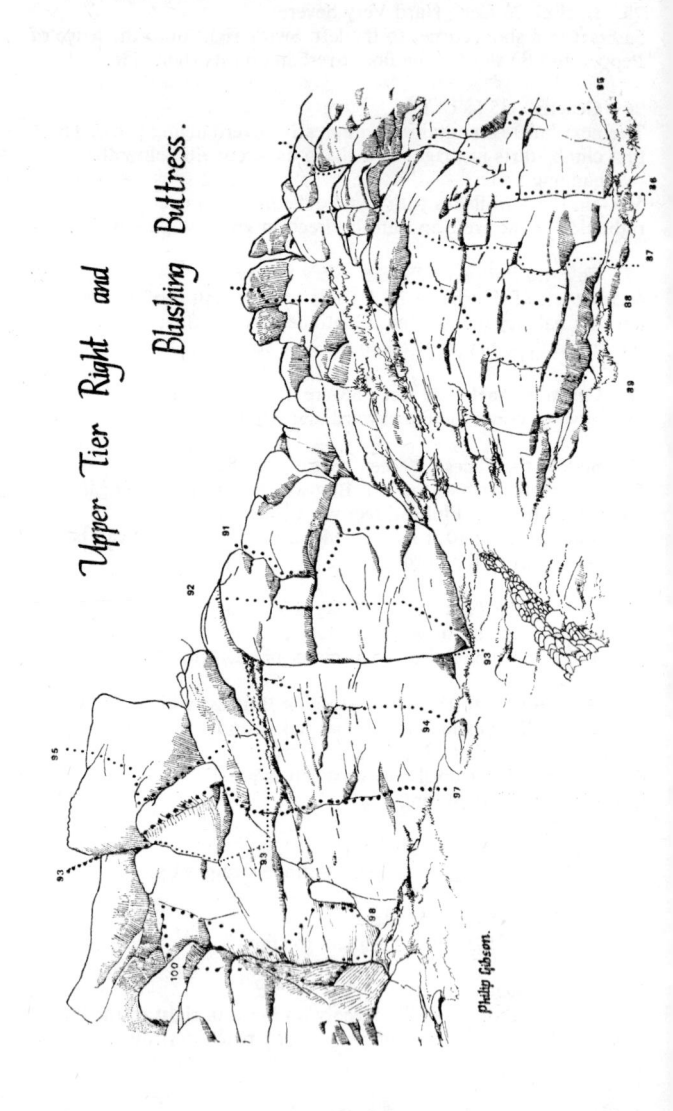

## THE ROACHES 151

**85 Gully Wall**  30 feet  Very Severe
4b. Ascend the large flakes to an awkward exit left onto the nose of Righthand Route.

**86 Righthand Route**  40 feet  Hard Very Difficult  ★★
On the front face is a polished layback crack. Go desperately up the crack to a small ledge on the right. Follow cracks to the protruding nose which is attacked direct.

**87 Lefthand Route**  40 feet  Very Difficult  ★
6 ft left is another crack undercut at its base. Ascend to a good hold, then follow shallow cracks to a move over a bulge. Go delicately to a wide crack and so to the top.

**88 War Wound**  35 feet  Hard Very Severe
5b. Start 3 ft left of Lefthand Route. Pull up (hard) and continue to the ledge. Traverse left to finish up the slabby arete.

**89 Scarlet Wall**  35 feet  Severe
4a. Strenuously up the crack near the left end of the buttress to gain a ledge on the right. Step up carefully to an exit left.

**90 Aperitif**  80 feet  Severe
This interesting girdle traverses the buttress from left to right.
4a. Start in a cave 5 yards left of Scarlet Wall. Traverse right above the lip to the crack of Scarlet Wall. Hand-traverse into Lefthand Route. Follow it for a few moves until it is possible to reach the ledge on Righthand Route. Swing right strenuously to reach the gully. Continue right across the next buttress.

Above and left of Blushing Buttress are three jutting prows. The centre one, by swinging right and over the lip, is a good 5a problem. A short wall 15 yards right provides further worthwhile problems. The keen boulderer will discover many hidden delights within the complex assortment of rocks in this particular area.

### UPPER TIER—MAIN SECTION
A drystone wall runs from the top of the steps towards a rock face. The main section of the Upper Tier starts here and continues left for several hundred yards until another wall provides a boundary between this main section and the Skyline Buttresses.

**91 Hangman's Crack**  35 feet  Severe
The righthand side of the first wall contains a large roof flake. From the right corner of the wall climb direct to the roof. Step left then go boldly up the wide crack. Protection difficult.

**92 Babbacombe Lee**  35 feet  Hard Very Severe
5b. To the left is the prominent undercut crack of Crack and Corner. Start just right of the crack and make hard moves to gain a ramp. Continue to a short crack and finish boldly over the nose.

**93 Crack and Corner**  115 feet  Severe  ★★
1. 30ft. Ascend the undercut crack to a large ledge. The initial overhang, 4c, can be overcome by bridging, pure strength or controlled temper. If all these fail traverse in from the right.
2. 40ft. Stroll left along the ledge to belay at a large block.
3. 45ft. Up the wall above via long pockets then left onto a ledge. Follow the corner and take the overhang on surprising holds.

**94 Roscoe's Wall**  25 feet  Hard Very Severe  ★
10 feet left of Crack and Corner is a line of weakness.
5b. A crafty heel hook enables a small niche to be gained. Either finish over the bulge slightly left or easier, to the right. From the grassy ledge a good continuation is to follow the righthand of two leaning breaks. This is:

**95 Round Table**  35 feet  Hard Very Severe
5a. Steeply up to a bold move into a wide crack. Swing across the bulge to the right and continue more easily.

**96 Magic Child**  20 feet  Hard Very Severe
5a. The left side of the lower wall contains a thin crack (Jelly Roll). 5 ft right are flakes low down. Start at the flakes and pull up to holds leading right. Up again via a pocket. Move left then right.

**97 Jelly Roll**  75 feet  Hard Severe
1. 20ft. 4a. The thin tiring crack. Belay at the block.
2. 55ft. Up the wall via long pockets to move right into the sloping crack. Follow this to the overhang of Crack and Corner. Finish airily over this.

**98 Easy Gully Wall**  70 feet  Very Difficult
1. 20ft. Follow a blunt rib 10 ft left of the thin crack to a block.
2. 50ft. Step left onto a steep wall climbing leftwards to a sandy ledge. Climb the short layback crack and bulge. Traverse left across a slab below the overhang. Finish up a gritty crack.

**99 Destination Venus**  80 feet  Hard Very Severe
5b. A traverse of the lower wall is possible from right to left. From below the short crack on Babbacombe Lee hand-traverse left into Crack and Corner. Step down then left again, crux, to reach the obvious traverse line into Jelly Roll.

To the left is **Easy Gully** (which definitely isn't easy) and left again an overhanging wall; here lurks:

**100  Bed of Nails**  40 feet  E2
5b. Somehow reach the crack over the roof and follow it to less strenuous ground. Continue left, then up to belay.

**101  Antithesis**  50 feet  E3 †
6a. The concave wall left of Bed of Nails. Work up left towards the exposed lip by an inventive series of finger changes and heel hooks. Finish up the front face. On the first ascent a small wire runner was placed in Bed of Nails at 12 ft.

**102  Kelly's Shelf**  55 feet  Hard Very Difficult  ★
The slanting ledge on the front face of Kelly's Buttress is often the scene of humorous fiascos (and the odd complete botch). Gain the left end of the ledge from below and follow it rightwards to a crack finish, or harder, from the right end pull over the bulge to pockets and so to the top (Hard Severe).

Kelly's Buttress has two other climbs: **The Direct**, Hard Very Severe, 5a, which goes straight up from the left end of the ledge to a large pocket and the top. **The Connection**, Hard Very Severe, 5a, is a strenuous traverse line from the roof of Righthand Route to meet The Direct at the pocket.

To the left is the Great Slab which is capped by a huge overhang overlooking a large perched flake; The Pedestal.

**103  Right Route Right**  50 feet  Mild Very Severe
4b. Climb the extreme right side of the slab past a short crack to a roof. Finish over this and climb the corner above.

**104  Right Route**  80 feet  Very Difficult  ★★★
1. 45ft. Follow worn holds near the right side of Great Slab to a roof. Step delicately left then go up to a large ledge on the right.
2. 35ft. Make an ascending and very exposed traverse leftwards to a crack and the top. A fine climb needing good footwork.

**105  Central Route**  50 feet  Mild Very Severe  ★
4a. Climb the slab between Right Route and The Pedestal on small holds. Quite bold. Traverse right below the overhang to belay.

154 GRITSTONE AREA

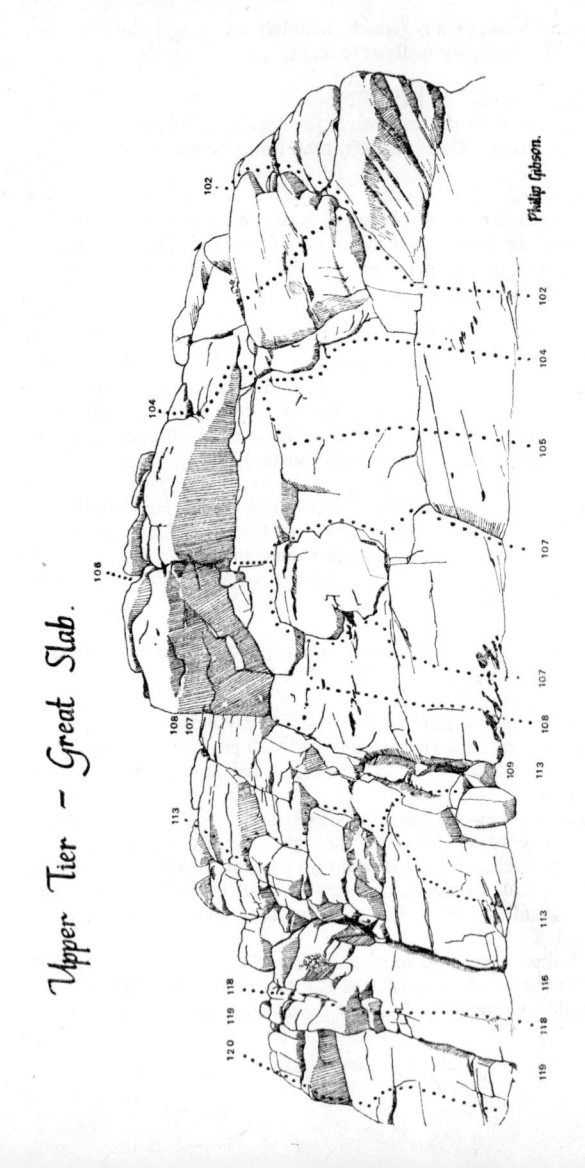

*Upper Tier – Great Slab.*

Philip Gibson.

## THE ROACHES 155

**106 The Sloth** 80 feet   Hard Very Severe ★★★
5a. A milestone in any leader's roof-climbing career. From the top of The Pedestal climb the short wall to a block, then launch out across the roof using flakes and adrenalin to a strenuous pull into a wide crack and so to the top. A direct approach to The Pedestal flake is possible together with its front face, 5b.

**107 Pedestal Route** 90 feet   Hard Very Difficult ★★★
1. 40ft. Either climb a short ramp then move left to the crack forming the right edge of the flake, or harder, climb the steep wall direct to the left crack and strenuously follow it to The Pedestal. Belay.
2. 50ft. Tiptoe left across the slab and into a corner, possible belay, then go up to and over a small overhang to an easier corner finish. A strategically placed nut prevents the rope jamming at the overhang.

**108 Technical Slab** 75 feet   Hard Severe ★
4a. Start 10 ft right of Hollybush Crack. Climb the steep slab with long and committing reaches. Traverse left below the overhang and into a corner. Continue over the small overhang above and finish up the final corner.

**109 Hollybush Crack** 90 feet   Mild Very Severe
To the left a narrow boulder rests at the foot of a chimney containing a holly bush.
1. 45ft. 4a. Bridge up above the holly until it is possible to step right into a wide crack. Belay a bit higher.
2. 45ft. 4b. Follow the crack over the small overhang and up the corner to a thread. Step down, then quiver rightwards across the steep exposed wall to finish near the right arete.

**110 Gillted** 100 feet   E3 †
5c. From below the thread of Hollybush Crack move down then blindly swing round to the very lip of the great overhang, (crux) and in a few feet the 'cave' under the roof. A hole above and right of this extricates the climber lucky enough to find it. A somewhat exposed route!! On the first ascent a second runner was placed in the lip of The Sloth.

**111 Diamond Wednesday** 85 feet   Mild Very Severe ★
4b. Follow Hollybush Crack but continue up the thin crack on the left to a small triangular roof. Go over this. Climb the wall above.

156  GRITSTONE AREA

**112  Black Velvet**  90 feet  Hard Very Difficult  ★★
Start as for Hollybush Crack but swing left into the corner of Black and Tans. Climb this and the roof above to continue up the easier final crack. A direct and enjoyable climb.

**113  Black and Tans**  100 feet  Severe  ★★★
1. 50ft. Start as for Black Velvet. Swing left into the obvious corner. Follow it until a ledge on the left can be gained. Plod across to a belay in the corner.
2. 50ft. Go up the corner above then left onto the nose. Continue direct to the top by three increasingly precarious and unprotected mantleshelf moves.

Scoffing experts may wish to do the Very Severe variation; start 12 ft below and left of Black Velvet at some long pockets. Step up then left to flake holds. Go up again then right to follow the original to the stance. Climb the wall on the right and climb the overhang direct, 5a, to finish up the wall above.

**114  Ruby Tuesday**  100 feet  E2  ★
A varied and technical expedition.
1. 40ft. 5b. Start as for Black and Tans variation but continue direct to the overhang, pull over this into a delicate groove then stretch up right and belay as for Black and Tans.
2. 20ft. 4b. Swing up and left round the rib to belay below cracks.
3. 40ft. 5b. Go up the cracks for 10 ft then cross left to the arete overlooking Jeffcoat's Chimney. Interesting moves up this lead to the top.

**115  Hanging Around**  80 feet  Hard Very Severe
5b. Start 10 ft left of Ruby Tuesday and climb a bulging wall. Continue direct to the large cracked roof above. Hard moves lead over this to the Buttress route. Finish up this.

**116  Jeffcoat's Buttress**  90 feet  Severe  ★★
Start just right of the chimney. A desperate few feet lead to easier moves up to a little corner left of an overhang. Pull up using a hidden hold, then traverse awkwardly right above the large roof to a belay below two cracks. Follow these cracks to the top.

**117  Jeffcoat's Chimney**  80 feet  Very Difficult  ★★
A classic and justifiably popular climb.
1. 60ft. Climb the chimney direct to a cave and go out over its roof to a vast stance. There are two variations for the lower chimney: either climb the wall on the left then move right to the cave, Severe, or follow the chimney for 10 ft, step right then up to where the wall steepens and left to the chimney. Difficult.

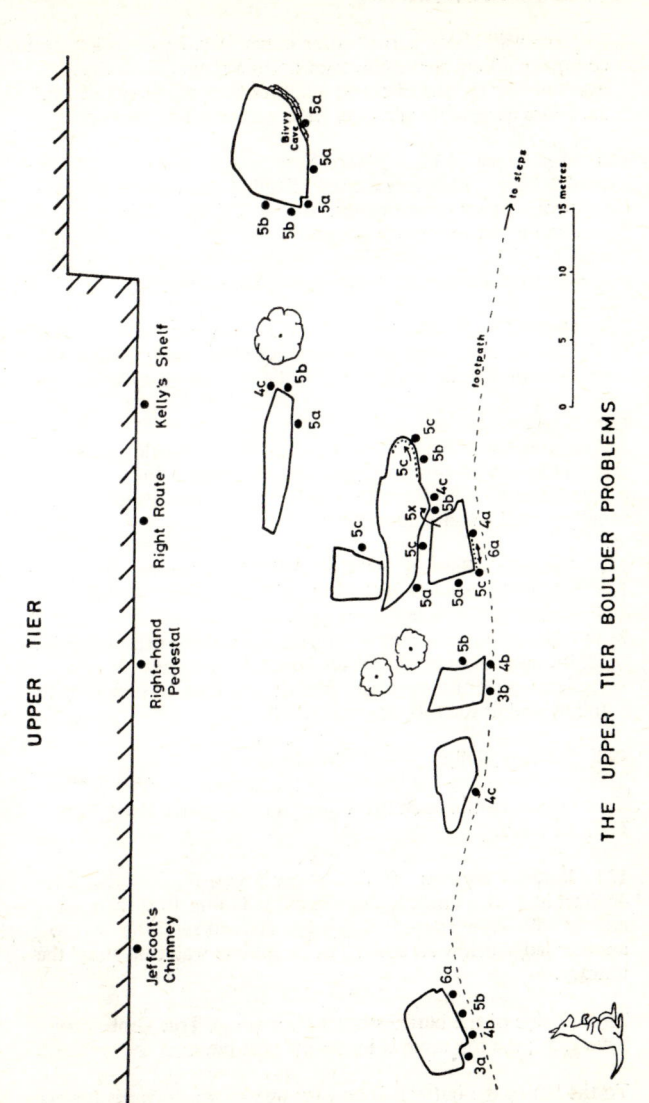

THE ROACHES 157

**UPPER TIER**

Jeffcoat's Chimney

Right-hand Pedestal

Right Route

Kelly's Shelf

Bivvy Cave

THE UPPER TIER BOULDER PROBLEMS

158  GRITSTONE AREA

2. 20ft. The wall above is frustrating either way. From its lefthand end make a long step right, then up to a move left at the overlap. The righthand corner requires strong fingers to start, 5a. More acceptable climbing leads across left to the top.

**118  Humdinger**  60 feet  Hard Very Severe  ★

Left of Jeffcoat's Chimney a crack, Saul's Crack, cleaves a steep path through a set of overhangs. Start 5 ft right of this.
5b. Ascend direct to a move left above the first overlap of Saul's Crack. Lurch up for a tauntingly distant hold over the roof and pull over to easier climbing, in a direct line to the top.

**119  Saul's Crack**  60 feet  Hard Very Severe  ★★★

5a. Follow the crack past an overlap to a strenuously baffling move over the roof. Continue more easily. Direct and absorbing.

**120  Gypfast**  60 feet  E3  ★★

5c. The roof left of Saul's Crack. Ascend the slab below its left side and follow ever-weakening flakes across right to its widest point. Pull over onto Bachelor's Buttress to finish. Protection is usually placed either side of the roof.

**121  Bachelor's Buttress**  60 feet  Mild Very Severe  ★

1. 30ft. Start 5 yards left of Saul's Crack and climb the slab diagonally left to belay in the gully.
2. 30ft. 4a. Make an ascending traverse right to the exposed arete. Finish up a short crack. **Direct Finish**, Very Severe, 4c. Go straight up from the crux of the original. Easy to find, easy to follow and at the top, easy to fall off.

**122  Rotunda Gully**  50 feet  Moderate

The gully bounding the left side of the buttress. A crack in the right face of Rotunda Buttress gives an alternative Hard Very Difficult pitch.

**123  Rotunda Buttress**  60 feet  Very Severe

4c. Start at a wide crack left of the gully. Go up 10 ft then left and up with some concern to a ledge. Ascend right then left to another ledge below an arete. The steep final wall can 'sting' the unwary.

The left side of the buttress has a poor route, **True Grot**, Very Severe, 5a; the top arete is by far the best bit.

To the left of the buttress is an easy way down. 10 yards further left the rocks begin again. Their right side consists of an arete

# THE ROACHES 159

*Upper Tier – Central Massive Area.*

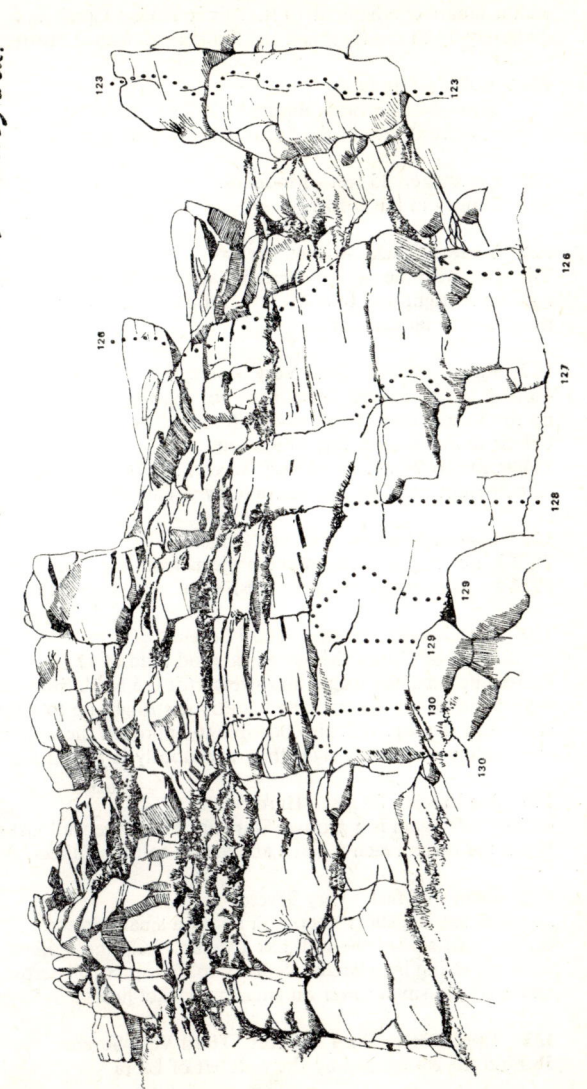

with a square overhang at 10 ft. This is Tealeaf Crack and
discretely up to the right is a small diamond-shaped buttress.

**124  A Short Trip to a
         Transylvanian Brain Surgery   25 feet   Mild Severe**
Climb the front face of the buttress on surprising holds.

**125  Cornflake   25 feet   Moderate**
The chimney in the corner.

**126  Tealeaf Crack   40 feet   Severe**   ★
The arete with the square overhang at 10 ft. Move round the
roof on its right side to a crack and difficult move. Step left and
finish up the pleasant arete.

**127  Aqua   40 feet   Mild Very Severe**
4b. 10 ft left of Tealeaf Crack is a roof split by a thin crack. Go
up to this and over it strenuously (either direct or slightly right).
Continue in the same line to the top.
**Public Enemy No. 1**, Hard Very Severe, 5a. The overhang 5 ft
further right can also be overcome by strenuous climbing.

**128  Central Massive   50 feet   Difficult**   ★
10 ft left of Aqua, a large flake projects from the face. Climb up
to this and continue direct to finish right of a steep wall.

**129  Lone Ascent   60 feet   Hard Severe**
5 yards left of Central Massive is a good hold at 12 ft.
4c. Step up on small ledges and stretch for the hold. Swing up
right to reach a wide crack and continue straight up to a final
crack and the top. It is also possible to approach the wide crack
from below by moving right then strenuously left to its foot.

**130  Joe Public   60 feet   Hard Severe**
4a. 10 ft left again is a groove. Start up this or the wall just right.
From the break reach a crack above and continue direct.

**131  Libra   45 feet   Very Severe**
20 yards left is a short steep wall above a small terrace.
4c. The right side of the wall has a vague crack line. Follow this
with increasing interest and delicacy to its top. Stroll across left
and ascend a small tower on amazing pocket holds.

**132  Third Degree Burn   30 feet   Hard Very Severe**
5b. Find the easiest line up the wall left of Libra.

## 133  Damascus Crack   40 feet   Hard Severe   ★
4a. 5 yards left is a crack on the right side of a slab. Follow this to a ledge and use flake holds to climb the small buttress above; alternatively take a short crack in a tower over to the left (Mild Very Severe).

## 134  Runner Route   35 feet   Severe   ★
From the left corner of the slab pad up rightwards with increasing delicacy. Mantleshelf then move back left to a holly. Finish up the crack behind this. Nice climbing.

The sharp arete to the left, **Dawn Piper,** gives an acute problem of Hard Very Severe, 5b, standard. Further left is a corner with a chimney and overhang above.

## 135  Broken Slab   40 feet   Severe
Ascend direct for 25 feet then bear right to a crack. Enter this with difficulty and follow it to the top. An inferior variation start is up the groove on the right and a direct finish to the original approach proves to be Mild Very Severe, 4b.

## 136  Reset Portion of Galley 37   40 feet   Hard Severe
4a. The corner with the chimney and overhang above. Ascend until forced to move awkwardly right below the roof. Finish up the crack.

## 137  Contrary Mary   60 feet   Very Severe
4b. To the left an oak grows out of a vegetated slab. Climb a short steep corner just right of this then go easily up to a final steep wall which gives a delicately exciting finish.

Left again is a clean slab overlooked by a steep wall. The right side is taken direct by **Lybstep,** Very Severe, 4b.

## 138  Maud's Garden   70 feet   Very Difficult   ★★
1. 45ft. Start below the centre of the slab. Nimble footwork for a few feet wins the obvious crack. Continue direct to a sandy ledge. Belay on the right.
2. 25ft. Puff up the chimney above the right side of the ledge then step left onto the exposed wall. Up this on good holds. It is possible to pull over the roof from the left side of the ledge but this is Severe.

## 139  Beckermet Slab   50 feet   Very Difficult   ★
Start at the foot of the gully left of Maud's Garden. Bridge against the slab to reach a horizontal crack and swing left to the arete; hard. Gain a higher ledge to finish up the slab and arete above.

# 162 GRITSTONE AREA

*Upper Tier – Maud's Garden Area.*

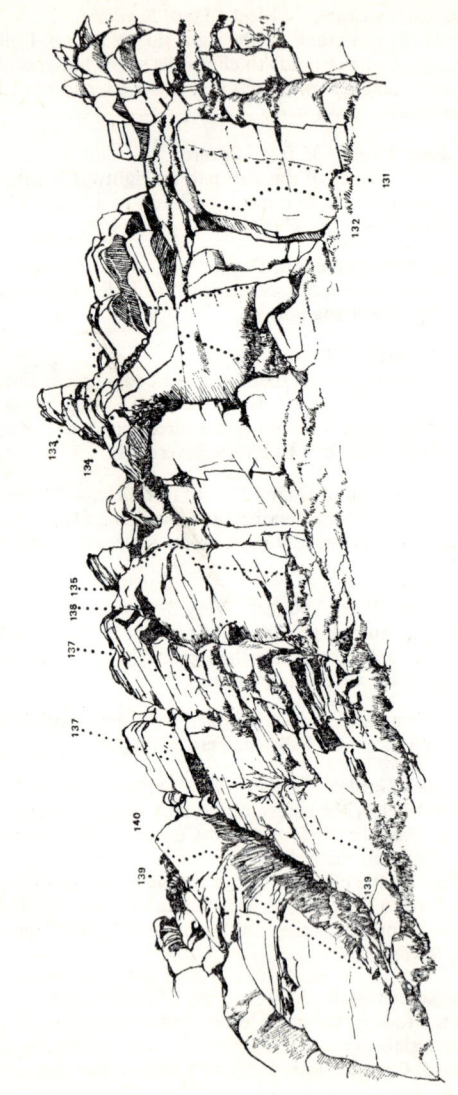

Philip Gibson.

## THE ROACHES 163

**140  The Valve**  50 feet  E2
5b. Start round the arete left of Beckermet Slab. With one long reach climb up to the ledge on Beckermet Slab. Cross the undercut wall to the right then ascend the steep top wall by moving first up then left to the arete. Layback up this.

**141  Late Night Final**  65 feet  Hard Very Difficult
10 ft left and at a lower level is an overhung buttress with a prominent narrow chimney on its right side.
Squirm and curse up the tight chimney until it eases to a stony gully. Continue up this to the top.

**142  West's Wallaby**  75 feet  Very Severe  ★
4b. Balance up a slanting crack to a block wedged under the right side of the overhangs. Swing wildly right across this and continue horizontally to the gully. Move up then left to finish up slabs.

**143  Wallaby Direct**  65 feet  Hard Very Severe  ★
5a. From midway along the traverse of West's Wallaby pull up the steep wall above, passing a short crack on the right. Continue direct.

**144  Walleroo**  65 feet  E2  ★
5c. As for West's Wallaby to the right side of the block. Make difficult fingery moves up and left over the bulge to an easier slab finish.

**145  The Wombat**  65 feet  E2  ★★
5b. Start off a boulder and climb direct to a thread under the roof. This leans menacingly above but a good flake carries the climber to flat holds and an isolated feeling over the lip whilst clutching a blind crack. Continue up the slabs above.

**146  Wrong Way Round**  65 feet  E2
5b. Climb up to and follow dirty flakes in a groove on the left side of The Wombat roof. Step left to attack other larger flakes then wander up the arete above. Unquestionably mediocre.

**147  Capitol Climb**  65 feet  Hard Severe
4a. Near the left of the buttress is a short corner crack capped by an overhang. Go up to this and step right between roofs to a nose, crux. A crack on the right, then slabs above, complete the climb.

**148  Heather Slab**  45 feet  Hard Very Difficult
To the left a vegetated slab forms the back wall of a large recess.

# 164 GRITSTONE AREA

*Upper Tier – Chicken Run Area.*

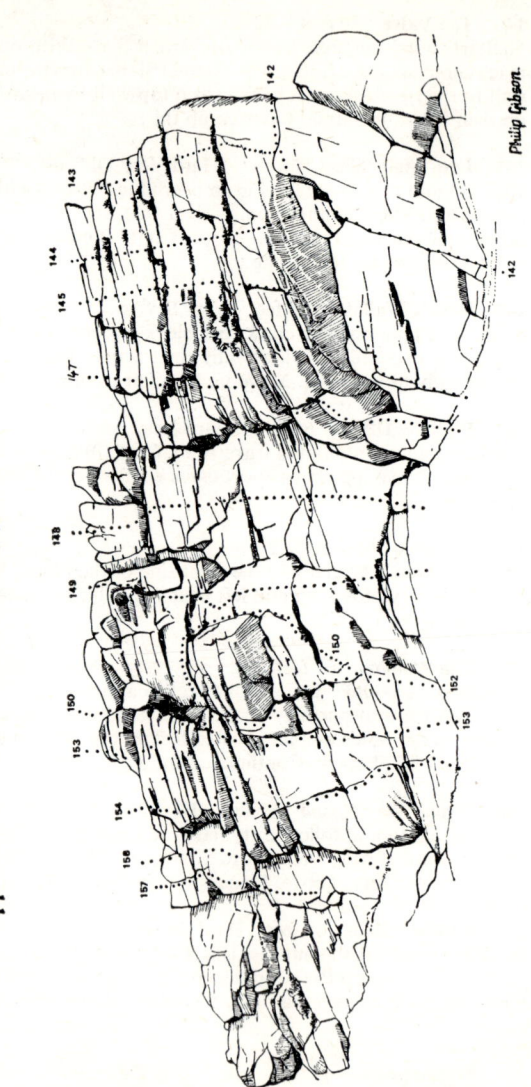

Philip Gibson.

Climb the centre of the slab direct finishing a few feet left of a short wide crack.

The left side of the recess is bounded by a short wall high up. This offers two lines.
**Crenation,** Hard Very Severe, 5a, is up the centre of the wall.
For **The Sublime,** Hard Very Severe, 5a, move left and climb the arete. It is possible to approach the arete from below and left, but this makes the climbing harder and somewhat artificial.

**149   The Tower of Bizarre Delights**   50 feet   E3   ★
5c.Climb a blunt undercut rib to the left of Heather Slab and work up the grooved, overhanging tower above by a series of intense and exciting moves.

**150   Inverted Staircase**   70 feet   Difficult   ★
1. 50ft.Start at the lowest point of the buttress and move up to the right to climb a groove at the right end of the big overhang. From the groove an alternative is to move left to the arete.
2. 20ft.Wriggle up through the boulders covering a short chimney at the back of the ledge.

**151   Simpkin's Overhang**   45 feet   E4
5c.The large roof to the left of Inverted Staircase. Gain the roof and cross it by an impressive hand-traverse using the curving flake. Pull up to safety at its end. A route to tire the mind and body at an alarming rate. From the sandy ledge it is possible to climb a thin crack; **Fantasy Finish,** 5b.

**152   Perverted Staircase**   40 feet   Very Severe
5a.The obscene crack splitting the left side of the overhang brings heavy breathing from most leaders.

A sandy terrace at 10 ft is the start of the next three climbs.

**153   Demon Wall**   50 feet   Hard Severe
1. 30ft.Left of Perverted Staircase is an undercut sandy corner. Go up to the roof below the corner and pull over on pockets. Continue up to the right to a spacious ledge.
2. 4b.Climb polished holds left of the chimney; hard.

**Heartbleed,** Very Severe, 5a†, is 5 ft left of Demon Wall pitch 1. Unfortunately the rock is extremely dirty.

## 166  GRITSTONE AREA

**154  Fern Crack**  60 feet  Very Difficult  ★
1. 30ft. Start below a crack line above the terrace. Strenuously climb the undercut pockets until a long flake can be grasped on the left. Continue to a thread, then go up and left to a ledge. Mantleshelf onto the next sloping ledge to belay. Alternatively from the thread, move right to a small notch then go up.
2. 30ft. Plod left round the corner into a recess to climb a crack or sloping holds on its right wall.

**155  Freak Out**  50 feet  Hard Very Severe
5b. Start below the left arete and use pockets to reach a break. Outwit the bulge by one antic or another and continue to a sloping ledge and finish up the rounded arete above.

**156  Chicken Run**  40 feet  Hard Difficult  ★
Up and to the left two slabby blocks rest against the foot of a slab.
Step up to a long pocket then follow obvious footholds to a ledge. From its right end step left then go precariously up to good handholds and the top.

**157  Rooster**  40 feet  Difficult
Climb the slabby boulders and continue direct to a ledge. Go up again to a jam crack and so to the top.

The Roaches Upper Tier has not escaped the inevitable girdles and the Great Slab area offers no fewer than three. In order to economise these are described without pitches or numerical grades which should maximise adventure possibilities.

**158  The Girdle Traverse**  250 feet  Severe
Start in Rotunda Gully and traverse right to Hollybush Crack. Cross 'Absolom's Gap' keeping tender parts well away from the holly and assemble left of the ramp of Kelly's Shelf (best soloed as it rarely gets 10 ft off the deck). Shuffle across this then, from its top ledge, slide down right and follow Crack and Corner to finish.

**159  The High Crossing**  240 feet  Very Severe  ★
Climbed from right to left. From Easy Gully hand-traverse beneath the roof to climb Kelly's Shelf with the Buttress finish. Cross left to The Pedestal and into Hollybush Crack. Swing left and across to meet Black and Tans at its stance. Go up then left to Jeffcoat's Buttress below the twin cracks. Reverse down left to a holly just left of the chimney. Climb to the top of Saul's Crack then descend diagonally to the ledge on Bachelor's Climb. Hand-traverse left into the gully.

**160  The Waistline**  200 feet  Hard Very Severe  ★
From Rotunda Gully cross beneath Gypfast roof into Saul's
Crack then go right to Jeffcoat's Chimney. Traverse right below
the roof of Hanging Around to swing across to Black and Tans
stance. Move down to Hollybush Crack and cross the Great Slab
at mid-height. Finish across Kelly's Connection.

## THE SKYLINE AREA
by Nick Longland

---

O.S. Ref. SK 005625 to 001635

SITUATION
The Skyline Area forms the natural continuation of the Roaches
Upper Tier, towards the north-west.

APPROACHES and ACCESS
As for the Upper Tier of The Roaches. The area can also be
reached by a path from the Five Clouds, or from the north along
the ridge from Roche End.

CHARACTER
The Skyline Area consists of about half a dozen distinct stretches
of rock set at a fairly amenable angle. Though clearly lacking the
size and majesty of the Upper Tier, the nature of the climbing is
similar; slabs, some of which are very holdless, predominate and
alternate with aretes and corners which in general yield routes
requiring more balance than brawn. It is primarily a place for
the seeker of solitude and anyone prepared to spurn the fleshpots
of the Upper Tier for a while may be rewarded by the quality of
the many little gems which a bit of persistence will uncover.
They may even see a wallaby.

THE CLIMBS are described from Right to Left.
10 yards beyond the gully bounding the left end of the Upper Tier
is a small square-cut buttress.

**161  The Pugilist**  20 feet  Very Severe
5b. The thin crack near the arete, through 2 overhangs, has an
enigmatic start. Unfortunately an escape right half-way up is
inviting.

## 168  GRITSTONE AREA

*Skyline Area – Condor Buttress.*

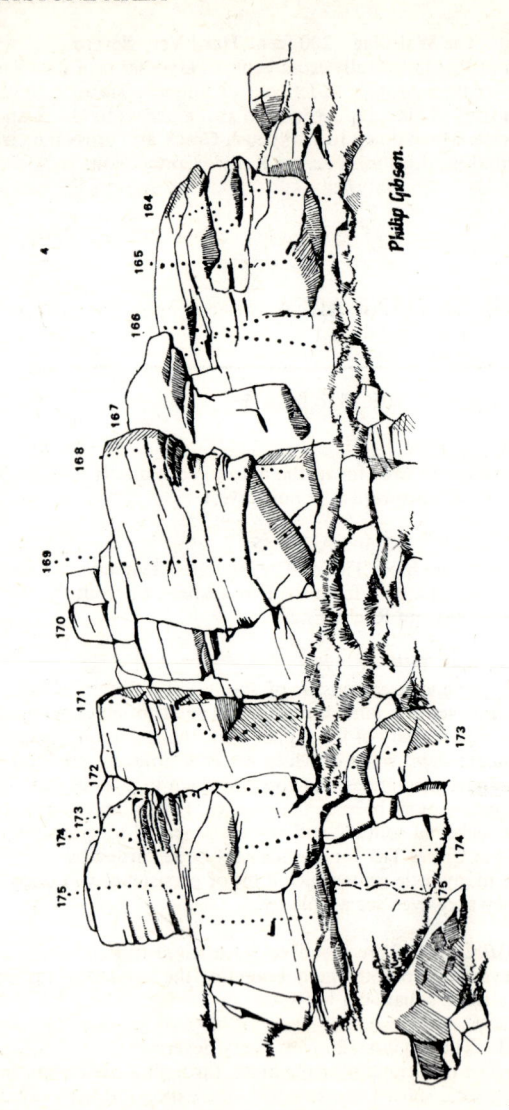

Philip Gibson.

**162 Happy Hooker**  25 feet  Hard Very Severe
5b. Climb a crack through the lower undercut 4 ft left. Move left and go up the slab on sloping holds. A more direct start is 5c.

**163 Southpaw**  20 feet  Severe
Climb the next crackline which widens to a slot at half-height. There is a short crack of Very Difficult standard 5 ft further left.

100 yards on is CONDOR BUTTRESS. At the righthand end is:

**164 Lung Cancer**  20 feet  Severe
Starting just right of a block, thread through the stepped overhang.

**165 Chicane**  20 feet  Very Difficult
Step off the block and follow the arete above.

**166 Navy Cut**  20 feet  Difficult
Gain a niche on the left (several approaches). Continue up behind, or to the right of the large prow.

**167 Bruno Flake**  20 feet  Severe  ★
The corner and awkward flake crack through the overhang above.

**168 Fagash Lil**  25 feet  Very Severe  ★
4c. Start up a little arete. Pull onto a ledge on the left. Climb diagonally right keeping close to the arete on the right. Exposed.

**169 Tobacco Road**  25 feet  Very Severe
4c. Go directly up the wall starting at a hold above the undercut.

**170 Time To Be Had**  25 feet  Very Difficult
The meandering crack left of the undercut, and right of an easy corner.

**171 Nosepicker**  25 feet  Hard Very Severe  ★
5b. Climb the blunt arete to the left. Make a thin move round the left side of the overhang to rejoin the arete leading to the top.

**172 Condor Chimney**  25 feet  Very Difficult  ★
The wide chimney just to the left provides satisfying bridging.

**173 Cracked Arete**  40 feet  Hard Very Difficult  ★★
Climb an arete, at a lower level, on polished holds to the base of Condor Chimney. Climb the slab and crack on its left.

170   GRITSTONE AREA

**174   A.M. Anaesthetic**   25 feet   Very Severe
4c. Balance up the blunt arete to the left on rounded holds. A lower but dubious start is feasible just right of the groove of Condor Slab.

**175   Condor Slab**   35 feet   Very Severe   ★
4a. The slab on the left has a hole in its centre. Below it a shallow groove leads to a ledge. Continue past the hole almost onto another ledge. Move right and up the middle of the buttress.

**176   Chicane Destination**   120 feet   Very Severe
4b. A girdle from the hole of Condor Slab to Chicane.

40 yards along the ridge are 3 buttresses known as THE TRIO. At the righthand end of the first buttress is:

**177   Ralph's Mantleshelves**   25 feet   Very Difficult
Follow a series of ledges leading slightly left.

**178   Lighthouse**   30 feet   Difficult   ★
Climb straight up from the lowest point of the buttress.

**179   Substance**   25 feet   Very Severe
4c. Left is an arete. Climb it on its leaning left side. Fingery.

2 rather scruffy corners at the back of the recess provide:
**180   Trio Chimney**   20 feet   Very Difficult

**181   Square Chimney**   25 feet   Difficult

**182   Left Twin Crack**   30 feet   Hard Severe
The groove and crack diverging leftwards from Square Chimney.

**183   Shortcomings**   30 feet   Hard Very Severe   ★
5c. Go straight up to the righthand end of the flake near the top. The tall can place a runner in the flake for the very thin move up to it. Ingenuity and faith may be critical for the less tall.

**184   Safety Net**   30 feet   Hard Very Severe   ★★
5b. A fine series of moves up the broad undercut rib and crack through the overhang above.
**Central Traverse**, 4c, is a line above the initial undercut.

**185   Hank's Horror**   25 feet   Hard Very Severe
5b. Go up the hanging corner round to the left. Swing right precariously to enter the wide crack. **The Direct Start** is reportedly 5c.

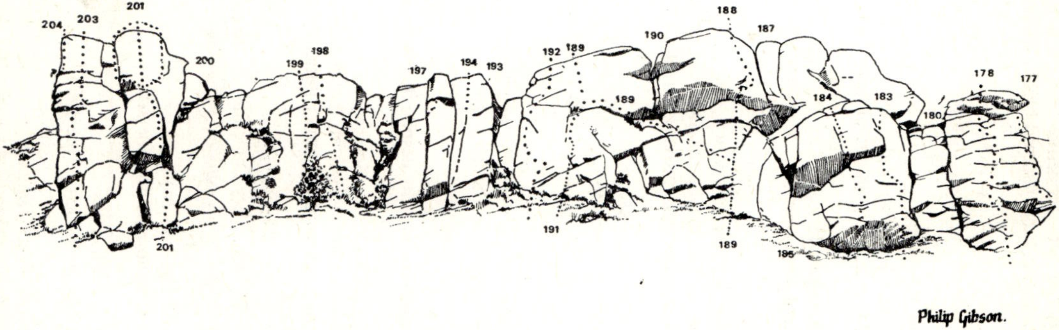

THE ROACHES 171

Philip Gibson.

Skyline Area ~ Tower Buttress and the Trio.

## 172  GRITSTONE AREA

**186  Letterbox Gully**  30 feet  Moderate
The slab and hole below the huge jammed block. Useful descent.

**187  Letterbox Cracks**  20 feet  Very Severe
4c. The cracks either side of the block, as a pair or individually.

**188  Topaz**  30 feet  E2  †
5c. Follow the blunt arete left of the gully up to a thin crack above the overhang. Use this to gain a final ramp.

**189  Rowan Tree Traverse**  45 feet  Very Difficult
Take the initial arete of Topaz for 15 ft. Traverse left, past a cave, to exit up a layback crack at the end of a bilberry ledge.

**190  Middleton's Motion**  30 feet  Very Severe
4b. Climb up to the cave. Thrutch up the awkward crack above; the coffin-shaped cave on the right provides a rest for the needy.

**191  Spectrum**  25 feet  Very Severe
4c. Delicately up a slight groove and slab just left of a detached block. Finish up the layback crack of Rowan Tree Traverse.

**192  Bad Sneakers**  25 feet  Hard Very Severe
5c. Pad up the very thin slab on the left converging with, but avoiding the edge of the gully to the left.

**193  Spare Rib**  25 feet  Severe  ★
The next rib. Interesting and worthy despite its cramped location.

**194  The Black Pig**  25 feet  Very Severe
4b. The incipient crack slanting away from the chimney. Poorly protected. Use may be made of the chimney initially, to get established in the crack.

**195  Ogden Recess**  25 feet  Very Difficult
The chimney/groove. Beware of its contents which might avalanche.

**196  Ogden Arete**  25 feet  Severe  ★
The next arete has a strenuous undercut start.

**197  Ogden**  30 feet  Difficult
Climb the obvious crack to the left of the arete.

**198  Oversight**  30 feet  Very Difficult
The blunt arete left of a little stony gully is climbed direct.

**199 Bad Poynt**  20 feet  Difficult
10 ft left is a perched block. Up this and the slab and crack.

10 yards on is the more imposing TOWER BUTTRESS.

**200 Thrug**  25 feet  Very Severe ★
4b. The steep crack slanting up the right wall of the buttress. Sustained.

**201 Perched Block Arete**  60 feet  Very Difficult ★
Starting from its lowest point, follow the arete mostly on its right side to the top block. Step left, exposed, to the final chimney. There are 2 other finishes from the top perched block:
(a) Very Severe, 4b. Climb straight up.
(b) Hard Very Severe, 4c. Move right to a layback flake. Ascend this.

**202 Tower Chimney**  50 feet  Difficult
The prominent chimney up the front of the buttress.
Another start, **Lefthand Start,** Very Difficult, is up the V-groove on the left which converges with the chimney at 25 ft.

**203 Tower Face**  45 feet  Hard Very Severe
5b. From the foot of the V-groove, go straight up the shallow crack system to a hold on the right at the top. Finish above.

**204 Tower Eliminate**  45 feet  Hard Very Severe ★
5b. Go up steep layaway cracks just left of the arete to a hold. Reach left to the base of a crack. Climb this to a niche. Continue up the crack, or, better, traverse right and up the arete.

**205 Sorcerer's Apprentice**  30 feet  Very Severe
4c. The wall to the left until forced left to sloping ledges and a crack.

50 yards left is CAVE BUTTRESS. 20 yards right of its high-arched cave is a fine arete. This is:
**206 Joiner**  30 feet  Very Difficult

**207 Connector**  30 feet  Very Severe
4b. The wall to the left starting up a flake. Scrappy top half.

**208 King Swing**  25 feet  Very Severe
5a. Swing round the hanging arete just right of the smaller block in the cave. Follow the arete and slab above.

## 174 GRITSTONE AREA

**209 Cave Crack** 20 feet Hard Very Severe
5a. The roof crack above the smaller block, on widening jams.
Bridging out right at the lip reduces the grade to Very Severe, 4c.
**Mousetrap Start**, 5a. Traverse in below the roof from the left.

**210 Stephen** 25 feet Very Severe
5a. The strenuous crack and V-chimney above the left edge of the cave.

**211 Cave Arete** 50 feet Mild Severe ★
From the lowest point of the buttress go up an arete to a ledge.
Step left and go up the slab until a hard move right leads to the exposed final arete.
**Distinction Finish**, Severe. Step further left from the ledge and go up the slab. A gap filler.

**212 Cave Buttress** 40 feet Difficult
Up a short corner to the ledge of the Arete. Wander diagonally left to finish up a broken crack. Scrappy.

70 yards left is the next buttress.

**213 Capstan's Corner** 25 feet Difficult
The righthand edge of the buttress gives a good clean route.

**214 Mistaken Identity** 30 feet Hard Difficult
Go up the middle of a slab left of a grassy groove. Surmount the overhang on the right or by a wider crack on the left; harder.

**215 Sally James** 30 feet Very Severe
4c. The arete of the buttress 10 yards left involves well-rounded pulls.

50 yards left is the best and largest expanse of rock, SKYLINE BUTTRESS. The crack on the right wall is too close to broken ground to warrant the status of a climb. Round the corner is:

**216 Skytrain** 45 feet E2 ★
5b. From the undercut base of the arete a thin crack leads left.
Move 5 ft right at the top and go up the slab trending slightly left, with mounting concern, to the overlap and final flake.

**217 Slab and Arete** 55 feet Severe ★★★
Start 8 yards left at 2 small pockets. Use these and the corner to the left if necessary and go up the slab for 15 ft. Traverse right to the exposed arete and go up on rounded holds. Classic.

# THE ROACHES 175

*Skyline Buttress.*

*Philip Gibson.*

## 176  GRITSTONE AREA

**218  Acid Drop**  45 feet  E4  ★★★
5b. A direct line above Slab and Arete start. Up on diminishing holds to a crucial long reach for a hold on the arched overlap. Finish up the final crack above the roof. An excellent but virtually unprotectable route.

**219  Karabiner Crack**  40 feet  Moderate
Any of several cracks lead, without interest, to a final chimney.

**220  Abstract**  40 feet  Hard Very Severe
5a. A rather artificial and somewhat harder finish to Karabiner Crack, up the hanging crack 5 ft right of the final chimney.

**221  Karabiner Slab**  35 feet  Very Severe
4c. The centre of the slab to the left. Finish up the crack.

**222  Karabiner Chimney**  35 feet  Very Difficult  ★
The chimney on the left. Pleasant climbing to a thrutchy exit.

**223  Enigma Variation**  30 feet  Hard Very Severe  ★
5a. Start up Mantleshelf Slab and follow the delicate right arete to a flake. Move left and up the slab. Quite bold.

**224  Mantleshelf Slab**  30 feet  Hard Severe  ★
From the base of the slab left of the Chimney trend slightly right to a mantleshelf. Continue to a flake and the top. A delicate pitch.

**225  Bilberry Traverse**  100 feet  Hard Severe
A mid-height traverse from the gully bounding the buttress on the right to Mantleshelf Slab. The crux is crossing Enigma Variation.

**226  Come Girl**  40 feet  Hard Severe
Up a square-cut rib 5 yards left of Mantleshelf Slab. Layback the next arete just right of an oak sapling. Finish up a crack right of the top bulge.

**227  Go Girl**  40 feet  Hard Very Difficult
A vegetated line up cracks 6 ft left. Exit as for Come Girl (crux).

**228  Pinnacle Slab**  45 feet  Hard Difficult
To the left and at a lower level is The Pinnacle.
Climb the slab right of The Pinnacle, by its righthand side.

The leaning crack on the right side of The Pinnacle has been climbed.

**229 Pinnacle Arete**  25 feet   Very Severe ★
4b.The right arete of The Pinnacle's front face. Satisfying moves.

**230 Split Personality**  25 feet   Hard Very Severe
5b.Climb the arete for 5 ft, then diagonally left across the slab to a hairline crack which is ascended using tiny fingerholds.

**231 Pinnacle Crack**  20 feet   Difficult
The wide crack on the left side of the front face.

35 yards left is ALPHA BUTTRESS. Towards the righthand end is a crack leading to a chimney. This is Righthand Route. 10 ft right is:

**232 Looking For Today**  20 feet   Hard Very Severe
5b.Climb a blind crack in the wall to a bulge. Stretch over for a thin flake and pull up to easier ground.

**233 Righthand Route**  35 feet   Severe ★
Jam the crack and go up the chimney for a few ft, then traverse left and climb the righthand of 2 flakes. Continuously interesting.

**234 Definitive Gaze**  30 feet   Hard Very Severe
5c.The wall immediately left. Turn the initial scoop on the left, avoid Wallaby Wall with difficulty and finish right of Righthand Route flake. Another gap filler but not without interest.

**235 Wallaby Wall**  30 feet   Severe ★
The next crack past a ledge and up the tricky lefthand flake.

**236 39th Step**  25 feet   E1 to E3
6a.The very thin shallow groove and slab 10 ft left. The crack on the left is mostly within arm's reach and determines the grade.

**237 Sennapod**  20 feet   Very Difficult
The corner on the left.

**238 Mantis**  25 feet   Hard Very Severe ★★
5a.The arete to the left gives a fine exercise in layaway technique.

**239 San Melas**  25 feet   E3 ★
6a.The slab to the left starting just left of centre. The upper section is both desperate and committing. A fairly mobile second may be an advantage.

## 178 GRITSTONE AREA

*Skyline Area – Alpha Buttress.*

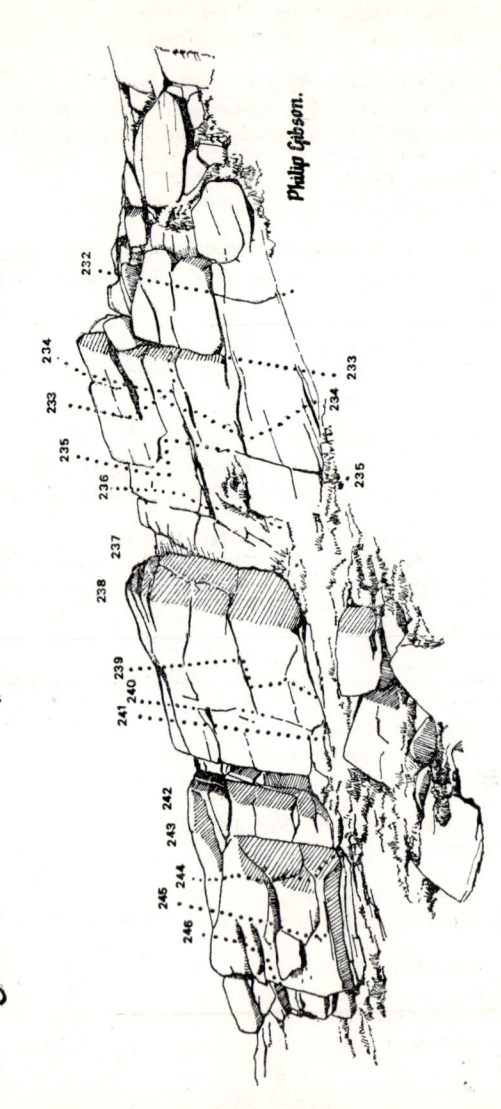

*Philip Gibson.*

**240  Days Gone By**  20 feet  Severe
The righthand of 3 close parallel cracks.

**241  Breakfast Problem**  20 feet  Very Difficult
The 2 lefthand cracks which merge into one.

**242  Alpha Arete**  20 feet  Hard Difficult
The pleasant arete left of the green corner.

**243  Alpha**  20 feet  Difficult
The V-groove just left, finishing over a small overhang.

**244  Devotoed**  20 feet  Very Severe
5a. The blunt undercut arete, gained from the right, has a sloping top.

**245  Melaleucion**  20 feet  Very Severe                           ★
4c. The middle of the front face, through the overhangs. Strenuous.

**246  Omega**  20 feet  Very Difficult
Pull over the bulge on the left to an awkward mantle on the right.

**247  Bone Idol**  110 feet  Very Severe
4b. Traverse from Omega to Righthand Route at roughly half-height.

The edge now deteriorates, the next significant buttress being FAR SKYLINE CRAG, 400 yards further along the ridge. Many small buttresses lurk in the intervening ground on which short routes and problems can be contrived.


**FAR SKYLINE CRAG**
This is a slabby buttress with a battlement-like top. It has a nose of rock near its centre forming a roof 5 ft above the ground. 10 yards right of the roof is a short flared chimney slanting leftwards.

**248  The Black Ram**  35 feet  Very Difficult
Climb a thin crack 5 yards left of the chimney to a square-cut groove. Ascend this and the steep cracks above.

**249  Black Ram Arete**  35 feet  Very Severe
4c. 10 ft left is a small ledge at 4 ft. From this move up and step right on small holds to a faint crack. Climb this and the left side of the arete above.

## GRITSTONE AREA

**250 Dangler**　35 feet　Mild Very Severe　　　　　　　　　★
4b. From the ledge at 4 ft, take a thin crack above to a bulge.
Pull rightwards over it and up the hairline crack and slab above.

**251 The Chimney**　35 feet　Severe
The blocky chimney just right of the roof. Leaving the ground,
either on the left or right side of the undercut is troublesome.
Bridging helps.

**252 Honky Tonk**　40 feet　Severe　　　　　　　　　　　★★
Climb a V-groove just left of the roof. Make a vast step right
above the lip and potter up the right arete of the slab.
**Direct Start**, 5a. Overcome the roof using holds on its right arete.

**253 Steeplechase Crack**　30 feet　Very Difficult
Climb a square-cut crack to a niche. Surmount the overhang
above on big holds and follow the crack to the top.

**254 Dazzler**　25 feet　Severe
Climb faint twin cracks in a shallow corner to a ledge at 10 ft.
A hard move up leads to easier ground and the top.

**255 Mudhopper**　20 feet　Very Difficult
The grassy leftwards slanting groove on the left.

**256 Slither**　25 feet　Severe
Climb the slab 10 ft left and the deceptive hanging corner above.

**257 Steeplechaser**　25 feet　Hard Difficult
Climb the large corner to the overhang. Traverse left to avoid it
and trend back right above.

**258 Tree Grooves**　20 feet　Difficult
The groove (or slab on its left) round the corner and 8 ft right of
a dead tree. Continue up the grassy groove.

**259 Tree Corner**　20 feet　Difficult
Up the corner behind the tree and through the gap in the
overhang. The arete on the left of the corner provides a pleasanter
start.

**260 Chronicle**　20 feet　Very Severe　　　　　　　　　　†
5b. The overlap and slab just right of Flutterbye Grooves.

## THE ROACHES 181

**261 Flutterbye Grooves** 20 feet Severe
From the base of the lefthand end of the crag gain wispy cracks from the left or direct; harder and better. Follow the cracks.

**262 Microcosm** 20 feet Difficult
The groove up on the left. Move right onto the buttress front at the top.

**263 The Girdle Traverse** 105 feet Severe
A traverse rarely more than 15 ft from the ground, the exact line of which is left to the adventurous to find.

220 yards on is the last group of rocks worthy of description. Although not high the climbing on them is very good.
The first is an undercut slab with a toppled flake on its right side, called VERY FAR SKYLINE CRAG.

**264 Mild Thing** 20 feet Difficult
Start up the flake until a crack in the slab can be ascended.

**265 Wild Thing** 20 feet Hard Very Severe ★★
5b. The faint groove in the slab 5 ft from the left arete, has an undercut start. A nice mixture of strenuous and delicate moves.

**266 Curvature** 20 feet Very Severe
30 yards left is an arete on a large boulder.
4b. The arete starting on its left side.

40 yards further on is a larger slab, steep and undercut and with a short chimney on its right. This is the aptly named HARD VERY FAR SKYLINE CRAG.

**267 Prelude To Space** 30 feet Very Severe ★★
4c. The blunt arete just left of the chimney. There is a balancy semi-mantleshelf near the top. Quite a serious route.

**268 Wings Of Unreason** 35 feet E2 ★★★
5c. The slab slightly left of centre contains some pockets. Pull over the undercut with difficulty and up the slab to the top line of pockets. The tall can reach the top. A further diabolical move or jump is necessary for the short, E4, 6b.

**269 Track Of The Cat** 35 feet E5 ★★
6a. The hanging left arete of the slab by its right side and starting directly below or by a flaky cutaway on the left. The final move is similar to that on Wings though the top is marginally less distant. Poorly protected.

**270 Inspiration Point** 60 feet  Hard Very Severe
5b. A problem traverse starting up the cutaway of the last route and crossing the slab just above the undercut to finish up Prelude To Space.

The ridge continues, albeit set back further to the east, to Roche End. The rocks along it yield many problems, the best being on some steep slabs between the last crag and the Trig. Point and on a pinnacle 250 yards north of the Trig. Point and 50 yards further than a Winnie-the-Pooh-shaped pinnacle. Its south-east side and an undercut wall a few yards south give problems of 5a/b.

# THE FIVE CLOUDS and Nth CLOUD
by Dave Jones

---

O.S. Ref. SK 001625

SITUATION
The crags are on the south-west flank of the Roaches ridge. They are midway between Upper Hulme and Roche End and about one hundred and fifty yards up the slope from the minor road that runs between these two points.

APPROACHES and ACCESS
From the Roaches lay-by pass through the gateway and immediately turn left to follow a track running almost parallel to the road. Follow this track for one third of a mile, past the old Roche End Quarries, until it peters out below the crags.
It is not possible to make a direct approach up the slope from the road as the area by the cottages is private land. In view of this climbers are asked to minimise noise and disturbance in order to preserve the good relations currently existing with the occupants. An approach from The Roaches is possible by following the path down the slope from the far left of the Upper Tier. Pass through the wood and over the moor until the path cuts through a scarp. Turn right here and follow the crest until the top of the crags can be seen to the left.

CHARACTER
The outcrops lie along a subsidiary scarp of the Roaches ridge and form five conspicuous humps. The Third Cloud presents the largest rock face, the Second and Fourth have smaller faces and the First and Fifth Clouds virtually no significant routes of any length. The climbs are very enjoyable and offer a pleasant alternative when the more popular areas are being used to capacity. The Third Cloud offers the finest climbs with Rubberneck, Crabbie's Crack and Flaky Finish being of classic status. Appaloosa Sunset will almost certainly become a popular route in the future.
It is also worth noting that the climbs still start and finish on ground not yet denuded of vegetation.

HISTORY
One of the early references to the Five Clouds concerned Harry Scarlet who had the misfortune to stumble over the top of one on a dark night, breaking a rib and nearly biting off his tongue. R. O. Downes visited the area in the early 50s and climbed

Crabbie's Crack, however it wasn't until the Spring of 1968 that the Clouds' full potential was realised. Martin Boysen free-climbed the thin crack in the Fourth Cloud to give Boysen's Delight but was unwittingly beaten to the first lead of Rubberneck by the Barley Brothers who, in fact, had led it some twelve months previously. Rubberneck became an instant classic and should be on any competent gritstoner's shopping list today. Boysen finally added the committing Flower Power Arete which needed the encouragement of a pre-placed runner to protect the crux; a few minutes later Colin Foord discovered the delicate Flaky Wall finish to Crabbie's Crack. 1968 also saw John Yates solo the Lefthand Variant; in 1969 he led Fifth Cloud Eliminate and a year later produced Private Display.

A period of inactivity followed until 1977 when Dave Jones noticed a line of holds in the blank-looking wall between Rubberneck and Crabbie's Crack. The lichen was vigorously removed and Appaloosa Sunset proved to be a fine route. Some months later Al Simpson forced the technically interesting top arete of Icarus Allsorts after several flying retreats. Jones returned with Simpson in 1978 and crossed the main face of the Third Cloud to effectively finish off the possibilities on the largest face of these crags.

Several minor climbs have been added since by various teams but the last major line to fall was climbed in 1979 as a solo ascent by Andrew Woodward. The result, Mirror Mirror, is a route very much in the modern idiom.

Nth Cloud, as it was originally known, has received relatively little attention and records of early climbing activity were non-existent. In the 60s, however, members of the North Staffs M.C. climbed most of the lines which included Plumbline by John Yates and Mayhem by Colin Foord in 1968. Colin Foord's prediction that the 'pebble age' of gritstone climbing was getting under way was totally justified by the first lead of The Pillar of Judgement by John Allen in 1977.

THE CLIMBS are described from Right to Left as one approaches.

THE FIRST CLOUD
There are no climbs of particular significance although a few interesting problems can be found.

THE SECOND CLOUD
This consists of two small buttresses. The righthand one is split by a fierce curving crack. The first route is up the steep wall to its right.

**1 Marxist Undertones**  25 feet  Very Severe
5a.Start at the undercut arete. Climb the wall to finish delicately up the slab above.

**2 Communist Crack**  25 feet  Very Severe ★
5a.The crack direct. A fine exercise in laybacking.

The lefthand buttress has a slab on its right arete and three cracks on the front face.

**3 K.G.B.**  20 feet  Hard Very Severe
4c.Climb the slab to a step left. Chicken out or finish boldly.

**4 Yankee Jam**  25 feet  Very Severe
5a.The flared righthand crack. Strenuous.

**5 Lenin**  25 feet  Hard Difficult
The central crack, which is hard to start.

**6 Legends of Lost Leaders**  25 feet  E1
5c.Gain the obvious sloping ledge by a precarious mantleshelf manoeuvre. Reach for the right arete and climb it quickly. It is also possible to climb the left side of the steep slab at HVS, 5b.

**7 Stalin**  25 feet  Very Difficult
The lefthand crack on beautiful jams.

**8 Jimmy Carter**  20 feet  Hard Very Difficult
The flakes and arete left of Stalin are quite pleasant.

## THE THIRD CLOUD
This outcrop comprises a large steep wall with a smaller face set back on its righthand side.

**9 Pointless Arete**  20 feet  Hard Severe
4b.Climb the right edge on layaways.

**10 The Big Flake**  20 feet  Hard Difficult
A good chimneying exercise.

**11 The Little Flake**  20 feet  Very Severe
5a.Green and trying.

**12 Tim Benzadrino**  20 feet  E1
5c.Start at the foot of No. 11. Ascend the wall above on small holds.

# 186 GRITSTONE AREA

*The Third Cloud*

**13  The Bender**  20 feet  Very Severe
4b. Follow the thin crack forming the right corner of the gully.

**14  Icarus Allsorts**  50 feet  E3  ★
6a. Make an unusual move through the roof of the cave to a standing position on the big flake. Step left and move up the slab to a ledge. Gain and use a flake on the left to reach holds to the right. Finish precariously. From the ledge the right arete is **Waxwing Finish**, HVS, 5a, which is more in keeping with the lower arete.

**15  Flower Power Arete**  50 feet  E1
5c. Follow the left rib of the cave to a ledge. Continue up until a stretch left enables a layback crack to be reached. Follow it to a ledge and final wide crack.

10 ft left is a green groove with a crack above.

**16  Crabbie's Crack**  55 feet  Very Severe  ★★★
4c. Go up the green groove to a crack; follow this to a ledge. Either climb the cracked wall above, or better, the superbly delicate rib on the right; **Flaky Wall Finish**, HVS, 4c.

**17  The Lefthand Variant**  55 feet  Very Severe
4c. Follow the green groove to the bulge where a move up and left enables flakes to be reached and followed to the ledge. Finish up the cracked wall.

Left again is a scoop, left of a 'burial chamber'. Just right is:

**18  Appaloosa Sunset**  55 feet  E2  ★★★
5c. Follow a shallow corner to finger holds leading rightwards; make a very long reach to gain a good hold in the middle of the wall. Continue up to a pocket and finish direct. Superb climbing. A nut is usually placed in Rubberneck to protect the crux.

**19  Rubberneck**  55 feet  Hard Very Severe  ★★★
5a. Climb the scoop to a short crack. Follow it to a tricky bulge. Once over this trend rightwards to a ledge. A short wall above completes the route. Sustained and immaculate climbing.

**20  Blue Bandanna**  80 feet  Hard Very Severe  ★
5a. The girdle traverse of the main wall. Start on the large flake above and right of the cave. Swing above the lip onto Flower Power Arete; cross into Crabbie's Crack and follow it to the flakes of the Lefthand Variant. Immediately move leftwards

across the steep wall (shaky flakes) to meet Rubberneck below the bulge. Follow the thin cracks direct or climb the slab to the left.

**21  Elastic Arm**   15 feet   Hard Very Severe
Two short crack climbs start from a terrace left of Rubberneck. 5b.The wide crack. Telescopic arms are an advantage.

**22  Glass Back**   15 feet   Very Difficult
The steep crack above the left end of the terrace.

Below this terrace is a short wall problem, **Persistence**, 6a.

## THE FOURTH CLOUD
The first climb starts from a rock shelf on the right of the crag.

**23  Roman Nose**   20 feet   Hard Very Severe
5b.The undercut slab. A 'bolder' problem.

**24  Chockstone Corner**   20 feet   Difficult

**25  Mantleshelf Route**   25 feet   Difficult   ★
Gain ledges leading left to a corner. Follow this.

**26  Mirror Mirror**   30 feet   E2
6a.Climb flakes in the steep wall just left to reach a thin crack near the right edge. Move up to a ledge and easy climbing.

**27  Boysen's Delight**   30 feet   Hard Very Severe   ★
5c.The thin crack; difficult moves at 10 ft constitute the crux.

**28  Private Display**   25 feet   Hard Very Severe
5b.The thin crack behind the large boulder; continue over the nose moving rightwards to gain a ledge. Finish slightly left.

**29  Righthand Block Crack**   15 feet   Severe

**30  Lefthand Block Crack**   15 feet   Severe

**31  Smun**   30 feet   Very Severe
4c.Follow the cracks to an awkward move. Finish to the right.

**32  Strangle Hold**   30 feet   Hard Very Severe
5b.Follow the layback crack 20 ft left up and rightwards to finish up Smun or just left. Rather devious.

# THE CLOUDS 189

*The Fourth Cloud*

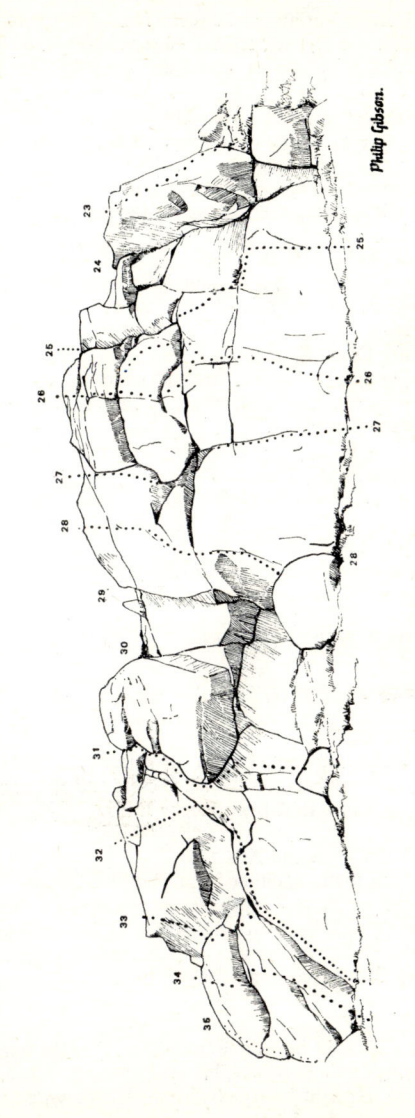

Philip Gibson.

**33 Meander Variation**  30 feet  Hard Very Severe
5b. Follow the layback crack to a move left onto the slab; go up this until it is possible to attack the steep right wall.

**34 Meander**  25 feet  Very Difficult  ★
Ascend to a bulge, go over it leftwards and onto the upper slab.

**35 Wander**  15 feet  Hard Difficult
The crack splitting the left side of the slab.

### THE FIFTH CLOUD
The only climbing of any value is to be found on a large fallen block forming an undercut slab.

**36 Fifth Cloud Eliminate**  30 feet  Hard Very Severe
5a. Swing up to a ledge on the left arete. Cross the slab to a shallow corner and finish direct. It can be started on the right side; Very Severe, 5a.

**37 Cloud Nine**  30 feet  E1
5b. Start as for the Eliminate but continue directly up the arete.

**38 Foxy Lady**  20 feet  Very Severe
5a. Follow cracks in the steep left wall to finish up the arete.

### Nth CLOUD (ROCHE END)

O.S. Ref. SK 998635

#### SITUATION
The outcrops are situated on the south-west flank of the Roaches ridge, midway between the ridge crest and the minor road, and just over half a mile from Roche End.

#### APPROACHES and ACCESS
Approach the crag either from The Five Clouds or the Skyline Area. Please do not approach the crag from directly below as this is causing problems with the farmer. The access situation here is very delicate at the minute and climbers are urged strongly not to do anything which might jeopardise any future negotiations.

#### CHARACTER
The crag is split into three buttresses, the righthand one, a steep wall split by three cracks, being the largest. The rock is sound and climbing pleasant in dry conditions but it can be greasy in the wet.

THE CLIMBS are described from Left to Right.

**1  Grenadier**  40 feet  Hard Difficult
Start at the lowest point of the front face of the lefthand buttress.
Climb into the sentry box and out via a crack; go up to a broken
corner crack and the top.

**2  Slanting Crack**  40 feet  Hard Very Difficult
Climb the lefthand of two slanting cracks on the righthand face
to a ledge at 20 ft. Finish up a shallow scoop.

**3  Mayhem**  40 feet  Very Severe
5a.The righthand crack to the overhang. Swing round to the left
to meet Slanting Crack.

**4  Green Chimney**  35 feet  Difficult
The leaning chimney bounding the right side of the buttress.
Finish over the chockstone.

A few good problems can be found on the central buttress.
The righthand buttress provides three crack climbs.

**5  Little Crack**  20 feet  Very Severe
5a.The lefthand crack until it fades. Finish slightly left.

**6  Rowan Tree Crack**  30 feet  Severe
Follow the centre crack all the way.

**7  Plumbline**  40 feet  Very Severe
4c.The righthand crack is most difficult at half-height.

**8  The Pillar of Judgement**  54 feet  E4                        ★
5c.Step off a huge boulder at the foot of the Pillar and ascend
to a ledge. Continue precariously to a wide crack at the top. A
bold undertaking.

**9  Barbeque Corners**  60 feet  Hard Very Difficult
Right of the main face a pinnacle rests at the foot of a corner.
Follow the groove formed by the right side of the pinnacle.
Traverse left and continue up the corner.

**10  The Pinnacle Start**  50 feet  Hard Severe
4a.From the foot of the pinnacle climb to a slanting ledge.
Follow this to the left then make an awkward move to the summit.
Leap off the top.

## HEN CLOUD
by Dave Jones

> *'Serious grit is like cornering a car right on the limit—commit yourself, keep the power down and it will see you through; hesitate or lift off and you're in for a big accident.'*
>
> Anon.

O.S. Ref. SK 008616

### SITUATION and APPROACHES
Hen Cloud is a very conspicuous hill overlooking Tittesworth Reservoir and the tiny village of Upper Hulme, 4 miles north of Leek.
Approach as for The Roaches as far as a gateway cutting through a line of trees on the right of the road and directly below the crag. Parking is allowed on the grass verge in the vicinity of the gateway but access must not be impaired. Follow the drive, through the gate, until it curves to the right. At this point strike left up the gruellingly steep path to the crags.

### CHARACTER
Hen Cloud is possibly the most majestic of all the gritstone cliffs. Standing alone, above a steep, fern-covered hillside, it dominates the surrounding area. The steep walls are broken by vertical cracks, corners and chimneys. This tends to make the climbs generally more difficult than those of The Roaches; a determination of attack being very much a prerequisite of successful ascent.
The rock is everywhere sound but unfortunately being in the direct path of the westerly airstream it catches any bad weather going. In these conditions climbs can become very slippery due to that gritstoner's green nightmare . . . lichen.

### HISTORY
The Kyndwr Club, in the persons of J. W. Puttrell, E. A. Baker and W. J. Watson, visited Hen Cloud at the beginning of this century but did not make any ascents of any importance.
In 1909, John Laycock and A. R. Thomson arrived at the foot of the main buttress quite late one evening. Laycock attacked the awkward crack which was to become the first pitch of Central Climb and managed after a great struggle to reach the ledge at its top. Thomson, after many attempts, had to admit that he was unable to follow and Laycock climbed on alone up the second crack and small corner above in the last of the daylight. He reached the large ledge below the final wall and sat beneath a

starry sky not daring to move in any direction until Thomson appeared above him with a sturdy chauffeur. They lowered a rope and hauled him up to safety. He later wrote 'the episode is delightful to me in retrospect: gritstone has its romance no less than granite'.

Stanley Jeffcoat and Siegfried Herford climbed Great Chimney shortly before the Great War of 1914-18. Jeffcoat in fact wrote the first guide to Hen Cloud in the Rucksack Club Journal of 1913. It included Central Climb, The Arete, Rib Chimney, Great Chimney, Footpath Chimney, Thomson's Buttress, Tree Chimney and the Inaccessible Pinnacle which then still lived up to its name, although the crack on the east face had been climbed to the ledge. Hall Cracks 'A' and 'B', which are now known as The Nutcracker and Deceiver, were described as 'extremely stiff 25-feet problems'. This is still very true, especially of Deceiver. Bow Buttress was climbed by 1924 and November Cracks together with the direct finish to Central Climb succumbed to a lead by 1927. Arthur Burns, junior, arrived on the scene to add K2, En Rappel (then known as Blizzard Buttress) and a line to the right of Reunion Crack. This latter route would seem to include some of The Pinch and he probably failed on the enormous reach for the top preferring to hand traverse left into Reunion Crack instead.

During the 30s access to the crags was difficult and many stories have been related of encounters with keepers armed with shot guns, and with the various animal inhabitants of the open-air zoo which used to flourish beneath the crags. The war years led to a relaxing of the difficulties and by 1947 Bachelor's Climb had been led.

In 1951 Climbs on Gritstone, Vol. 3, included Hedgehog Crack and Rainbow Crack but its major significance was to stimulate interest in the area. Inevitably Hen Cloud felt the force of Brown and Whillans and by 1957 Brown had notched up the left finish to Bachelor's Climb, Second's Retreat and En Rappel variants and by 1961, Main Crack, Delstree, Reunion Crack, Slimline and Hen Cloud Eliminate had all succumbed to him. Whillans countered with the magnificent Bachelor's Lefthand.

In the early 60s Tony Nicols and the Black and Tans Club were active in the area and produced some excellent routes including Encouragement, Long and Short, and Chicken. The North Staffordshire Mountaineering Club had climbed on Hen Cloud since the club's formation in 1957 when Clive Shaw made the first ascent of Bulwark. In 1963 Bob Hassall led Second's Advance thinking it would be an easy variant to Second's Retreat but he found it harder than the original. He also found Crispin's Crack and Rib Chimney crack, which is now the finish to Charisma.

Colin Foord led High Tensile Crack, a short but very strenuous route. Peter Ruddle did The Ape in a style in keeping with the name of the route, and Dave Salt led the overhanging crack above the variant start to En Rappel making a direct line of considerable difficulty. A nut had to be used for aid and this gave it the name The Bitter End. In 1969 John Yates found Shortbread and two years later added Songs of Praise.

Little else was established until 1975 when John Allen and Steve Bancroft decided to visit the area. They were climbing a few years ahead of their time and forced an increase in standards. Initially Allen liberated Bitter End of its aid point then the pair swung leads on Anthrax. A year later Bancroft overcame the obvious lines of Comedian and Corinthian whilst Allen stepped over the threshold of the possible to force the superbly positioned Caricature, after several airborne retreats. 1976 also saw John Gosling re-emerge to get tangled up in Anaconda; he left suitably mauled. The northern raiders continued to come; Nick Colton added Heart of Gold whilst Jim Campbell found Short Man's Misery and the devitalising Shortcake. A year later Steve Bancroft returned to climb the bold Helter Skelter and produced the immaculate Chameleon to bring Hen Cloud well in line with the standards being achieved on the eastern edges.

1978 saw unprecedented activity with the number of climbs swelling drastically owing to keen competition between rival factions; people were even forced to take days off work to protect their lines. Dave Jones just beat Jim Moran to Slowhand but Moran quickly replied with Electric Chair and Gallows. The same day Simon Horrox created Nutted by Reality and Pullet. A week later he cheekily added 'Apology' knowing that Jones had failed to lead it previously. However he did not know that Jones had returned 3 days earlier to lead it as Short'n'Sharp.

Meanwhile Gary Gibson, considered then to be a rather radical character, had started his career with Face Value and Bitching. Mid-week visits saw Jim Moran and Al Evans produce the compelling Borstal Breakout, The Raid and Sorcerer. The locals replied with The Monkey in Your Soul by Al Simpson whilst Jones produced Quantas and Press on Regardless. Jones also led Broken Arrow and strung together Standing Tall during this period. The routes continued to fall (along with the leaders) to visiting parties, the culprits this time being the Berzins brothers who forced the powerfully steep Caesarean, which was later to be straightened out by Jonny Woodward. They didn't see The Pinch though, which finally gave in to John Holt.

The pace of development was gradually waning and only a few important additions followed in 1979 with Phil Burke's ascent of Levitation and Jonny Woodward's ascents of Mandrake and

Space Probe, the latter needing pre-placed runners on the first pitch. Gary Gibson was gaining momentum by now and invented a plethora of routes on the smaller buttresses; Cold Sweat, Triumph of the Good City and the hazardous Jellyfish being the best of the bunch. Guidebook work uncovered a few crumbs with Solid Geometry and the discreet Whisper but the major events had passed, or had they (?) for Nick Postlethwaite found his Charisma, possibly a pointer to future development. Some powerful lines still exist, especially the one just right of . . ., but these are for the keen to discover and the brave to climb.

THE CLIMBS are described from LEFT to RIGHT as one faces the crag.

**1  The Aiguillette**  20 feet  Severe
A small isolated pinnacle quite close to the road and near the col between Hen Cloud and The Roaches. Wander up the right front arete.

**2  Zoom Wall**  20 feet  Very Severe
The lefthand end of the crag proper forms a short steep wall facing The Roaches. Three lines are possible; to the left, 4c, centre, 4c, and right edge, 5a.

**3  Nutted By Reality**  20 feet  Hard Very Severe
5c.10 yards right of Zoom Wall is a small rippled face. Fierce finger pulls gain better holds slightly right. Continue somewhat stunned.

**4  Slipstreams**  20 feet  Hard Very Severe
5a.The twin shallow cracks and flake finish just left of No. 5.

**5  Little Pinnacle Climb**  20 feet  Very Difficult
10 yards right of Nutted By Reality is a small corner. Climb up into a deep corner then left to a ledge and go up to the top.

**6  November Cracks**  40 feet  Hard Very Difficult
Vigorously follow two parallel cracks in the front face of the large pinnacle. From a ledge on the left continue up the corner.

**7  Bulwark**  50 feet  E1                                            ★
5a.Start on the right face of the pinnacle and ascend awkwardly until the left arete is gained, runner. Continue gracefully up this. Bold, airy climbing.

196 GRITSTONE AREA

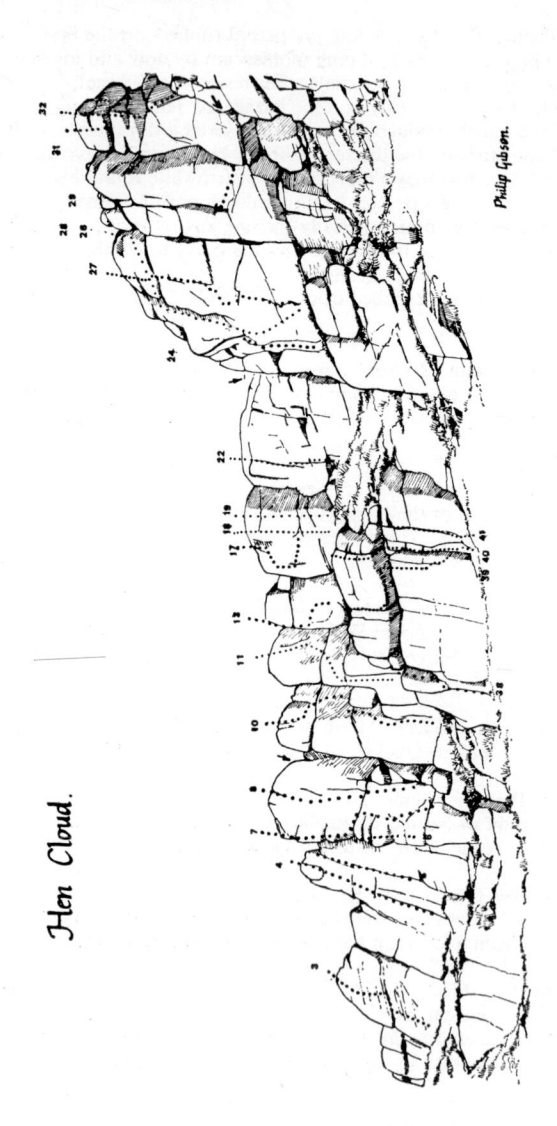

Hen Cloud.

Philip Gibson.

**8 Slowhand** 45 feet E1 ★
5b.5 ft right of Bulwark is a crack. Follow this and one above to its conclusion where a cautious move brings gratifying holds.

**9 Chockstone Chimney** 30 feet Moderate
The corner, which is also a convenient way down.

**10 The Notch** 40 feet Very Severe
4c.Between the Second and Third pinnacles are two cracks: Take the left one to the top of a block, move up a shallow corner then go left to climb a short crack near the arete. A much harder start is from right to left into the notch; 5b.

**11 Chicken** 45 feet Hard Very Severe
5a.The thin crack right of The Notch is followed steeply until moves right gain a ledge. Step delicately left to a groove and the top. It is possible to gain the ledge directly from the wall below it. This is **Pullet**, Hard Very Severe, 5b.

**12 Piston Groove** 25 feet Very Severe
4c.The deep V-groove succumbs to 'udging' or bridging.

**13 Mandrake** 35 feet E3 †★
6a.Start below an overlap 10 ft right of Piston Groove. Go up to and over this on small holds to gain a flake near the left arete. Finish direct or on the right.

**14 Victory** 25 feet Very Severe
4c.The exhausting crack which leans left at its top.

**15 Short'n'Sharp** 25 feet Hard Very Severe
5b.The crack 5 ft left of Green Corner has hard moves to reach it.

**16 Green Corner** 20 feet Hard Very Difficult
The often greasy corner right of the last climbs.

**17 Electric Chair** 25 feet E2 ★
Round the arete to the right of Green Corner is a short wall.
5c.Start just right of centre. From the ledge traverse left on pockets to a short crack, then go up to a groove and the top. Strenuous in execution.

**18 Bad Joke** 20 feet E2
6a.The wall directly above the ledge is hard at mid-height.

**19 Gallows** 20 feet  Hard Very Severe
5b. Carefully follow the right arete to moves on its right wall near the top.

**20 Recess Chimney** 25 feet  Hard Difficult
The wide chimney with a block low down. Finish right or, harder, left.

**21 The Sorcerer** 25 feet  E2 †
5c. The shallow crack on the bulging face to the right. Devilish start.

**22 High Tensile Crack** 25 feet  Hard Very Severe
5a. The crack and small corner 5 ft right of The Sorcerer. Interesting but tiring.

**23 Chockstone Crack** 35 feet  Difficult
12 yards right is a short crack in a small recess. Climb the crack to a chimney finish. The slab to the left can be used, together with the lower crack, as a way down.

**24 The Bitter End** 40 feet  E2
5c. 10 ft right again is an overhanging corner crack. Climb this to a sloping ledge. 'Barn door' laybacking remains; crux.

**25 The Raid** 45 feet  E3
6a. Climb the shallow scoop in the arete right of Bitter End (some seepage). Move left to a short crack and go up to a good ledge. Climb the thin cracks in a direct line moving left to finish.

**26 En Rappel** 50 feet  Very Severe ★
4b. Right of The Raid is a steep face. Teeter up this, via ledges near its left edge, to a cracked slab. Follow this then cross 15 ft right to a chimney finish. From the top of the cracked slab it is possible to move left then up at Hard Very Severe, 5a.

**27 Caesarean** 50 feet  E4 ★★★
6b. 5 ft right of En Rappel is a blind flake. Technically interesting moves lead up the flake to a horizontal break. Move right then go up to a crack, crux. Continue with haste. Strenuous but well protected.

**28 Main Crack** 50 feet  Very Severe ★
4c. The obvious wide crack 5 yards right of En Rappel needs little thought but much application.

**29  Delstree**   75 feet   Hard Very Severe   ★★★
5a.Start from a chimney below and 10 yards right of Main Crack.
Climb this, heave over the roof then delicately left to the shallow
corner where steep moves lead to a balding finish. Brilliant.

**30  Levitation**   75 feet   E3
6a.Follow Reunion Crack to the slab. Search for holds on the left
wall and rise steeply right then left to a spike and arete finish.

**31  Reunion Crack**   70 feet   Very Severe   ★
4c.Start as for Delstree. Climb the chimney and overhang to a
slab below the corner, ponder, then ascend convincingly to good
holds.

To the right is a wide slab-filled gully, **Slab Way**, which can be
used by the more gallant as a way down. Above is a black tower.

**32  The Pinch**   70 feet   Hard Very Severe
5a-z.Follow Slab Way for 20 ft then ascend a V-slot above to the
foot of the tower. Wander past two breaks to an impasse. Make a
giant reach for the top of the arete or step left then up; 5b.

**33  Fat Old Sun**   170 feet   E2
5c.A left to right girdle is possible from the ledge on Bitter End,
crossing En Rappel, then the obvious break into Main Crack.
Climb this then follow the prominent overlap into Delstree. Go
up this a few ft to a break. This leads right to the finish of The
Pinch.

**34  Slab Way**   45 feet   Moderate
Climb the gully moving right onto the slabs. Choose an exit.

**35  Quantas**   25 feet   E1
10 yards right of Slab Way and facing The Pinch is a short steep wall.
5c.Start in the centre of the wall. Move up to a small deep groove.
Pull across right to a baffling move and thin crack finish.

**36  Press On Regardless**   30 feet   E1   ★
5b.Start as for Quantas but after 10 ft veer right to the arete.
Ascend this on its left, or easier and protectable right side.

To the left of Slab Way and at a lower level, is a lower tier
consisting of a smooth face about 30 ft high capped by an
overhang.

200 GRITSTONE AREA

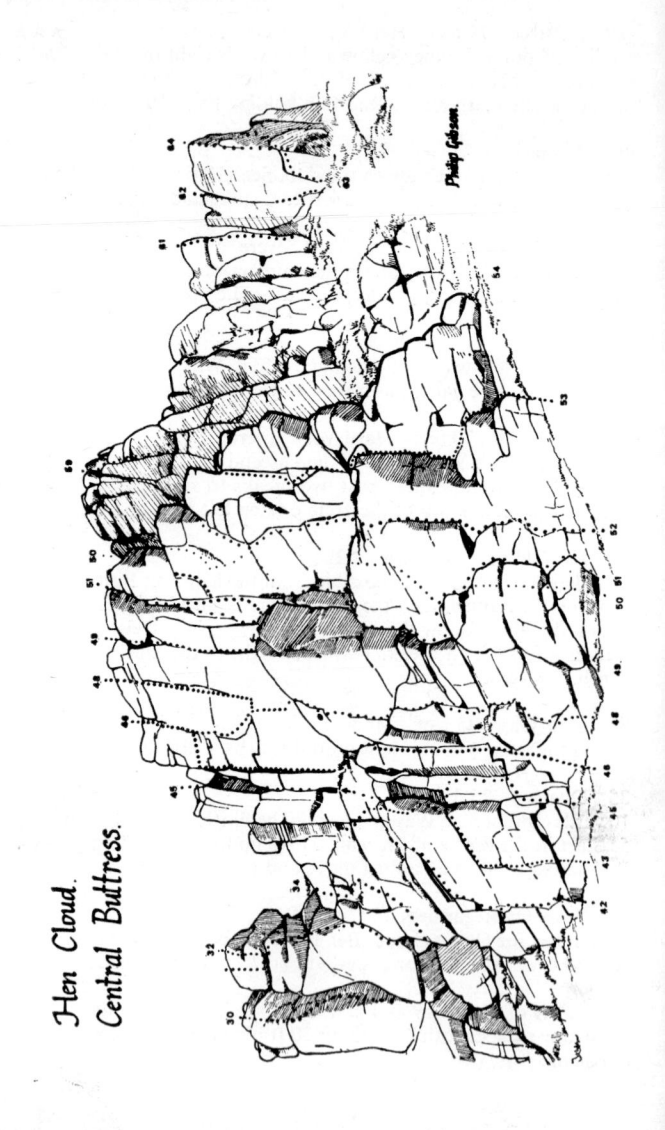

Hen Cloud.
Central Buttress.

Philip Gibson.

**37 Buster The Cat**  25 feet  Hard Very Severe
5b. The thin crack left of Pug.

**38 Pug**  25 feet  Very Severe
4c. The crack and groove up the lefthand end of the buttress.

**39 Anthrax**  45 feet  E2
5c. Just left of Lum is a thin crack. Up this to belay on a ledge. Stomach-traverse 15 ft left. Go over the roof via a widening crack.

**40 Lum**  25 feet  Very Severe
4c. The square recess on the right of the buttress. Go left to a flake and the top.

**41 Bantam Crack**  25 feet  Very Severe
4c. The obvious crack to the right of Lum.

**42 The Ape**  35 feet  Hard Very Severe
10 yards right of Slab Way and starting below a terrace is a green wall with dirty broken cracks on the left side.
5b. Jam the cracks to the high traverse line. Swing right across this.

**43 The Monkey In Your Soul**  40 feet  E3
5c. A similar but lower line than The Ape. Climb the thin crack to reach the hand-traverse. Cross this step right then left and go up the arete.

**44 Broken Arrow**  35 feet  Hard Very Severe
5b. Ascend past hollow flakes to the end of Monkey's hand-traverse. Step right then back left onto the arete. Finish over the prow.

**45 Roof Climb**  100 feet  Very Severe
To the right of Broken Arrow is a series of cracks and grooves.
1. 50ft.4b. Go 15 ft up the lefthand crack. Move right and climb a groove. Step left to a ledge, hard. Climb the wide groove to the terrace.
2. 50ft. Amble up the stone-filled chimney above.

**46 The Long and Short**  85 feet  E1
1. 30ft.5b. Start on a grass ledge 10 ft right of Roof Climb. Tentatively climb the steep green groove to the terrace.
2. 55ft.5b. Thrash up the wide crack to its top. Move right to a good hold and continue more easily.

## 202 GRITSTONE AREA

**47 Anaconda** 90 feet  E4     ★
1. 40ft.6a.Start 5 ft right of the green groove. Follow the rightwards-slanting groove to the overhang. Swing left then go up and right to a flake. Climb this to a mean exit.
2. 50ft.6a.Start by a thin crack line above the terrace and work towards the black curving flake above. Continue steeply to join Long and Short.

**48 Borstal Breakout** 110 feet  E3     ★★★
1. 20ft.4b.Climb an awkward crack to the grass ledge.
2. 40ft.5c.Take the hand-jam crack until it narrows and disappears. Steep fingery moves lead to a pocket then go right to the top.
3. 50ft.6a.Start up Anaconda but continue up the crack line to a good ledge and easier wall above. A fine, exhilarating climb.

**49 Central Climb Direct** 115 feet  Very Severe
1. 55ft.4c.Grunt up the bulging, twisting crack to a ledge. Follow the next wide crack to another good ledge.
2. 15ft.The flake crack left of the corner to the grass terrace.
3. 45ft.4a.The wide crack left of the groove of Central Climb.

**50 Standing Tall** 110 feet  Hard Very Severe
1. 25ft.4c.The blunt arete directly above the small cave.
2. 30ft.4b.Climb the wall on flakes to the next ledge.
3. 55ft.5a.Go up the corner of Central Climb for 10 ft then hand-traverse right to Encouragement. Climb steeply up the wall first left then right up a shallow corner. A worrying pitch.

**51 Central Climb** 120 feet  Severe     ★★★
1. 25ft.4a.The wide crack right of the cave to a difficult finish.
2. 30ft.From the left end of the ledge struggle up the next crack.
3. 25ft.The small corner above to a grassy terrace.
4. 40ft.Ascend the obvious groove moving right towards its top. It is also possible to enter the groove directly or to finish up a crack right again. A classic expedition.

**52 Encouragement** 100 feet  E1     ★★
1. 45ft.5b.There is a small shallow groove a few feet right of pitch 1 of Central Climb. Reach and follow the groove to a ledge.
2. 55ft.5b.The curving crack is best done quickly to good holds and an easy open corner. Varied and interesting.
The green arete right of the initial groove is reported as E2, 5c.

**53 K2** 100 feet  Hard Very Difficult     ★
1. 55ft.Climb up to a corner to the right of Encouragement. Follow this, with a move left at the top.

2. 45ft. Strenuous. The Y-crack requires determination from the leader. Pull into a groove and finish up The Arete.

**54 The Arete** 100 feet Very Difficult ★★
The prominent stepped arete is climbed to a steep little wall. Climb this on its left side which, for one move, is sensationally exposed. Continue easily to the top.

**55 Arete Wall** 60 feet Hard Severe
4a. Start right of the arete at the foot of the gully. Pursue the steep crack with some urgency over a block. Move right then go up.

**56 Easy Come** 40 feet Hard Severe
4a. The thin crack 10 ft right of Arete Wall for 30 ft to a block. Continue diagonally right up the green slab to meet The Arete.

**Easy Gully** divides the crag here and provides a good way down.

**57 Songs of Praise** 50 feet Hard Very Severe
5b. The flake on the right wall of the gully is climbed to a move out right. Follow the arete above.

**57a Loose Fingers** 30 feet Hard Very Severe †
5c. The crack 5 ft right with a finish up indefinite and dirty cracks.

**58 Prayers, Poems and Promises** 35 feet Hard Very Severe
5b. The arete to the right of the last climb. Ascend to a hole and continue on the right side past a sloping ledge to the terrace.

**59 Modern** 55 feet Severe
The hanging flake above a platform is followed with some trepidation to a little terrace. Finish up the thin and difficult righthand crack.

**60 Ancient** 55 feet Very Difficult
The broken wide crack right of Modern leads to the same terrace. Finish up the lefthand crack.

**61 Small Buttress** 20 feet Hard Very Severe
5a. Amble up the right edge of the small buttress left of Bow Buttress.

At the head of the amphitheatre is a completely detached buttress.

**62 Bitching** 25 feet Hard Very Severe
5b. The widening crack left of Bow Buttress start.

## 63  Bow Buttress  40 feet  Very Difficult
Start at a short crack to the left of the arete. Go up a little then swing right onto the front face. Gain a ledge, step right then go up a crack to the top. A good route spoilt by the removal of a flake by vandals

## 64  Solid Geometry  30 feet  E1
5b. The arete direct is hardest in the middle.

The long, steep, tapering wall to the right provides the next group of climbs, all of them good, some classic, but none of them easy. The three small ribs in the wall left of Stokesline are **Fingerythm**, 5b.

## 65  Stokesline  20 feet  Hard Very Severe
6a. The first thin crack gives a problem of initial projection, the rest being just plain hard.

## 66  Slimline  30 feet  Hard Very Severe
5b. The second crack. Trouble to start with more to follow.

## 67  Hedgehog Crack  40 feet  Mild Very Severe  ★
4b. The third widening crack is followed to a squeeze chimney finish. It is possible to finish left from below the chimney by gaining the obvious crack; Hard Very Severe, 5b.

## 68  Comedian  45 feet  E3  ★★
5c. Start below the crack line. Follow holds leading steeply right to a horizontal break. Enter the crack and climb it to finish directly over an exciting bulge and humourless groove.

## 69  Second's Retreat  50 feet  Very Severe
4c. The slanting green groove proves awkward.

## 70  Second's Advance  55 feet  Hard Very Severe
5a. Start right of the groove with a mantleshelf. Continue up to the wide crack, climb it, then exit left to a chimney.

## 71  Corinthian  65 feet  E3  ★
5c. 10 ft right of Second's Retreat is a vague crack line (old peg). Reach the crack from the left and follow it direct. Sustained.

## 72  Hen Cloud Eliminate  60 feet  Hard Very Severe  ★★
5b. Follow the crack system to the right of the last climb. Entering the groove is hard and feels easy to fall off.

## HEN CLOUD 205

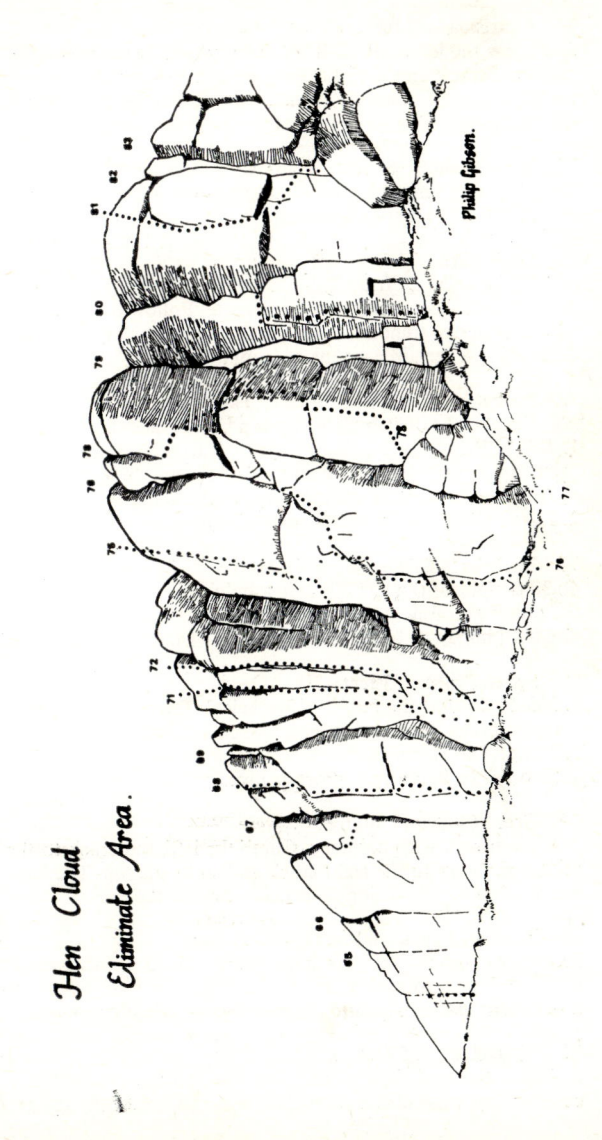

*Hen Cloud*
*Eliminate Area.*

Philip Gibson.

**73 Charisma** 65 feet  E3 †
5c. Follow the left arete of Rib Chimney until it is possible to reach the crack on the right. Jam up this. No-one has yet plucked up the courage (or suffers a sufficient cerebral deficiency) to lead the top arete, although this has been ascended on a top rope.

**74 Rib Chimney** 65 feet  Hard Very Difficult ★
The obvious chimney is awkward low down but succumbs to more traditional tactics higher up.

**75 Caricature** 70 feet  E5 ★★★
6a. From a belay 20 ft up Rib Chimney traverse right using pockets to a short crack round the arete. Follow the faint line of weakness above trending slightly left at the top. Superb climbing demanding a certain amount of 'cool'.

**76 Bachelor's Lefthand** 80 feet  Hard Very Severe ★★★
A few feet right of Rib Chimney is a short crack. Start below it.
1. 45ft.5a. Reach the crack and ascend it to a hard move right at its top. A hole above is then used to reach a 'thank God' flake. Traverse the slab rightwards and so to the upper crack.
2. 35ft.4c. Climb the crack. A magnificent route.

**77 Bachelor's Climb** 40 feet  Mild Very Severe ★★
4b. 30 ft right of the last climb is a bulging crack. Climb this to the pulpit and follow the upper crack to a platform. Finish up Great Chimney or better, the top crack of Bachelor's Lefthand.

**78 Space Probe** 55 feet  E3 ★
1. 30ft.5c. Start at the pulpit of Bachelor's Climb and traverse right to the arete. Ascend this, past a break, to the platform.
2. 25ft.5c. The Helter Skelter finish. Boldly attack the left arete. Step left to finish up a short groove.

**79 Great Chimney** 60 feet  Severe ★★
The prominent wide chimney. Climb the lefthand crack to the platform. Cross to the right crack and so to the top. The left crack is harder and bridging brings a tear to the eye.

**80 Rainbow Crack** 60 feet  Very Severe ★★
5a. Either climb the thin crack on the right wall of the chimney or the wider crack round the arete. The flake above only yields to a tenacious leader. A route deserving more attention.

**81 Chameleon** 35 feet  E5 ★★
6a. Reach the roof right of Rainbow Crack from the right and continue up finger flakes above. Superb and frantically sustained.

## HEN CLOUD

**82 Left Twin Crack**    30 feet    Hard Severe
4a. To the right and at a higher level is a smaller replica of Great Chimney. This climb is up the left crack.

**83 Right Twin Crack**    30 feet    Mild Very Severe
4b. The right crack with some difficulty.

**84 Footpath Chimney**    60 feet    Hard Difficult
Way over right, and much lower, a chimney starts from the path.
1. 25ft. The chimney passing the bulge with difficulty.
2. 35ft. Follow slabby boulders and the cracked arete above.

**85 Thomson's Buttress Route One**    45 feet    Very Difficult    ★
20 yards right is Thomson's Buttress. On the right side is a series of rocky steps and in the centre, a steep corner crack.
Go up the corner crack to a ledge. Climb the cracks in the wall.

**86 Thomson's Buttress Route Two**    45 feet    Difficult
Follow the rock steps to the ledge and finish up the obvious wide crack.

**87 Tree Chimney**    50 feet    Hard Very Difficult
Right of Route Two slabs lead to an undercut chimney. Climb the flake on the right until a hard move left gains the chimney finish.

**88 Tunnel Vision**    40 feet    Hard Very Severe
5b. Ascend the slabby face to the right of Tree Chimney directly up its centre with one long reach for a bilberry break. Totally escapable.

Further right is the Inaccessible Pinnacle. It has a large detached block leaning against its right edge, forming a crack up either side. Escape from the top is easiest by leaping (the short side being an infinitely less serious proposition).

**89 Cold Sweat**    20 feet    E1
5b. Climb the steep gully wall near its right side, studiously avoiding any moves right onto easier ground. Finish up a short crack.

**90 Pinnacle Face**    40 feet    Very Severe    ★
4b. Climb the left crack of the block to a short crack on the face. Climb this to continue near the left side, with delicacy, to a short crack on the left.

## GRITSTONE AREA

**91 Face Value** 40 feet Hard Very Severe
5a. Climb the front of the block. From the short crack move directly up to the summit. Thin, with meagre protection.

**92 Pinnacle Rib** 35 feet Very Severe
5a. The crack on the right of the block. Continue up the arete.

**93 Delusion** 25 feet Hard Severe
4a. On the right face of the pinnacle is a short V-chimney. Follow this and the groove above. Step right then left and so to the summit.

**94 Short Side** 12 feet Very Difficult
The shelf on the back is only gained by considerable effort.

The Innaccessible Pinnacle has also been traversed at half-height, 5a. To the right and at the same level is a group of three pinnacles.

**95 Shoe Shine Shuffle** 20 feet Hard Very Severe
5b. The righthand crack on the left face of the first pinnacle. Exit right to a rounded finish.

**96 Diagonal Route** 40 feet Very Difficult
Climb bulging ledges on the left front face and follow the flared cracks diagonally right to the top.

**97 Triumph of the Good City** 35 feet Very Severe
5a. On the right side of the first pinnacle the rounded arete is undercut. Pull over this and continue up the slabby arete above.

**98 Jelly Fish** 20 feet E2
5c. Shiver up the curving ramp and short wall up to the right of the last climb. Short but hazardous.

**99 Pete's Backside** 20 feet Very Severe
5a. Climb onto a pulpit below the scooped crack. A queerish move gains better holds and the top.

**100 Central Tower** 25 feet Very Difficult
The narrow face left of Nutcracker.

**101 The Nutcracker** 25 feet Severe
The third pinnacle has a wide corner crack. Climb this vigorously.

**102 Heart of Gold**  35 feet  E1  ★
5b. The arete right of Nutcracker is climbed via flakes and an unusual pocket at 25 ft.

**103 Deceiver**  20 feet  Very Severe
4b. The crack just right is difficult to finish.

50 yards directly below the first pinnacle and in line with the Rock Inn are three small buttresses.

**104 Hal's Ridge**  35 feet  Very Difficult
Start at the lowest point of the central buttress and follow the broken ridge, with interest, to a final steep wall which is taken direct.

**105 Shortman's Misery**  30 feet  Hard Very Severe
5a. The arete left of Crispin's Crack, climbed on its left side.

**106 Crispin's Crack**  35 feet  Very Severe
4c. The obvious crack on the front of the righthand buttress. Climb this to a glacis, step right to an arete and finish straight up.

**107 Duck Soup**  30 feet  Hard Very Severe
5a. The flake 10 ft right of the last climb with the same finish.

25 yards right is a small buttress in the trees. Several lines have been done here but possibly the best is **The Whisper**, 5b, a curving crack starting from a sharp arete.

Further round the hill to the right of the three pinnacles are some small buttresses which face the Mermaid Inn across the valley. The first buttress has a pleasant 20-foot chimney up its front face. Round to the right is a peculiar hole.

**108 Last View**  20 feet  Very Difficult
Climb the wall left of the chimney. Move left into a groove finish.

**109 The Weirdy**  35 feet  Very Difficult
Climb up past the hole and follow a ramp up to a large ledge. Move left along this to finish up the short wall right of the chimney.

A further fifty yards down the hill is another buttress with a rectangular block at its foot.

## 210 GRITSTONE AREA

**110 High Energy Plan** 25 feet Hard Very Severe
5a. Take a direct line through the 'crisp' roof and finish direct.

**111 Shortbread** 35 feet Hard Very Severe
5a. Start 10 ft right of the block. Climb up to a groove then traverse left to black flakes. Heave over the roof and continue direct.

**112 Shortcake** 25 feet Hard Very Severe
5b. A direct finish to the groove of Shortbread. The short diagonal crack and anything else that comes to hand.

**113 Gingerbread** 20 feet Hard Severe
4a. The obvious steep slab right of the last climb. Delicate.

**114 Ginger Biscuit** 25 feet Mild Very Severe
4b. Climb the arete on small but adequate holds.

There remain a few smaller buttresses and the old quarry walls, none of which warrant description. However as climbers' attitudes change, some rock insatiated desperados may need to explore them in the future.

# RAMSHAW ROCKS
by Nick Longland

---

> *'Arrive there on a warm summer evening, fighting fit and determined—preferably with a few preliminary bouts under your belt—crash the jams in, move quickly and the climbs submit. Arrive on a bad day, and it is a different story; the rock will maul you and you will retire bloodied to lick your wounds.'*
>
> Martin Boysen

O.S. Ref. SK 019622

## SITUATION
The Rocks run NNE-SSW and overlook the Leek-Buxton road, the A53, about 4 miles from Leek.

## APPROACHES
The PMT Route 208 between Sheffield and Stoke-on-Trent runs along the A53. The nearest official stops are some distance either side of the crag but the driver will usually drop passengers close to the rocks on request. Cars may be parked by the A53 or at a few places along the narrow lane skirting the southern end of the crag.

## ACCESS
The main crag is owned by Harpur Crewe Estate and there are no problems of access apart from the 'Winking Eye' which some selfish climbing vandal has partially destroyed and climbers are requested to avoid the routes which are on this unique gritstone formation. The Lady Stone is on private land and climbers should seek permission from the farm 200 yards to the north-east.

## CHARACTER
The Rocks form an exposed ridge of rough natural gritstone which has been highly eroded into a series of distinct buttresses and pinnacles. Although quick-drying, not very high and with the appreciable inward dip of the strata favouring the climber, the lack of sun, the overhangs and the abrasiveness of the many pebble-lined cracks can make the place seem inhospitable at times, particularly on first acquaintance. Nonetheless there is much to tempt, puzzle and delight, not least of which are the boulder problems. Because many of the best of these are easily missed by the occasional visitor, their whereabouts and brief descriptions (plus technical grade) have been included.

## HISTORY

The striking setting of the Rocks and quick approach must have attracted numerous climbers as they passed along the A53, but probably because of their small size, gamekeeper hazards and close proximity to more illustrious crags few records or route descriptions have survived prior to the 1970s. Predictably Ramshaw is mentioned in E. A. Baker's 'Moors, Crags and Caves of the High Peak', 1903, and A. J. Lowe wrote up some routes, the inclusion of which in 'Climbs on Gritstone', Volume 3, 1951, was prevented by lack of space.

No doubt the easier routes were all climbed in the first half of this century and it seems likely that Joe Brown, Don Whillans and others of the old 'Rock and Ice' climbed the majority of routes between 1950 and 1965. Certainly that trio of fine cracks on the Lower Tier; Brown's Crack, Prostration and Don's Crack were done during this period. Then in September 1964, during the almost obligatory hailstorm, Brown led the ferocious Ramshaw Crack, with some aid from a chockstone, to produce one of his last great gritstone routes.

In 1968, the North Staffordshire Mountaineering Club's interest, with a future guidebook in mind, expanded to include Ramshaw. They repeated the existing routes and over the next four years added several, probably new, routes of their own. Dave Salt led the alarming Alcatraz; John Yates led The Crippler; Bob Hassal produced an excellent route with The Press and with Norman Hoskins did Tally Not with an aid sling; Colin Foord excelled with The Untouchable and, on a wet day, kept the lads amused by engineering his way up Foord's Folly. This activity culminated in an exhausting week-end when Salt added The Undertaker (without the aid nut subsequently mentioned in the guide) and Extended Credit with various N.S.M.C. stalwarts commandeered to climb as many routes as possible in the course of manuscript checking for the 1973 guidebook, 'The Staffordshire Gritstone Area', Volume 9. This, the first comprehensive guide to the crag elicited disapproval from some Ramshaw habituees for being too thorough but showed to the uninitiated the wealth of good climbing available.

Unbeknown to the North Staffordshire group, Martin Boysen had already begun to adopt the crag and had climbed The Swinger and freed Tally Not before the appearance of the guidebook.

In 1973, John Allen, on a raid from Sheffield, scooped what was probably the first free ascent of Foord's Folly, after which a lull followed. Gabe Regan probably freed Ramshaw Crack and in 1976 Andrew Woodward climbed the short but technical Crystal Tipps. In 1977 Boysen, usually accompanied by Mark Stokes, returned with a vengeance and produced a crop of worthwhile

routes, mostly led on sight. First to go was the impressive and
oft-tried Gumshoe, followed shortly by Overdrive, Handrail,
Midge, Escape, Overdraught and culminating in two superb routes
at either end of the crag. Jumbo and Old Fogey. Regrettably,
controversy arose over several of these routes, notably Jumbo,
with rival first ascent claims and names by the Woodward brothers.
In 1978 Jonny Woodward continued his explorations and climbed
two fierce horrors, National Acrobat and Electric Savage and
Gary Gibson added English Towns the following year. 1979 also
saw the disappearance of Ramshaw's single (and arguably
harmless) peg from above the hard part of Foord's Folly. In the
course of guidebook work the author added a few titbits including
the start to Elastic Limit, the first pitch of Electric Savage and
after much time and several twisted joints, solved Tierdrop.
Finally Jonny Woodward, after top rope practice led the
desperately thin Direct Start to Old Fogey.

THE CLIMBS are described from Left to Right.
150 yards south of the bend where the lane passes through the
southern end of the crag is a pinnacle with 3 routes and problems.

**1 East Face** 20 feet Moderate
The slab moving left to a notch and the top.

**2 After Eight** 25 feet Severe
Directly up the wall to the nose on the south-east corner.

**3 Southern Crack** 25 feet Very Difficult
A crack on the left is gained by rounded holds and leads to an
awkward pull onto the fluted top.

**Playaway**, 5a, a layback crack towards the left end of the south
face.
**The Whale**, 5c, 4 ft left. Use the mouth and eye to gain the brow.
Round the corner a shallow runnel gives a further problem, 4c.

40 yards north of the bend in the lane is a curious-shaped
pinnacle called the Loaf and Cheese. Its only worthwhile route
starts at the righthand end of the still unyielding front face.

**4 Loaf and Cheese** 35 feet Very Severe
4c. Climb a slanting crack awkwardly to a ledge. Scramble to the
final tier and take it direct or on the more exposed front face.

**5 Green Crack** 25 feet Very Severe
5a. The green groove and wide crack through the bulge 15 ft right
of the short gully. Precarious despite the chockstones.

## 214 GRITSTONE AREA

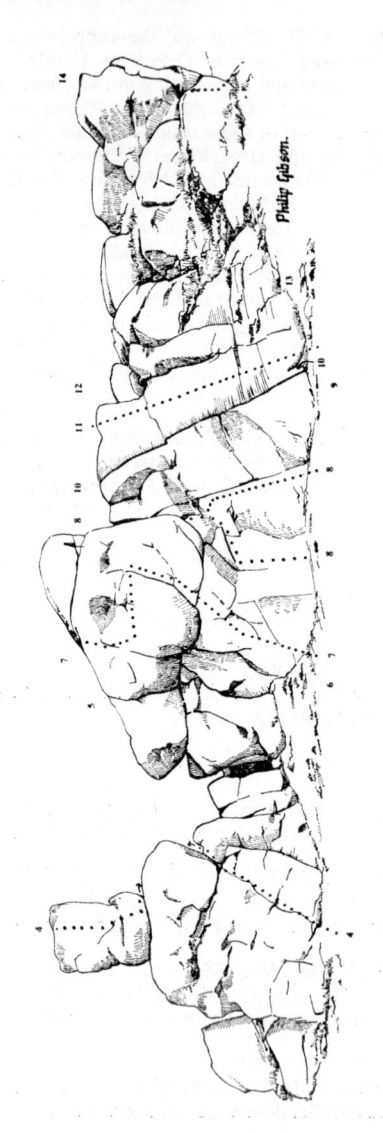

*Loaf and Cheese – Ramshaw Rocks.*

Philip Gibson.

**6 National Acrobat** 25 feet E4 †
6b. The blind crack through the overhang 4 ft right. Finish up the shallow water-worn runnel.

**7 Jumbo** 35 feet E4 ★★
6a. A few ft right is a hanging flake. Climb to, and up this. Swing left and mantleshelf precariously onto a flake. Move left to finish up National Acrobat. An intimidating route.

**8 Wall and Groove** 30 feet Very Difficult
Go up under the prow left of The Arete moving right to a ledge or gain this direct—easier. Climb the chimney above. Harder than it looks.

**9 The Arete** 30 feet Severe
Climb the overhanging start direct to a ledge. The rib above, once gained, succumbs to layaway or 'a cheval' tactics.

**10 Louie Groove** 25 feet Hard Very Severe ★
5a. The clean-cut groove on the right. Straightforward to the elegant but friable top part which is slowly being eroded by abseilers.

**11 Leeds Slab** 25 feet Hard Severe
Ascend the slab centrally to finish up the notched rib.

**12 Leeds Crack** 20 feet Difficult
The crack right of the slab provides introductory hand-jamming.

**13 Honest Jonny** 20 feet Difficult
Immediately right is a pleasant groove.

**14 The Undertaker** 20 feet Hard Very Severe
15 yards right and higher up is a blunt-nosed pinnacle with a thin curved crack on its front face.
5c. Climb the finger-wrecking crack to a long reach for the wider slot above.

The righthand wall of the pinnacle gives 3 problems.
**Pink Flake**, 4c, the obvious hollow flake from the right.
**Pink Flake Direct**, 5a. Approach the flake from the left.
**Mantle**, 4c. The rounded shelf to the right, then the wall on the right.

**15 Overdrive** 25 feet Hard Very Severe
15 yards right is a small buttress with a triangular roof on the

left and two cracks low down.
5c. Climb the roof on the left side to a rounded finish.

**16  Twin Cracks**  20 feet  Difficult
The lefthand crack is slightly easier. Finish up the groove.

**17  Double Chin**  20 feet  Severe
The rounded prow 10 ft right and the friable nose above.

Right again is a buttress with a prominent recessed crack on its left. Round the arete 10 ft left is a faint water-worn groove.
**Equilibria**, 4c—pad up the groove. The arete gives another start.

**18  The Great Zawn**  25 feet  Very Severe  ★
4c. The wide mean-looking crack.

**19  Broken Groove**  25 feet  Moderate
Climb the crack on the buttress front and the groove above.

**20  Broken Groove Arete**  25 feet  Difficult
The arete to the right of the crack.

**21  Wellingtons**  25 feet  Very Difficult
15 yards right, beyond a double V-shaped gully two prominent cracks breach a two-tiered overhang.
The wide lefthand crack direct or start by the slab on the left.

**22  Masochism**  30 feet  Hard Very Severe
5a. The righthand crack. Painful jamming leads to the upper crack which is awkward and strenuous round the chockstone.

**23  Trivial Traverse**  20 feet  Very Severe
4c. Traverse the righthand wall of the buttress using a horizontal crack just below the top to a foothold. Then go up. Fun.

**24  Sneeze**  20 feet  Hard Very Severe
To the right is a wall above a grassy terrace.
5b. Layback the wall's left edge to gain an incipient crack system.

**25  The Crank**  20 feet  Very Severe  ★
4c. The crack near the righthand end of the wall gives excellent jamming to a thought-provoking finish. May be started on the scruffy lower wall.

The crag now reaches full height, as SOUTH BUTTRESS, with an impending wall bounded on the left by a chimney.

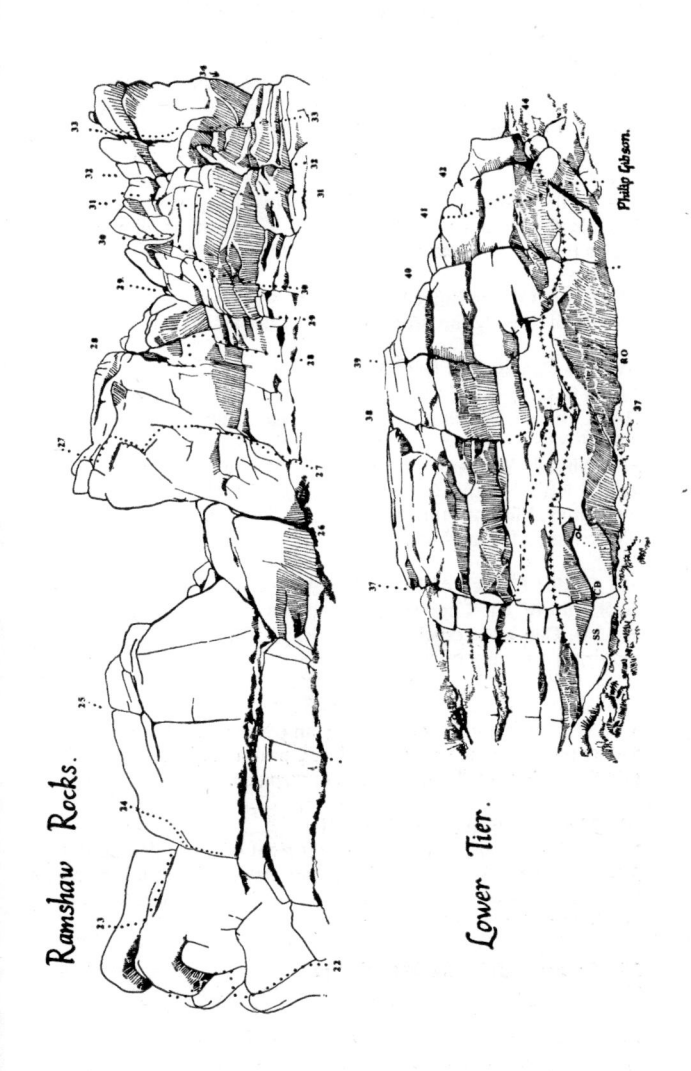

## RAMSHAW ROCKS 217

Ramshaw Rocks.

Lower Tier.

Philip Gibson.

## GRITSTONE AREA

**26 Chockstone Chimney**  25 feet  Very Difficult
The chimney relents above the huge chockstone.

**27 Gumshoe**  45 feet  Hard Very Severe  ★★★
5b. Ascend the shallow groove in the centre of the wall to a ledge. Go left up the bulging wall to finish left with a long reach. An improbable route with some pleasant surprises.

**28 Tally Not**  45 feet  Hard Very Severe
The wall is terminated on the right by two hanging corners.
5c. Gain the lower corner from the left. Go up it, hard, and swing left to the other corner which still warrants care to the top.

**29 Battle Of The Bulge**  30 feet  Very Severe
4b. Attack directly the prominent crack immediately right.

**30 The Cannon**  45 feet  Hard Severe
Climb flakes 3 ft right until a crack/groove on the right leads to 'The Cannon'. Finish direct or up the easier glacis on the right.

**31 Whilly's Whopper**  45 feet  Very Severe
4c. Just left of Phallic Crack is a faint groove above the initial overhangs. Pull into this, move left up the slab and go over the 'Policeman's Helmet' to the top.

**32 Phallic Crack**  45 feet  Hard Very Difficult  ★★
20 ft right of The Cannon a conspicuous crack passes a rock prow at 15 ft. Climb the crack and its sides all the way. A classic, requiring a variety of techniques.

**33 Alcatraz**  50 feet  Hard Very Severe
5b. Just right is a corner capped by an overhang. Go up this and follow the widening crack line above, past a distinctly unhelpful middle section, to the top. Protection sparse.

**34 The Untouchable**  35 feet  E1  ★★
Round the corner is a crack, a few ft right of the undercut arete.
5b. Gain the crack from the right, via a flexible flake: a long reach helps. Venturesome jamming leads to the top. A fine route with an air of seriousness.

**35 Corner Crack**  25 feet  Severe
The steep corner on the right has a traditional flavour.

**36  The Rippler**  25 feet  Very Severe ★
4c. Right of Corner Crack is a small buttress crossed by protruding veinlets. Use these to reach a small ledge at half-height. Move right to finish by a carved hold. A neat little route unfortunately showing signs of wear. Please treat the ripples gently. The ledge can be gained by starting just left of the right arete.

Below The Rippler is a smooth undercut face with a problem at each end.
**Midge**, 5c, is the strenuous bulge and twin cracks on the left.
**Cleg**, 4c, the hanging groove on the right leads to a tricky landing.

At a still lower level and 100 yards further right is the LOWER TIER. The lefthand end is scruffy but yields a few problems, the best is up two overlaps and a rib 8 ft right of a short corner. Near the centre of the Lower Tier a scoop breaches the initial overhang.

**37  Crab Walk**  50 feet  Severe
Pull into the scoop and make an ascending traverse left to exit up a crack on the left of the upper overhang.

**38  Brown's Crack**  45 feet  E1 ★★
5b. Master the roof crack directly above Crab Walk start.

**39  Prostration**  45 feet  Hard Very Severe ★★
5a. This is the blind crack 10 ft right of Brown's Crack again starting as for Crab Walk. The horizontal slot is surprisingly accommodating but is tricky to leave.

A number of good problems tackle the initial overhang of this section of the Lower Tier and can be used as independent starts or rival cruces to the routes above.

**Sensible Shoes**, 5a. Skirt the left end of the Crab Direct overhang to a sloping ledge and shallow corner.
**Crab Direct**, 5b. The uncooperative crack below Crab Walk finish.
**Overlap**, 5b. Surmount the overhang on undercuts 6 ft to the right.
**Roll Off**, 5b. A rounded mantleshelf below the crack of Prostration.

**40  Don's Crack**  35 feet  Hard Very Severe ★
5a. 15 ft right of Prostration is a crack splitting an overhang at 15 ft. Climb it on widely-spaced jams. Large nut belay.

## 220 GRITSTONE AREA

**41 Tierdrop** 25 feet E2 †
6b. Gain the runnel on the lip of the overhang right of Don's Crack via 2 pinch grips. Lunge for a small jug far above. Frustrating.

**42 Tier's End** 25 feet Very Severe
5a. Pull gymnastically over the overhang to the right, to a slanting runnel and the break above. Continue straight up a shallow groove.

**43 Abdomen** 110 feet Severe
The upper girdle of the Lower Tier. Follow the marked line of weakness about half-way up the crag.

**44 Hem Line,** 5c on 1 move, is an entertaining traverse never exceeding 10 ft above the ground. Start up Sensible Shoes (or further left and higher) and continue, past the crux right of Don's Crack, to step off the righthand end of the crag.

At the same level and 100 yards right a small undercut buttress has 3 greenish problems at 4b, left, right and centre, **The Doleman**. Above, by the path along the ridge top are 2 boulders. On the larger, up flakes on the south corner, is **Ossie's Bulge**, 5a.
A classic. The edge commences again with two isolated buttresses.

**45 The Comedian** 30 feet Very Severe ★
4b. Go directly up the front of the lefthand buttress until forced to stomach traverse right into a break. Exit precariously. Inferior finishes exist to the left, 4a, or straight up, 5a.

**46 Camelian Crack** 20 feet Very Difficult
The layback crack on the left side of the righthand buttress.

**47 Elastic Limit** 30 feet Hard Very Severe
5a. The overhang guarding the front face has a crack at its lip. Deft footwork enables this to be reached. Swing up and right to a ledge. Finish direct; a long reach probably essential. The ledge can also be gained by traversing from right, Very Difficult or left, Severe.

A more continuous stretch of rock begins 20 yards right with two wide problem cracks facing along the edge. The slabs to the west also afford some good sport for the diligent searcher.

**48 Wriggler** 20 feet Hard Severe
The first crack on the front face. A steep awkward finish.

# RAMSHAW ROCKS 221

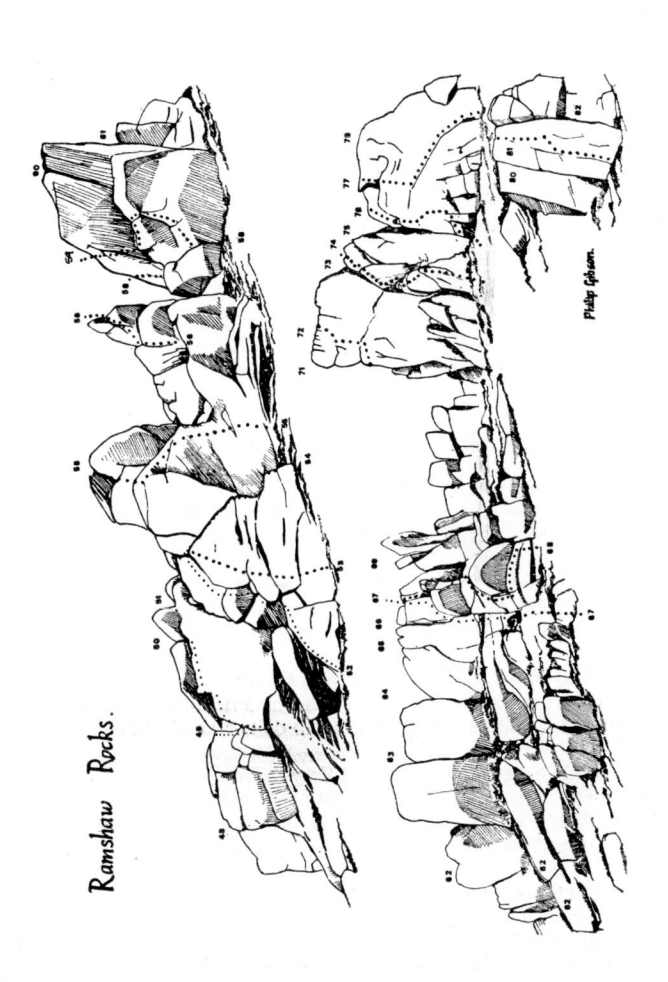

Ramshaw Rocks.

Philip Gibson.

## GRITSTONE AREA

**49  Arete And Crack**  45 feet  Very Difficult
Take the blunt arete left of a cave. Move left and up a crack. Exit left.

**50  Handrail**  40 feet  E2
5c. Near the top of Arete & Crack a rising hand-traverse leads out right on dwindling holds to a short crack before the prow. Strenuous.

**51  Assegai**  35 feet  Very Severe
4c. The corner crack above the cave is hard where it steepens.

**52  Bowrosin**  40 feet  Very Severe
4c. Climb the slab right of the cave, then the awkward bulging crack.

**53  English Towns**  40 feet  E3
5b. The wall on the right leads to a fierce mantleshelf (to avoid Bowrosin). Continue directly up easier-angled rock. Protection in Bowrosin reduces the grade but increases the peace of mind.

**54  Boomerang**  40 feet  Very Difficult  ★★
The beautiful diagonal flake crack 40 ft right of the cave.

**55  The Watercourse**  50 feet  Hard Severe
Up the right side of an often wet groove to a ledge. Scramble up a second groove and traverse left to finish up the cracked nose.

**56  Dan's Dare**  30 feet  Mild Very Severe
4b. At a higher level. An awkward flaky groove just right of a short chimney. Continue up the arete on the right.

**57  Gully Wall**  30 feet  Hard Very Severe
5a. The left wall of the next gully, starting 5 ft from the arete. A thin move near the top adds zest to quite a good route.

**58  Little Nasty**  45 feet  Hard Very Severe
1. 4c. The undercut crack 10 ft right of the gully to a wide shelf.
2. 5a. Walk back 10 ft and gain a shallow crack (balancy) in the right wall leading to a sloping shelf and the top.

**59  Electric Savage**  50 feet  E3  †
1. 5b. From 10 ft up No. 58 finger-traverse right and up to the shelf.
2. 5c. Pull up to the hanging flake at the left end of the shelf to a scary rounded finish.

**60 Ramshaw Crack** 45 feet E3 ★★★
1. 4c. For purists. A crack on the right of the lower overhang.
2. 6a. The progressively widening crack splitting the upper overhang provides a 'tour de force'.

The thin crack to the right awaits the future.

**61 Green Corner** 20 feet Severe
Climb the angle right of the buttress. Not as poor as it looks.

**62 Zigzag Route** 35 feet Very Difficult
Begin up the first undercut crack right of a short gully, then the wide crack on the right moving right again to finish. Harder starts exist up twin cracks to the right, 4c, or a slanting crack further right, 4c.

For the next 30 yards the crag is in 2 tiers. The lower slabby part is disappointing. The next 4 cracks are in the upper tier.

**63 Imposition** 25 feet Hard Very Severe ★
5a. The steep undercut crack beyond an impressive leaning wall 30 ft right of Zigzag. A good test of crack technique.

**64 Iron Horse Crack** 20 feet Difficult
The friendlier crack 10 ft right.

**65 Tricouni Crack** 20 feet Hard Severe
The thin slanting crack 10 ft right again has an energetic start.

**66 Rubber Crack** 20 feet Very Severe
4c. The incipient flaky crack and groove 8 ft right. Tricky landing.

**67 Darkness** 30 feet Severe
Begin up the slab below Rubber Crack. Bridge the steep corner crack curving right (crux) and then go up the first crack on the left.

**68 Army Route** 40 feet Difficult
Start on the lower section. Traverse left below a small prow to a cracked rib and grassy ledge. Finish up the broken chimney above.

**69 Dusk** 40 feet Difficult
Go up the boulder-topped gully right of the prow to the ledge. There are various exits up the chimney and crack system above.

To the right is FLAKY BUTTRESS, a pinnacle with a fine-looking left wall.

**70 Flake Gully**  20 feet  Moderate
Climb the gully to the left of the wall.

**71 Flaky Wall Direct**  45 feet  Very Severe  ★★
4b.Go Steeply up the righthand side of the wall on good holds to a ledge. Climb leftwards past a wicked-looking spike which guards entry to the exhilarating final groove.

**72 Flaky Wall Indirect**  55 feet  Very Severe  ★
4c.As for the Direct to the ledge. Go rightwards up flakes, round the corner and go up the north face on small holds (crux).

**73 Cracked Gully**  40 feet  Difficult
The shallow groove on the front of the pinnacle.

**74 Cracked Arete**  40 feet  Very Difficult
The arete immediately right is taken direct to the top.

**75 Arete Wall**  30 feet  Difficult
The V-groove. The groove and rib on its left give another start.

A gully separates Flaky Buttress from the next slabby buttress.

**76 Crystal Tipps**  20 feet  Hard Very Severe
5c.Pull onto a slab just to the right and aim for the layback flake.

**77 Magic Roundabout**  30 feet  Severe  ★
From a niche 20 ft round to the right of the gully take the lower rising line leftwards across the slab to finish up a black flake.
There are two variation problem starts:
**The Direct**, 4b. A shallow groove 6 ft left of the niche.
**The Superdirect**, 5c. A layaway flake and slab 4 ft further left.

**78 The Delectable Deviation**  25 feet  Very Severe
4c.Start just right of the niche and from 6 ft up tiptoe along the upper crease to the black flake. A neat variation is possible up the green crack directly above the niche, 4c.

**79 Perched Flake**  25 feet  Difficult
Climb left, right or centre up a flake to the right. Go up a blunt arete.

Further right a solitary pinnacle, **The Finger**, provides amusement.

**80  Port Crack**   25 feet   Severe
Directly below Flaky Buttress is a small buttress with 3 cracks.
Start by bridging from below or from the slab on the left.

**81  Time Out**   30 feet   E1
5b.The middle crack moving right where it peters out, to another
crack.

**82  Starboard Crack**   30 feet   Hard Very Severe
5a.The hand-mauling righthand crack. Painfully steep to start.

At the same level and further right is the famous 'WINKING
EYE BUTTRESS'. At the left end is a small pinnacle.

**83  Owl'ole**   20 feet   Difficult
From just right of the pinnacle climb up past an eroded hole.

**84  Middle Route**   20 feet   Severe
The crack to the right through the bulges.

**85  The Shoulder**   20 feet   Hard Very Difficult
The corner left of the 'face'. Go straight up or move left at
half-height onto a protruding flake then go over a bulge.

Routes 86, 87 and 89 are included for completeness. Please avoid
them to prevent further damage.

**86  South Cheek**   20 feet   Hard Severe
Traverse right from the corner and awkwardly go up to the
'Winking Eye'. Step on the 'nose' and mantleshelf on the
'forehead'.

**87  North Cheek**   30 feet   Very Difficult
Climb the slab and corner on the right until a traverse left leads
to the 'Winking Eye'. Continue as for South Cheek.

**88  Collar Bone**   30 feet   Difficult
The pock-marked slab 10 ft right of the corner.

**89  The Veil**   80 feet   Hard Severe
The girdle which also crosses the 'eye' should be avoided.

Back on top of the ridge and 80 yards right of Magic Roundabout
is ROMAN NOSE BUTTRESS. Directly below the nose is:

# 226 GRITSTONE AREA

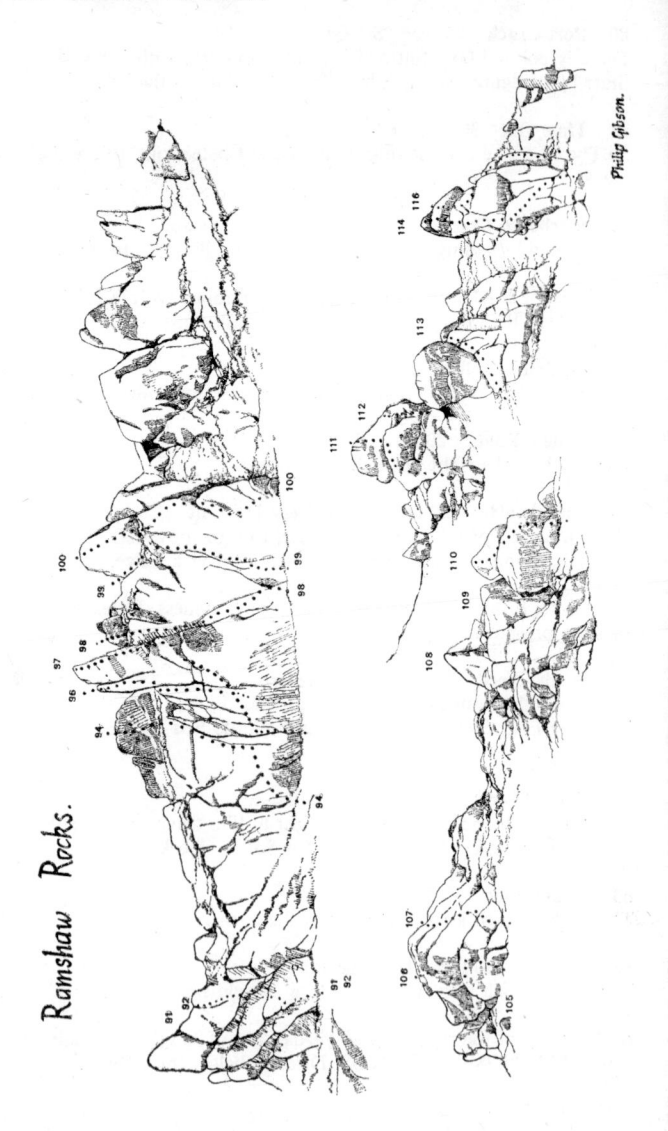

Ramshaw Rocks.

Philip Gibson.

**90 Big Richard**   35 feet   Severe
Climb direct, or from the right, to a spike at 10 ft. Squirm through the chimney above to a ledge. Go up the reachy wall on the right.

**90a The Proboscid**   35 feet   Hard Very Severe
5a. From the ledge of Big Richard layback the exposed nose. Serious. An independent start to the left is pointless.

**91 The Crippler**   35 feet   Hard Very Severe   ★★
5a. Start 15 ft right of the spike. Trend diagonally left under and round the main overlap to a delicate finish. One of Ramshaw's best.

**92 Escape**   25 feet   Hard Very Severe
The buttress is bounded by a man-eating chimney.
5b. Swing onto the wall between The Crippler and the chimney and go intricately up it. Difficult to avoid capture at the top.

**93 Mantrap**   25 feet   Hard Very Difficult
Climb the chimney.

The next buttress, THE PINNACLE, has a shallow undercut gully on its left. A jamming crack on the wall to the left overlooks this gully.

**94 Great Scene Baby**   35 feet   Severe
Gain the crack by traversing from the left. Climb it and the neb above.
**Direct Start:** a digit-distorting 5b if the gully is totally foresaken.

**95 Groovy Baby**   35 feet   Hard Severe on the first move
The gully is exasperating to start and disappointing to finish.

**96 Pile Driver**   55 feet   Very Severe   ★
4c. After 10 ft of Groovy Baby move right to a corner crack which is climbed to its top. Step right and go up a worrying crack on the exposed front face.

**97 The Press**   50 feet   Hard Very Severe   ★★
5a. As for Pile Driver to a swing right at 20 ft onto the leaning wall. Pull into the crack above and finish right of the arete.
**Direct Start**, 5c, is just right of the gully. A dynamic approach helps.

**98  Curfew**  40 feet   Hard Very Severe  ★
5a. The green undercut crack bounding the Pinnacle on the right. There is an improbable resting place in the lower part.

**99  Foord's Folly**  35 feet   E1  ★★
5c. The crack system up the bulging wall 5 ft right is continuously thought-provoking. A jamming testpiece.

**100  The Swinger**  45 feet   Hard Very Severe
5a. From the right end of the wall swing up left via 2 slanting rakes to a ledge on the blunt rib. Go up to a grassy ramp and follow the arete above. Cop out variations exist.

**101  Screwy Driver**  100 feet   Very Severe
4c. A rather contrived girdle, at about two-thirds height, from the gully left of Great Scene Baby to a crack right of The Swinger arete.

Up on the right several unappealing prows intervene. 40 yards on is an undercut nose with a short wall above and to the left.

**102  Slow Hand Clap**  25 feet   Hard Very Severe
5c. Climb the wall just right of centre, starting directly below. A long reach appears necessary for the final move.

**103  Modesty Crack**  25 feet   Difficult
Go up the crack on the left side of the nose and over blocks on the right.

**104  The Brag**  30 feet   Very Severe
5a. Enter the slanting undercut groove just right of the nose with difficulty. Move up and left along cracks to easier ground.

On the crest of the ridge to the right is the SHARK'S FIN. The roof flake, 5a, is a superb problem and a hand-traverse of the lip to the flake is worthwhile. Beware of the huge frog on top to the right.

**105  Early Retirement**  20 feet   Difficult
The next buttress 20 yards right, has a blocky groove on its left. Climb the groove to the slot on the right. Shuffle backwards to the top.

**106  Overdraught**  25 feet   Hard Very Severe
5a. Tackle the frontal overhang. Climb the right edge to a slab below the main roof. Surmount this from the left swinging right to a flake.

**107 Extended Credit**   25 feet   Hard Very Severe
4c.The interesting right wall of the buttress. Some suspect holds.

**108 Caramta**   40 feet   Severe
25 yards right is a buttress with a leftwards slanting crack. Jam up the crack and pull directly over the 2 noses above.

**109 The Prism**   30 feet   Very Difficult
Bridge up the undercut corner on the right and climb either the cracks on the left or the groove on the right.

**110 Lechery**   30 feet   Hard Severe
The overhanging arete to the right on spaced jugs. Continue delicately to the top block which gives a gymnastic finish.

30 yards on are 2 outcrops, one above the other. The upper gives:

**111 Ceiling Zero**   20 feet   Very Severe
4c.Gain huge jugs on the lip of the overhang starting on the left.

**112 Pocket Wall**   20 feet   Hard Severe
Climb the bulging wall just right of a large block on sufficient holds.

Further right is a problem crack, 3c, and slab, 4a. Below is:

**113 Curver**   30 feet   Hard Very Difficult
Cross the slab under the prow from left to right to a crack and flake.

**114 Old Fogey**   40 feet   E2                                    ★★
10 yards right is the last buttress bounded on the left by a gully.
5b.From 10 ft up the gully traverse right on a small ramp to the arete which is climbed on the right. An excellent route.
**Direct Start**, 6c†. The pebbly wall below the arete. Apparently desperate.

**115 King Harold**   30 feet   Severe
Climb the chimney on the right.

**116 Little Giraffe Man**   40 feet   Hard Severe
An amusing excursion. Climb the arete on the right, cross the chimney, continue left and airily up the thin crack in the roof above.

250 yards along the ridge is the LADY STONE. Permission should be asked at the farm 200 yards to the north-east. A short slab, 4a, is on the left side of the stone.

230  GRITSTONE AREA

**117 Lady Stone Chimney** 20 feet  Difficult
Climb the chimney to the right of the slab.

**118 Farmhouse Arete** 30 feet  Hard Severe ★
From the chimney, move right on parallel cracks to the arete.
Go up it.

**119 Childhood's End** 30 feet  Very Severe ★
5a.Start 10 ft right with a fingery move. Move up through
overhangs and go right to a final slab.

**120 Ladies' Route** 35 feet  Severe
The diagonal crack on the right is tricky to enter. Exit right.

**121 Evil Crack** 25 feet  Hard Very Severe
5a.Further right is a roof crack. Approach this via a pocket.
Climb the crack by standing on the nose on the left. Strenuous.

50 yards right is a small buttress with several little problems.


# NEWSTONES, BALDSTONES and GIB TORR
by Nick Longland

---

O.S. Ref. SK 019638 — Newstones
　　　　 SK 019644 — Baldstones
　　　　 SK 018648 — Gib Torr

SITUATION and APPROACHES
The rocks form 3 distinct outcrops on a small north-south ridge
about a mile north of Ramshaw Rocks, and 5 miles north of Leek.
The outcrops are best reached from the Leek-Buxton road, the
A53 (PMT Bus Route 208). For the Newstones end take the first
lane north of Ramshaw Rocks, leading to Allgreave and Gradbach.
The lane passes by a low ridge (the natural continuation of
Ramshaw) which has a few disappointing problems. Park near a
triangular junction after half a mile. The rocks are visible 200 yards
away beyond a cottage. For Gib Torr take either of the next
2 lanes off the A53 to the north (from the Royal Cottage or
Morridge Top). These join and then pass within 50 yards of
Gib Torr.

## ACCESS
The ownership is not known. No difficulties have so far arisen.

## CHARACTER
The outcrops face east, are mainly small and have been weathered into weird shapes by the elements. The rock is sound gritstone; some of the cracks and faces have a veneer of more resistant iron ore affording excellent holds. The result is a very good and varied boulderer's playground with some longer and more serious routes where a rope is advisable. Both problems and climbs are described, the distinction between them being somewhat arbitrary: problems have not been given an adjectival grade.

## HISTORY
These outcrops have been the solo playground of various groups over the years and their devotees have mostly been unconcerned, perhaps rightly, about recording who first did what and when, though each group had its own names for many of the problems. Perambulator Parade was described by A. J. Lowe in 'Climbs on Gritstone', Volume 3, 1951 and Graham Martin of the Mountain Club undoubtedly climbed many of the routes in the early 1950s. During the 1960s frequent visits by the Manchester University M.C. resulted in the addition of many popular problems such as Elephant's Ear and Martin Boysen added the old test piece of Original Route.
Later the NSMC attentions resulted in Baldstone Arete, The Ensign and The Gibbet. Around the same time, but quite independently, a loosely-knit group named the 'Altrincham All-Stars' (by Ken Wilson) made regular visits and added some of the harder routes. In particular Tony Barley climbed the spectacular Charlie's Overhang (also known as Barleymoon) and The Gibe. Boysen did All-Stars' Wall and Gib.
Problems such as Fielder's Corner, Itchy Fingers and Left and Right Fin were almost certainly first discovered by this group. In 1975 Jim Campbell led Trepidation and in 1976, with Nick Colton, produced the un-nerving Goldrush. In 1977 Ray Jardine, on a visit from the U.S.A., succeeded after several days in leading Ray's Roof which may prove to be the hardest roof on gritstone to date.

The outcrops are described from south to north and the routes from Left to Right.

## NEWSTONES
250 yards along the grassy track from the cottage and across the fence is the first buttress which sports a large roof.

## 232 GRITSTONE AREA

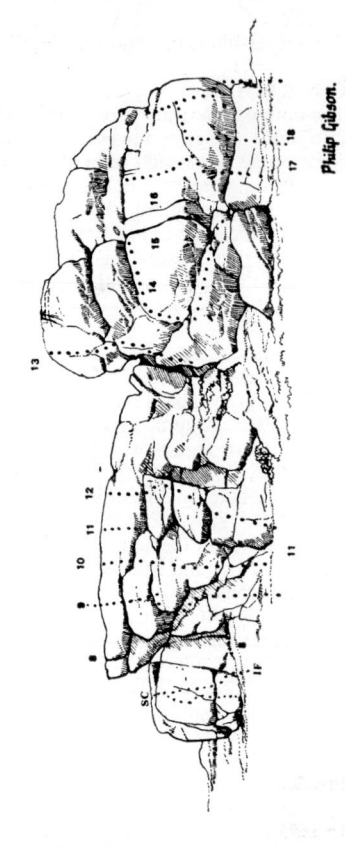

*The Newstones.*

Philip Gibson.

**1 Charlie's Overhang**  20 feet  E1  ★★
5c. The roof, from the right, on flakes to a hideous final mantleshelf. Short but exhilarating. The ground below is flat—and getting flatter.

**2 Newstone Chimney**  20 feet  Difficult
Either crack (left is harder) to the overhanging chimney.

**3 Moonshine**  20 feet  Hard Very Severe
5a. The middle of the bulging wall right of the chimney.

**4 Praying Mantle**  20 feet  Very Severe
4c. Mantle onto the prow 5 ft right and up the thin scooped wall.

A girdle is possible at 5a.

25 ft right is a small prow, 4c, and below and across the fence is a short slab with 2 close lines, both 5b on the first move.

On the left side of the next buttress are 2 rising lines:
**Ripple**, 6a. Finger traverse the vein near the top of the wall.
**Martin's Traverse**, 5a. The lower line, delicately up to the arete. It is easy to 'barn-door' off.
**Direct Start**, 5c, is straight over the undercut arete.
**Short Wall**, 5a. The undercut but juggy wall left of Short Chimney.
**Short Chimney**, 2a. Detour left near the top for more interest.
To the right the front of the buttress contains a crack and a groove.

**5 Hazel Barrow Crack**  20 feet  Hard Very Difficult  ★
The crack then slightly left over the bulge with a long pull.

**6 Hazel Barn**  25 feet  Very Difficult  ★
The shallow groove (or ripples on the right), then over the block.

**7 Nutmeg**  25 feet  Hard Severe
The undercut wall and perched arete 10 ft right is fun. Just left, a barely distinct eliminate, 5c, avoids the rugosities.

60 yards on, the next buttress has a smaller edition on its left.
**Scratched**, 5b. The bulge just left of Scratch Crack.
**Scratch Crack**, 4b. The jamming crack splitting the mini-buttress.
**Itchy Finger**, 5c. The fingery right wall of the buttress, gained from the right, should delight the connoisseur. A more direct approach, 6a, is possible just to the left.
**Bridget**, 4c the short steep slab at the back of the recess.
To the right is an overhanging wall with a crack at its lefthand end—**Peel's Problem**, 5c. Gain the crack from the right. Strenuous.

**8  Rhynose**  25 feet  Very Severe ★
4b. The hanging flake crack on the arete. Bridge airily left to finish.

**9  Hippo**  25 feet  Very Difficult
The groove and chimney just right of the arete. Continue direct.

**10  Rosehip**  25 feet  Severe
The bulge and wall above, immediately left of The Witch.

**11  The Witch**  25 feet  Difficult
Climb a corner to a 'tunnel', step left and go straight up.

**12  Candy Man**  20 feet  Severe
The slab and awkward double overlap, moving progressively right.

10 yards right is the undercut SLY BUTTRESS with a leaning left wall.

**13  Trepidation**  25 feet  Hard Very Severe †★
5b. From the gully, take the blind crack system rightwards to a horizontal crack. Go slightly right up the centre of the wall. Bold.

**14  The Snake**  40 feet  Severe
Make a contortionate move to gain the catwalk left of The Fox. Go along, up and stomach traverse right to a chimney. Good entertainment.

**15  The Fox**  30 feet  Hard Very Severe
5b. The lefthand of the twin cracks on the buttress front. The short-armed may find the chockstone tantalisingly distant.

**16  The Vixen**  30 feet  Very Severe
4b. The less obdurate (as befits a lady) crack and wall above and right.

**17  The Sly Mantleshelf**  30 feet  Hard Very Severe ★
5a. Mantle with considerable delicacy onto the left end of the line of ripples. Continue up the steep slab slightly to the left.
**Sly Superdirect**, 5b. Another pull and thin mantle onto the ripples a few feet right. Toe-traverse right to escape.

**18  Sly Corner**  30 feet  Very Severe ★★
4c. From 8 ft round the corner, traverse left to a delightful move round the arete onto the right end of the ripples. Go up the wall.
**Sly Direct**, 4c. Heave straight onto the right end of the ripples.

A few problems remain, the best being: a wall, 4b, above Sly Corner start, a rib further right, 5b and a crack, 4a, in the back wall.

## BALDSTONES
500 yards along the ridge is Baldstone Pinnacle.

**19  Perambulator Parade**  35 feet  Difficult ★★
From the ruin, take a slanting groove to a slab round the back. Go up this and step left over the bulge. Pull onto the summit block. The easiest descent is to jump from the bottom of the upper slab.

**20  Incognito**  30 feet  Very Severe
4c. Climb the centre of the steep slab to the right to an awkward exit.

The front face contains 3 fine routes.

**21  Baldstone Face**  35 feet  Very Severe ★
4b. Take the rake on the left. Continue up near the left edge. Exposed.

**22  Original Route**  30 feet  Hard Very Severe ★★
5b. The central groove. A puzzling start and a delicate finish.

**23  Baldstone Arete**  30 feet  Hard Very Severe ★★
4c. Swing up flakes, then right, thin, to the airy but easier right arete.

**24  Goldrush**  35 feet  E4 ★★
The upper overhangs of the next buttress are split by a crack.
5c. Left of the crack is a hanging scoop. Climb up to this and enter it from the left. Pull over the bulge above (crux). Unprotected.

**25  Goldsitch Crack**  40 feet  Very Severe ★
4c. The wide upper crack is reached from an undercut crack 5 ft further right.

**26  Blackbank Cracks**  40 feet  Very Difficult
Go up cracks left of the chimney. Traverse left to a wide final cleft.
**Direct Start**, 4b. The hanging crack and bulge 10 ft left.

**27  Forking Chimney**  30 feet  Difficult
Both forks are of equal difficulty.

# 236 GRITSTONE AREA

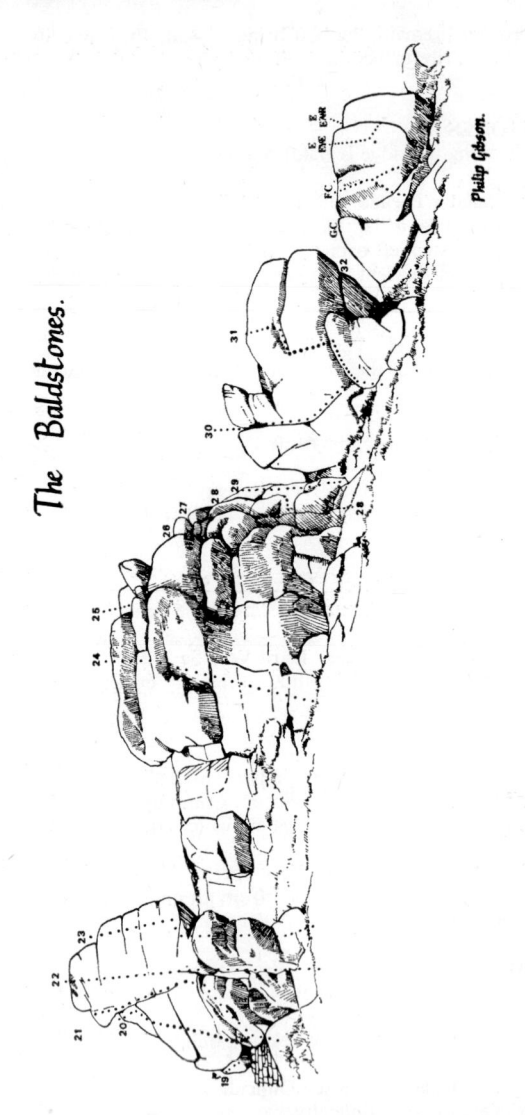

*The Baldstones.*

Philip Gibson.

**28  Bareleg Wall**  30 feet  Severe  ★
Climb a groove on the right. Traverse right, hard, and go up via a crack.

**29  Morridge Top**  30 feet  Very Severe
4b.The centre of the wall to the right.

**30  Minipin Crack**  20 feet  Very Difficult  ★
Follow the meandering crack on the facing wall with interest.

**31  All-Stars' Wall**  20 feet  Hard Very Severe
5b.The wall on the right. Reachy, despite the small pocket.

**32  Ray's Roof**  25 feet  5.11c  †★
The roof crack leading right awaits a first British ascent.

The next buttress is smaller but provides some superb problems.
**Ganderhole Crack**, 4a. The crack directly behind the boulder.
**Fielder's Corner**, 5a. From the corner just right, move right above a nasty landing, round the arete and up pockets on the front face. A harder, 5c, but less-enjoyable start takes a chipped layaway on the right.
**Elephant's Eye**, 5c. Start up the 'ear' then move left to the 'eyes'.
**Elephant's Ear**, 4c. A fine layback crack leads to a bald brow.
20 yards on is a small buttress with a Moderate chimney on the left.

**33  Pyeclough**  20 feet  Very Severe
4b.The crack splitting the nose is quite awkward.

**34  Heathylee**  20 feet  Difficult
The rake slanting to the right. Direct (Very Difficult) or lefthand (Severe) finishes offer alternatives.

**35  End Game**  25 feet  Hard Severe
40 yards right is a final wall. Start below its highest point. Climb the wall and prow above.

Two slanting cracks to the right and the wall between give problems up to 5a.

## GIB TORR
300 yards north-west, across Black Brook, are the 3 buttresses of Gib Torr. The lower buttress has a fin of rock at its lefthand end.

**Left Fin**, 4c. The dirty crack on the left side of the fin.
**Right Fin**, 5c. The right wall of the fin on barely sufficient holds.

**36   Gib Sail**   40 feet   Moderate
Follow the right edge of the grassy slab right of the fin.

**37   Gibber Crack**   20 feet   Severe
The twisting crack round the arete on the front face. Tricky exit.

**38   Montezuma's Revenge**   35 feet   E3   ★
5c. From the ledge of The Gibe go up and left on poor holds.
Exit through the top bulge by a blind crack and 'ear'.

**39   The Gibe**   35 feet   Very Severe   ★
4b. From a block 20 ft right, ascend to a ledge at 12 ft. Continue
steeply right to a catcrawl allowing escape round the corner. The
crack above the catcrawl has supposedly been climbed.

**40   Gibble Gabble Slab**   25 feet   Difficult
Diagonally up the green slab. Move right, long step, and up.

**41   Gibbon Take**   50 feet   Very Severe
4b. A girdle starting up Gibber Crack and finishing with The Gibe.

Several entertaining problems exist on the scattered boulders to
the left of the lower buttress.
The lefthand upper buttress has a ledge at 10 ft at its centre.

**42   Gibbon Wall**   25 feet   Very Severe
4b. Gain the ledge and climb the crack and bulge above.

**43   Gibing Corner**   25 feet   Severe   ★
The shallow Corner on the right moving onto the slab to finish.
A barely distinct finish over the bulge is harder, 4a.

**44   Gibeonite Girdle**   45 feet   Hard Very Severe
5b. Traverse from right to left at two-thirds height until forced
over the top above the overhang.

The righthand buttress has an easy cleft on its lefthand side.

**45   Gibraltar**   25 feet   Very Difficult
The corner and crack 8 ft to the right.

**46  The Ensign**   30 feet   Hard Very Severe
5a. Gain the overhanging corner right again, with difficulty. Often greasy.

**47  Gib**   30 feet   E2   ★
5c. Below the undercut crack on the right is a hold. Make fierce moves from left or right to reach this. Use it to gain the crack above.

**48  The Gibbet**   35 feet   Hard Very Severe
5a. Start up Giblet Crack and cross the wall on the left diagonally.

**49  Giblet Crack**   20 feet   Very Difficult
Climb onto the lower chockstone of the chimney and finish up the crack on the left.

# BACK FOREST and THE HANGING STONE
by Kevin Pickup

---

O.S. Ref. SJ 987653 to 974654

## SITUATION
These crags are near the crest of the northern continuation of the Roaches ridge. From Roche End the ridge runs north-west for ¾ of a mile and then curves to the west towards Danebridge.

## APPROACHES
For Back Forest crags continue along the minor road past The Roaches to where it crosses the ridge at Roche End. There is ample parking space here. Take a footpath going north-west keeping strictly to the ridge; after ¾ of a mile a wall crosses the path. The Main Area appears immediately after the wall on the left. A further ½ mile along the ridge is the Western Outcrop. The Hanging Stone, another ½ mile along the ridge, is best approached from Danebridge (O.S. Ref. SJ 965652) which can be reached from the Congleton-Buxton road or the Leek-Macclesfield road. From the bridge follow a wide track upstream for 50 yards on the Staffordshire side (right bank) of the river. Cross a stile on the right and follow a path through a little wooded valley (yellow marker posts) to another stile. Walk across a field to Hanging Stone farm, passing quietly through the farm buildings and up the hillside to the rock.

# 240 GRITSTONE AREA

## ACCESS
There have been no problems so far.

## CHARACTER
The outcrops provide interesting and varied climbing on good clean gritstone although in wet conditions they can become green. The Main Area comprises a series of well-named buttresses which although usually less than 25 feet high give a good range of routes to keep most climbers suitably extended. Many are soloable with good landings but beware of the long crawl back to the car park. Only 2 buttresses of the Western Outcrop yield climbs. The main feature of 2 large overhangs is on the extreme left and gives spectacular climbing. The Hanging Stone is an isolated buttress projecting from the hillside. Its summit prow provides an overhang forming a strenuous finale to all the routes. 2 plaques are secured to the buttress; one commemorating the death of a dog, and the other is a memorial to a notable member of the Brocklehurst family.

## HISTORY
The first mention of the Main Area of Back Forest was in an early guide to The Roaches. Subsequently in 1931 details of 16 routes and the buttress names appeared in the Rucksack Club Journal. These and other routes, particularly those further along the ridge, were described in the Staffordshire Gritstone Area guide of 1973. Since then The Keeper and Thin Wall by Tony Barley and Toe Rail by John Holt have filled in some of the blanker faces. The Double Overhang on the Western Outcrop probably first fell to Dave Salt in 1971, but has since been climbed without the use of a sling. The only other climb added here is Barley's The Nick. The impressive Hanging Stone has two additions to the climbs of the sixties; The Bridge Of Sighs by Dave Jones and Right Bow by Jon Woodward, both requiring the aggression this rock demands.

**THE CLIMBS** are described from Right to Left, except for the Hanging Stone.

## MAIN AREA (S.J. 987653)

The first buttress gives a series of 15 feet high problems.
**Unseen Face**, 4b. The blunt arete above a stone shelter. 3 ft left is:
**Contract Worker**, 4a. A strenuous finger crack with a small overhang at the top.
**Problem Arete**, 5c. The arete to the left with lefthand and righthand starts.

**Dog Leg Corner,** 2a. The wide corner crack left of the arete.
**Armstrain,** 5b. Just left of the corner. The undercut and wall above.
**Dog Leg Crack,** 2a. The crack bending left at the top.
**Harrop's Pride,** 4a. 6 ft to the left. Strenuous moves over the undercut to gain the arete.
**Simple View,** 5a. 5ft left. The thin crack and rounded wall above.

Beyond a narrow cleft, **Lair Gully**, is ROCKING STONE BUTTRESS which no longer has the stone for which it was named. The right edge gives a short Moderate problem, **Weathered Corner**.

**1 Rocking Stone Ridge** 20 feet Very Difficult
The lefthand arete provides easy climbing after assaulting the undercut problem start.

**2 Grasper** 20 feet Very Severe
4c. Climb the centre of the wall, finishing up 2 thin cracks.

**3 Requiem For Tired Fingers** 20 feet Very Severe
5b. The green slanting crack 5 ft left of Grasper requires fingery moves finishing slightly right at the notch.

**The Hanging Slab Crack,** Moderate, in the corner with capstone is the start of BROKEN NOSE BUTTRESS.

**Thin Crack,** 4a. The strenuous crack splitting the face 5 ft left.

**4 Not So Central Route** 20 feet Mild Severe
From the toe of the buttress climb the arete and traverse awkwardly under the first overhang to the right. Straight up to finish.

**5 Central Route** 20 feet Mild Severe
Climb the arete to the second overhang, avoiding it with technique and faith to the right.

**6 Green Shaker** 25 feet Very Difficult
As for Central Route to the first ledge. Move left onto the steep wall to a small flake in the centre. Go diagonally right to finish.

12 yards left is BASTION BUTTRESS. The small rounded buttress to the right has a Severe arete, **Filler In**.

**7 Bastion Face** 20 feet Difficult
This is the right face of Bastion Buttress on the right edge.

**8 Bastion Corner**  20 feet   Very Difficult
Start on the left face and climb sloping ledges rightwards and finish up the blunt arete. A good reach helps.

**9 Pseudo Crack**  25 feet   Hard Very Difficult   ★
The steep groove and crack separating Bastion from Bollard Buttress. Step right near the top, or for a strenuous and airy finish traverse left and go up the arete.

**10 Toe Rail**  25 feet   Hard Very Severe
5b. Climb the right face of Bollard Buttress by a flake hold and go direct over the top bulge.

**11 Bollard Edge**  25 feet   Hard Severe   ★★
At the foot of the buttress avoid the overhang via the left. A short crack leads to the top of the bollard. Continue up keeping slightly left of the arete.

**12 Capstone Chimney**  20 feet   Mild Severe
Climb the chimney to the left of Bastion Buttress facing left to squeeze awkwardly past the chockstone on good holds.

**13 Wrestle Crack**  20 feet   Hard Severe
The wide undercut crack 3 ft left offers hidden holds.

**14 The Saucer Direct**  20 feet   Severe
8 ft left is a small slab, The Saucer, below an overhang. Climb up to The Saucer. Move right past the overhang and go up a loosely wedged flake above. An alternative start to the right is harder.

**15 The Saucer**  20 feet   Hard Difficult
Climb The Saucer, move left round the corner and up via a crack.

**16 Keep Face**  20 feet   Severe
A short gully defines the right edge of the LOWER KEEP BUTTRESS. On the right mantleshelf onto the left side of a ledge and climb the L-shaped crack to reach a difficult move and mantleshelf finish.

**17 Portcullis Crack**  20 feet   Hard Very Difficult   ★★
Climb the left side of Keep Face via a crack with chockstones. Pass an overhang strenuously to a ledge. Finish up and left on the arete.

**18  The Keeper**  20 feet  Hard Very Severe
5a. Start below the overhang and pull up onto the steep left wall of the buttress to reach a ledge, then ascend the right arete.

HOLLY TREE BUTTRESS stands at a higher level across a sandy bank.
**Blow Hard**, 4a. A short flaky crack right of the niche in the right wall.

**19  Holly Tree Niche Right Route**  20 feet  Difficult
Climb into the niche in the right wall and go up the corner.

**20  Holly Tree Niche Left Route**  30 feet  Severe  ★
From the toe of the buttress climb the arete on the right side. Above the first bulge move left to awkward moves up the left side of the nose.

**21  Thin Wall**  30 feet  Hard Very Severe  ★★
5a. 6 ft left is a thin crack leading to a horizontal break. Unusual technique is required to pass the blank section to the next break, then go straight up via a blind flake.

**22  Twin Thin**  25 feet  Severe
The 2 thin vertical cracks one above the other in the centre of the left face, finishing left up a slight groove.

**23  Green Crack**  20 feet  Hard Very Difficult
True to its name is a curving crack. Start 4 ft left of Twin Thin.

100 yards left is another outcrop on the crest of the ridge.
**Racer's Rock**, 4c. The small pinnacle at the right edge, direct.

**24  John's Route**  20 feet  Hard Very Severe
5a. The wall and roofs just right of Rostrum.

**25  Rostrum**  20 feet  Severe  ★
Near the left edge of the buttress is a projecting platform called The Rostrum onto which an ungainly entry is made from the right on good holds. Finish left up the bulges.

THE WESTERN OUTCROP (SJ 981655)

**26  The Nick**  20 feet  Very Severe
5a. This is the obvious overhang split by a crack on an isolated buttress 60 yards right of Double Overhang Buttress.

**27  Double Overhang**   35 feet   Hard Very Severe   ★
5a. Start below the centre of the main buttress. The first roof is overcome by a long reach over to the left and the final roof is climbed just right of centre.

**28  Burnham Crack**   30 feet   Very Severe
4c. The steep corner crack and its continuation, left of the overhangs.

**29  The Gaping Void**   35 feet   Difficult
Start at the lefthand side of the buttress, traversing right to an exposed step across Burnham Crack. Continue right across a slab finishing right of the overhang.

## THE HANGING STONE (SJ 974654)

THE CLIMBS are described from Left to Right.

**30  Lefthand Crack**   25 feet   Very Severe
5a. Follow a corner right of the steps to a break. The continuation crack over the roof relents only after a great deal of effort.

**31  The Bridge Of Sighs**   40 feet   E2   ★★
5c. Ascend the wall just right of the lefthand plaque, with difficulty. Continue to the wide break, then wildly swing across left to climb a shallow groove above the roof. A climb for the committed only.

**32  Hanging Stone Crack**   35 feet   Hard Very Severe   ★
5a. Start right of the prominent arete. Pass the copper plaque with delicacy and a metal fingerhold and overcome the top crack by strenuous jamming or holds on the right.

**33  Right Bow**   25 feet   Hard Very Severe
5b. On the right side of the buttress is a flake high up. Ascend the bulging wall to the break then attack the flake on strength and wits. A climb not recommended for the highly strung.

No fewer than 3 girdles grace the buttress. **The Low Girdle** close to the ground is good but strenuous for Hard Very Difficult. **The Drifter's Escape** hand traverses the central break at Very Severe, 4c, and the **High Girdle** crosses the top break and crawls to safety at Hard Severe, 4a. All 3 are climbed from left to right.

# GRADBACH HILL
by Nick Longland

O.S. Ref. SK 001653

## SITUATION
These outcrops are near the crest of the ridge called Gradbach Hill about 1 mile east of Back Forest Crags and 2 miles north of The Roaches.

## APPROACHES
From the A53 Buxton-Leek road, follow either of the minor roads past Newstones (forking right at the triangle) or Gib Torr. These lanes join after a further mile and cars can be parked 130 yards on by a sharp righthand bend at SK 008651. From the west, turn off the Congleton-Buxton road at Allgreave towards Quarnford. Turn right again ¼ mile beyond the bridge over the River Dane and continue for a mile to the sharp bend (see map). From the bend follow a track due west until it begins to lose height and bear right along the top of the scarp to the rocks.

## ACCESS
Ownership unknown. No problems have so far arisen.

## CHARACTER
There is an atmosphere of quiet isolation about these rocks which emerge from the hillside with sufficient stature to present climbs in only a few places. The most conspicuous features are a large pinnacle easily visible from the Roaches/Back Forest ridge and 150 yards south, a substantial block on top of the edge known as the Yawning Stone. The rock is mostly sound natural gritstone and though west-facing, is somewhat lichenous.

## HISTORY
The majority of the routes of these easily seen rocks were almost certainly done long ago, exceptions being Barry Marsden's eponymous crack and The Phantom which required a bolt for aid inserted by a known member of the N.S.M.C. More recently Jon Woodward led The Phantom without using the aid bolt and Stoke Guidebook Writers Inc. added The Gape, Sense Of Doubt and John's Arete.

**THE CLIMBS** are described from Right to Left: i.e. as approached from the south. 100 yards south of The Yawning Stone are 2 short slabs.

## 246 GRITSTONE AREA

**1 Feed The Enemy**   25 feet   Hard Severe
The blunt arete of the righthand slab.

5 ft left the slab gives a 5a problem. On the lefthand slab the right edge and left side are about 4a and 4c respectively.
The Yawning Stone itself is best climbed up its front face, Severe and has just enough rock on its short side to provide a complete and quite fingery girdle, 5a.

Directly below the Yawning Stone is a small cliff with a prominent crack through an overhang towards the righthand end.

**2 Sense Of Doubt**   25 feet   Hard Very Severe
5b.Start through an undercut 6 ft right of the crack. Follow the blunt arete closely, with a hard move above a horizontal crack.

**3 The Gape**   25 feet   Very Severe
4c.As for Sense Of Doubt to the horizontal crack. Step left and go delicately up the front face past a short ramp.

**4 Chockstone Crack**   25 feet   Hard Very Difficult
The prominent crack. A big jug eases the passage of the overhang.

**5 Marsden's Crack**   25 feet   Very Severe
4b.The thinner crack through the overhang 10 ft to the left.

**6 Barbiturate**   20 feet   Severe
Left is a large corner. Up the slab on its right and the corner crack.

**7 Sleep Walker**   30 feet   Hard Severe
Climb a crack in the left wall of the corner to a double overhang. Traverse strenuously left and trend right up the delicate slab above.

**8 John's Arete**   30 feet   Hard Very Severe
5a.Climb the arete right of the oak tree, then directly up the slab.

**9 Oak Tree Crack**   20 feet   Very Difficult
The wide crack by the oak tree to an easier finish.

25 yards right is a small buttress with a thin crack, 5a up the front. 30 yards further on is another little buttress.

**10 Little Arete**   20 feet   Mild Very Difficult
The arete, skirting the overhang on the left.

90 yards on is THE PINNACLE. The short side is Difficult, or just to the left, Severe. A stone wall runs up to the front face.

**11  The Phantom**  50 feet  E4 ★
5c. From the wall go up a crack to a ledge. Move left onto the arete and up past a bolt. Move 10 ft left and over the top bulge by a thin crack. Superb but serious: the bolt is untrustworthy!

**12  The Cleft**  40 feet  Very Difficult
10 ft left of the wall. Climb first right then left into a cleft. Follow this past a chock and round to finish up the easy back route.

**13  The Cue**  20 feet  Hard Difficult
20 yards left is a buttress with a ledge at two-thirds height. The crack on the right, passing the right edge of the ledge. Thrutchy.

**14  The Chalk**  25 feet  Hard Very Severe
5a. Climb the wall just left to the ledge. Finish up the top wall.

**15  The Billiard Table**  30 feet  Severe
From the lowest point of the buttress climb a crack to a bulge. Go over this awkwardly to the ledge. Exit up the corner crack.

100 yards left of the pinnacle is CYNIC'S BUTTRESS.

**16  Old Son**  25 feet  Very Difficult
Climb a corner crack, right of the central arete, and the arete above.

**17  For Tim**  30 feet  Difficult
Climb the wide central crack.

**18  Fat Old Nick**  30 feet  Very Difficult
Up a crack on the left of an overhang. Move right and up the front slab.
**Al's Abdominal Start,** 5a. The overhang direct on big rounded holds.

# MISCELLANEOUS CRAGS IN THE GRADBACH AREA

### LUDCHURCH O.S. Ref. SJ 987656
This remarkable ravine, steeped in history, is on the north-eastern slopes of Back Forest ridge. Receiving practically no sun, its sides are clothed in vegetation and most of the rock remains wet and greasy except after prolonged dry spells. Ludchurch thus affords a rare environment for thirsty plants suffering from photophobia and as such, is thought to be of greater significance to botanists and ecologists than to climbers.

Although a few routes have been excavated in the past on the northern side, their descriptions are therefore not included in this guide. Climbers are URGED NOT TO CLIMB HERE.

### CASTLE CLIFF ROCKS   O.S. Ref. SJ 985658
These are several shattered gritstone pillars near Ludchurch. They offer a few problems barely worth climbers' attentions.

### GIBBONS CLIFF   O.S. Ref. 971664
Just south of Allgreave, Clough Brook winds through a steep-sided wooded valley. There are several vegetated outcrops, the cleanest being situated on the west bank above an old ruined mill. These are about 25 feet high, rather sandy and loose. The stone walls of the mill ruins look marginally more attractive.

### THE BALLSTONE   O.S. Ref. SK 013658
This large perched boulder is in the grounds of Green Gutter Stake Farm. The farmer does not wish it to be climbed on as it stands only a few yards from his house.

### FLASH BOTTOM ROCKS   O.S. Ref. SK 018657
These interestingly named rocks consist of 2 buttresses up to 25 feet in height. The southerly buttress has a crack up its front, Very Difficult, and a slab capped by an overhang a few yards to the left. The overhang gives a good 5a problem. The northerly buttress has a route up each edge of its front face, both Very Difficult, and a layback crack on its right, Difficult.

# BOSLEY CLOUD

O.S. Ref. Cloud End Crags: North Quarry SJ 903638
Secret Slab    SJ 901636
The Catstone SJ 898631

## SITUATION
This prominent hill is situated 3 miles east of Congleton.

## APPROACHES
The network of lanes in the area is quite complex. If a map is unavailable aim for the north end of The Cloud from Congleton or the Leek-Macclesfield road, and with luck arrive at a minor cross-roads immediately below the north end of the hill. The North Quarry can be reached by a strenuous path leading directly up the hill from here. However, since the routes are described from east to west round the hill, a better approach may be made by following the road round the east side of the hill from the cross-roads and taking a gently rising path which starts by the second farm.
For the Catstone, take the road skirting The Cloud on the west side towards Timbersbrook. About ⅔ of a mile from the cross-roads the buttress will be seen behind a large house on the left.

## ACCESS
Cloud End Crags are owned by the National Trust and its bye-laws should be observed. Permission to climb on The Catstone should be sought from the owner of the large house who is quite willing to let competent parties on his rocks.

## CHARACTER
The routes are on both natural and quarried gritstone. The natural rock is as solid and well-weathered as any. The quarries, whilst on the whole reliable, contain friable bands which require care. Although the crags have been known as a climbing ground for over 70 years, they remain unpopular and have their fair share of lichen. The climbs will prove most attractive for evening visits.

## HISTORY
The first record of climbing here was of Stanley Jeffcoat around 1908. He was later joined by Siegfried Herford and John Laycock, resulting in a short guide to Bosley which was included in Laycock's book 'Some Gritstone Climbs' in 1913. However the first routes of significance came in the 1920s when Morley Wood, A. Pigott and H. Kelly climbed Mutiny Chimney and Cat Crawl

## 250 GRITSTONE AREA

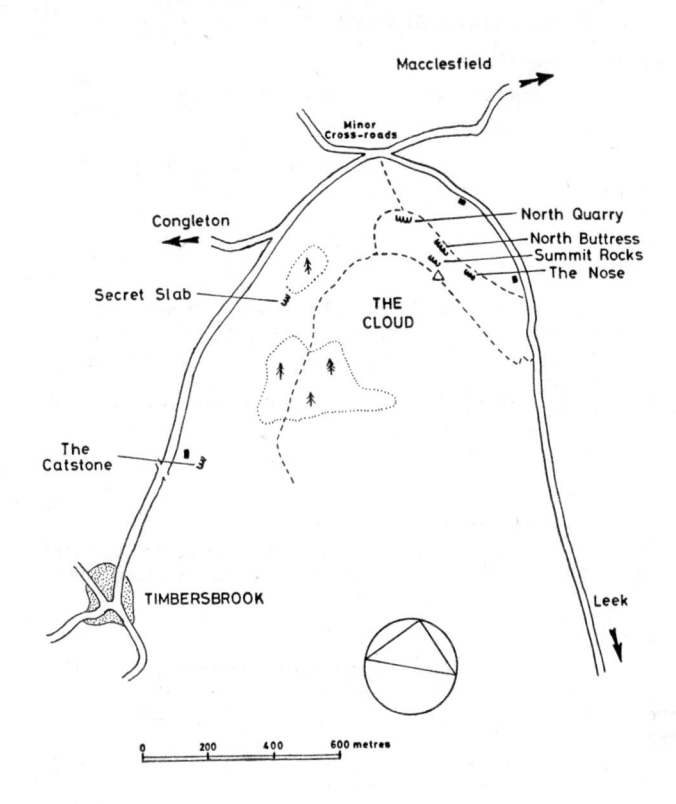

on The Catstone. By the 1940s Eric Byne and Mike Holland had
explored The Cloud and compiled a rough guide. V Chimney
belongs to this period and was a very fine lead for the time.
Byne's guide was given to A. Lowe of the M.U.M.C. who
compiled a complete guide intended for 'Climbs On Gritstone',
Vol. 3 in 1951. For reasons of space the guide was seriously
condensed and the full notes were lost. In 1963 Pete Bamfield,
with the aid of Byne's old guide, began to write up the area for
the new series 'Rock Climbs In The Peak'. Bulldog Flake was led
by a local teacher named Drummond, and other new lines were
added by Bamfield, E. Dance and Frank Johnson. Bamfield's
notes appeared in full in the M.A.M. Journal of 1965, but
P. Williams and friends were unaware of this when they produced
their script which appeared in the Staffordshire Gritstone guide
of 1973. Williams, with J. Amies and P. King climbed and named
the routes on Timbersbrook Quarry in 1969, and Hot Tin Roof
on The Catstone and Slab Wall are probably the results of this
trio's efforts. The publication of the 1973 guide led to the
rediscovery of Bamfield's notes which form the basis of this
present edition. In 1977 Jonny Woodward climbed Impact Two
up the arete right of Main Wall. The following year, with brother
Andy, Main Wall itself was free-climbed and other smaller routes
added to the same quarry. Then in the spring of 1979 they
climbed Slender Thread and Crystal Voyager on the previously
virgin Secret Slab. It was only due to the efforts of Byne and
Bamfield that the last 2 routes were discovered, and perhaps now,
with the complete guide recorded for the first time in guidebook
form, their work will be rewarded. Summit Arete, long done with
a point of aid, was freed by Jonny Woodward at a late stage of
the guidebook work.

THE CLIMBS are described from Left to Right. 200 yards along
the path is a tiny pinnacle in a hollow in the hillside. Below and
40 yards right is a green buttress with 2 short routes of
Moderate/Difficult standard. 100 yards further is a large buttress,
THE NOSE, on which the first described climbs are found. It has
a prominent overhang near the top with a broken chimney on its
left and a steep green groove on the right.

**1 Corner Route** 55 feet Very Difficult
Any one of several lines up the ledgy wall left of the Nostrils to
finish up the slabby corner left of Left Nostril's final chimney.
A harder finish is up the steep right wall of the corner.
The rock to the left contains one or two poor rambling routes.

## 252 GRITSTONE AREA

**2 Left Nostril**  50 feet   Very Difficult
Start below the broken chimney. Pull awkwardly out left onto a slab and climb a crack to a ledge on the right below the chimney. Climb this and go over the chockstone to finish.

**3 Right Nostril**  50 feet   Severe
Climb the steep jamming crack just right of Left Nostril to the ledge and common finish.

**4 V Chimney**  50 feet   Hard Very Severe
5a. Climb the steep green groove on small holds and exit right to a small ledge. Move up and left on the overhanging wall to the top.

**5 Green Gully Direct**  35 feet   Hard Severe
Climb the corner 20 ft right to a big grassy ledge on the right. Go back left and up the corner to mantleshelf on the right at the top.

60 yards right is a good natural buttress, NORTH BUTTRESS.

**6 Envy Face**  25 feet   Severe
15 yards left of this is a small wall. Go up a thin crack in the wall with a slightly overhanging start. Finish on the left arete.

There are 2 obvious flakes on the front face of North Buttress. Round the arete to the left is a shallow undercut corner.

**7 Fertility Rite**  25 feet   Hard Very Severe
5a. The corner. The section above the overhang is delicate.
**Lefthand Finish**, E1, 5c. From the overhang climb the vague blind crack just left, mostly using poor holds on the left wall.

**8 Slab Wall**  25 feet   Very Severe                    ★
4c. Climb the wall on the right near the arete.

**9 Bulldog Flake**  25 feet   Hard Very Severe           ★
5b. The fierce overhanging flake round to the right, climbed by slippery laybacking at the upper limit of its grade.

**10 White House Crack**  25 feet   Very Difficult        ★
The flake crack in the centre of the face. An old classic.

**11 Deception**  20 feet   Hard Severe
The undercut crack 5 yards right is rounded and hard to finish.

Above this buttress, on top of The Cloud are THE SUMMIT ROCKS. These give many boulder problems. However 2 on the main buttress are rather longer and deserve special mention.

## 12  Summit Arete  25 feet  E2
6b. The main arete of the buttress has a 10 ft overhanging base. Difficult dynamic moves lead to easier climbing.

## 13  Drystone Wall  30 feet  Very Severe
4c. Climb the thin crack 10 ft right of the arete for 15 ft, then move 3 ft left and finish up the centre of the wall.

Right of North Buttress and at the same level is **THE NORTH QUARRY**. Several diminutive routes have been climbed on the left half, but all the worthwhile routes are on the highest right half. The path from the cross-roads below arrives steeply at this end, and opposite the path is a narrow sharp-angled corner. Just left is a shallower corner and left again a blank-looking slabby wall.

## 14  Everdance  25 feet  Very Severe
4b. Climb the wall on surprisingly good holds.

## 15  Death Wish  25 feet  E3
6a. The shallow corner on the right is very fingery to holds on the right wall where the angle eases. Easily to the top. Quite serious despite the ledge.

## 16  Thin Finger Corner  25 feet  Mild Very Severe  ★
4b. The sharp-angled corner. Over ledges to the corner proper. Use the left arete to start some delicate moves up the corner. Belay up left.

## 17  The Lubricant  45 feet  Very Severe
About 15 yards right of the last climb the rock becomes higher and forms a corner on the left of an overhanging wall.
4c. Climb the broken corner until the crack forks. Follow the left fork boldly, then go over broken rock to the top.

## 18  Wet and Warm  40 feet  Very Severe
4c. The rather inferior right fork of the crack.

To the right is the highest buttress in the quarry. Both routes on it are very serious and difficult undertakings. The thin leftwards slanting crack up the overhanging wall was originally pegged.

## 19  Main Wall  50 feet  E5
6a. The crack direct. Very strenuous and sustained. Peg runners exist at 20 ft, poor, and 40 ft, but the hardest moves are at the top and a band of friable rock just below makes protection suspect.

## 20  Impact Two   40 feet   E5
5c. This takes the right side of the arete right of Main Wall. Gain it at half-height from ledges on the right. Make a difficult move left into the void and layback the smooth final arete.

10 yards right is a short smooth slab. A 5a problem takes the right side of this. Low walls occur to the right but the quarry soon peters out.

The remaining climbs are on isolated buttresses on the north-west side of the hill. About 450 yards from the quarry are 2 buttresses 30 yards apart; hidden by trees they are rather awkward to find, but are just beyond a junction on the road below. The left buttress, THE SECRET SLAB, contains 2 delectable routes, and it is well worth the trouble to find.

## 21  Slender Thread   30 feet   E4          ★★
6a. There is a very thin finger crack in the centre of the slab. Climb this with increasing difficulty until it ends. Make a long reach for an indefinite horizontal crack and move left to gain an arete for the last few feet. Unprotected. Inspection advised.

## 22  Crystal Voyager   30 feet   E2          ★★
6a. A delicate climb at the lower limit of its grade. Right of Slender Thread is a thinner crack system. Climb on small holds in the line of the crack to a good hold just left of a large grassy ledge; escape is unfortunately possible here. Stand on this hold and move left with difficulty into the short final groove.

## 23  Birch Tree Climb   25 feet   Severe
30 yards right is the other buttress. At the left side is a corner. Climb the corner to an old tree stump near the top. Make an exposed swing right to the arete to finish. Inferior finishes exist.

## 24  Sirloin   25 feet   Hard Severe
From the overhang on the right swing right onto the face and up the crack.

## 25  Anticlimax   25 feet   Very Severe
5a. Climb the wall right of Sirloin to a big ledge. Finish up the crack just right of the finish of Sirloin.

## 26  Bottle Crack   25 feet   Difficult
To the right is a gully containing the 'bottle' boulder. Above this climb the crack on the left wall.

About 250 yards right is a small face split down the front by a crack with a protruding chockstone.

**27  Minute Wall**  20 feet  Hard Very Difficult
Start 5 yards left of the crack. Go up the wall with a mantleshelf beginning at the cutaway.

**28  Key Green Crack**  25 feet  Very Difficult
Climb the chockstone crack direct.

400 yards right is THE CATSTONE, a fine tower-like buttress.

**29  Termination Crack**  60 feet  Severe
The corner crack left of the main buttress. Needs gardening.

**30  The Cat Crawl**  60 feet  Mild Severe                    ★
The left arete of the tower. 15 ft of easy rock leads to the arete. Climb this awkwardly at first, then on better holds to the top. Alternatively, take the upward curving ledge right of the upper part.

**31  Hot Tin Roof**  60 feet  E1                              ★
5a. A bold lead, especially if runners are not placed in the chimney. Climb the crack 6 ft right of Cat Crawl. Move right along 2 ledges to a point overlooking Mutiny Chimney. Follow a line of small sharp pockets with difficulty.

**32  Mutiny Chimney**  60 feet  Hard Severe
Climb a short wall to gain the chimney, which is climbed to a hard, unpleasant exit onto the hollybush ledge. Step left onto the face and finish nicely up the arete.

**33  Hollybush Wall**  30 feet  Very Severe
4c. Climb the wall below the hollybush ledge using thin indefinite cracks and the arete to the right at the top. A good finish is the arete of Mutiny Chimney.

## TIMBERSBROOK QUARRY
Owing to frequent landslides, creeping vegetation and restricted access this quarry is not considered worthy of climbers' attentions at present and is therefore excluded from this guide.

# KNYPERSLEY ROCKS
by Stephen Dale

O.S. Ref. SJ 900557

## SITUATION, APPROACH and ACCESS
These rocks are 1½ miles south-east of Biddulph, in the wood on the east side of Knypersley Reservoir. The best approach is from the north. Take Rock End road (Park Lane) from Knypersley cross-roads on the A527. After 1¼ miles turn right down an unmade road (Lodge Barn Road). This is followed for 300 yards until it forks (limited parking space). A footpath bisects the fork and leads to a stile; turn right here. Several small crags will be seen on the ridge to the right, the first reasonably high ones being in the vicinity of a wall which crosses the path. If the wall is followed up right it ends in a stepped slab. This is Green Slab and 50 yards right is Small Slab. Several parties have been approached by various people not wishing climbing to take place.

## CHARACTER
The rocks are of fairly sound gritstone but their situation in the woods tends to make some of the crags a little green. Most of the climbs are worth doing and it is a pleasant evening crag.

THE CLIMBS are described in the order in which they would be met using the approach described, i.e. from Right to Left.

## SMALL SLAB
**1 Right It** 30 feet Very Difficult
Climb directly up the front of the slab.

**2 Left It** 25 feet Very Difficult
Start to the left and climb direct to a large shelf, finishing more easily.

## GREEN SLAB
**3 Twinkle Toes** 35 feet Very Difficult
From the left corner of the easy-angled green slab traverse delicately right to the right arete and climb this to the top.

**4 Two Step** 30 feet Severe ★
From the left corner climb direct to the top. Interesting.

**5  The Jug Jam**   40 feet   Very Difficult ★★
150 yards left of Green Slab is The Pinnacle. The front of the crag is barred by overhangs which are split by a crack. Use either of the twin cracks to gain a chimney at the overhang. Climb the chimney to the top. A superb climb on excellent rock.

**6  Scorpion**   35 feet   Very Severe ★
4c. Start round the corner to the left and make a hard traverse to gain the left arete. Climb the arete delicately to the top.

**7  Logos**   30 feet   Hard Severe
Climb the shallow groove to the left and make an awkward move onto the arete. Move right along a ledge and finish straight up.

**8  Grassy Slab**   40 feet   Very Difficult
To the left of The Pinnacle are some cleaned slabs. Climb either of two cracklines on the slabs and finish up the front of the steep tower above. Many variations are possible.

At the bottom of the ridge on the opposite side of the valley is the last crag. It has a natural arch in its right end. The climbs on this buttress are described from right to left.

**9  Gryphon**   35 feet   Very Difficult
To the right of the arch is a small low overhang. Climb out of the left corner of the overhang to the final vague crackline. At the level of the arch it is possible to traverse right to a large ledge below a steep corner and finish up this.

**10  Briar**   30 feet   Very Severe
4b. Gain the cracks left of the arch by climbing the green greasy wall.

**11  Christmas Cracker**   30 feet   Hard Very Severe ★
5a. A thin crack is gained from the broken chimney on the left and climbed with difficulty to the left and widest crack and the top.

**12  Misogynist**   30 feet   Very Difficult
The chimney is climbed direct.

**13  Halcyon**   25 feet   Very Difficult
The line to the left of the bulge to the left. Hard to finish.

**14  Northern Lights**   25 feet   Difficult
The thin crack to the left.

**15 Prometheus**  25 feet  Moderate
The wide crack to the left.

**16 The Common Good**  25 feet  Very Severe  ★
4b.Layback over the overhang to the left and make an awkward move right to a ledge. Finish easily up to the tree. Entertaining.

**17 Danera**  30 feet  Very Difficult
The crack to the left is climbed direct or by climbing the ramp that goes towards The Common Good.

**18 Keep Left**  25 feet  Hard Severe
The thin crack immediately left of Danera. Quite hard if the holds on Danera are avoided.

To the left is an excellent boulder with some good problems.

ROCK END    O.S. Ref. SJ 898570
This pleasant outcrop of rocks is situated at the southern end of the Biddulph Moor Ridge and is best approached by taking the Biddulph Moor road (Park Lane) out of Knypersley just south of Biddulph. The rock is good quality grit and in most places the low height and grassy landing combine to provide extensive bouldering terrain. The lefthand and highest part of the crag is on private ground and permission should be sought at the house at the lefthand end of the crag. A further outcrop occurs ½ a mile north and looks quite promising.

# MOW COP
by Gary Gibson

O.S. Ref. SJ 858576 — The Old Man Of Mow
SJ 858573 — The Folly Cliff and Quarries

## SITUATION
This rocky hill lies on the Cheshire-Staffordshire border 2 miles north of Kidsgrove and about 7 miles north of Stoke-on-Trent. Its folly castle on top is a prominent landmark from miles around.

## APPROACHES
A bus service runs from Stoke to Mow Cop village within 15 minutes walk of the rocks. For those with private transport, Mow Cop is well-signposted from Biddulph or Kidsgrove. There is adequate parking just below the castle on the west side. The Folly Cliff and nearby quarries are on the east side of the ridge crest. For the Old Man, follow the ridge northwards from the Folly to a lane. Cross this to a footpath leading round the side of some houses, until the pinnacle appears on the right.

## ACCESS
Permission to climb is not required but please do not damage the fence which has been erected round part of the base of the Old Man.

## CHARACTER
All the routes are in old quarries and have a brittle hold or two. Despite its unpopularity as a climbing ground there are a few gems and the routes on the Old Man are of high quality, especially Spiral Route.
It should perhaps be noted that the youths of the area tend regularly to get stuck half-way up the crag!

## HISTORY
The first route to be recorded was K. Maskery's ascent of the Old Man by the Spiral Route, which remains the best route here. Various other people visited and Harold Drasdo added two more routes to the pinnacle with Piton Route and Alsager Route, and together with G. Sutton, R. O. Downes and Tony Moulam completed its development with Cambridge Crack and the Direct Route. Since then records are scarce and the first ascents noted below may be incorrect. Castle Crack was established as were other routes. Several, including Carbonel and the foul Bow and Arrow were added by A. Taylor and P. Williams of the N.S.M.C.

around 1960. Later on P. Kenway of Alsager College M.C. and
J. Amies and J. Lockett of the N.S.M.C. added Hawks Hell,
Left Eliminate, Folly Berger, Man Mow and Right Tot. J. Amies
described the known routes in the 1973 Staffordshire Gritstone
guidebook.
The remaining rock now lay virgin until 1975 when the very
talented Woodward brothers, Jon and Andrew free-climbed
B.S. Mow, The Arete and Carbonel's direct finish and added
Captain Skyhook. John Holt was drafted in to write the guide and
added Special Branch. Sadly John was killed in 1979 and this sole
route stands as a testimony to his special talents. Andrew
Woodward returned in 1979 and led Silent Scream and finally
Gary Gibson in 'typical manner' added Crystal Voyager, The
Captain's Blood and Crystine.

## THE OLD MAN OF MOW

The climbs on this unique contorted gritstone pinnacle are
described in a clockwise fashion starting at a large step just right
of the fence round the rockfall remains on the front face.
N.B. Descent from the top is by precarious abseil; not
recommended for novices.

**1  The Spiral Route**   65 feet   Hard Severe                    ★★★
A unique climb. From the left end of the steps ascend up left to a
ledge at the base of a slab. Move left and down round the corner
and go up another slab to the left shoulder. Belay. Step up and
right onto the forehead and ascend direct to the top.

**2  The Direct Route**   55 feet   Hard Very Severe                  ★
5a. Starting just inside the fence climb the left-facing groove
through the overhangs to the first slab of Spiral Route. Step up
and left onto the forehead. Finish as for Spiral Route.

**3  Alsager Route**   55 feet   Hard Very Severe
5a. From the foot of Direct Route trend left across the rock scar,
then straight up to the left shoulder. Up a groove in the arete.

The back of the pinnacle has 3 routes. These are:

**4  The Lee Side**   65 feet   Hard Very Severe
5a. Climb the righthand side of the small pedestal to its top.
Traverse horizontally right across the leaning wall and round the
corner to the shoulder. Go diagonally back left to the top.

MOW COP 261

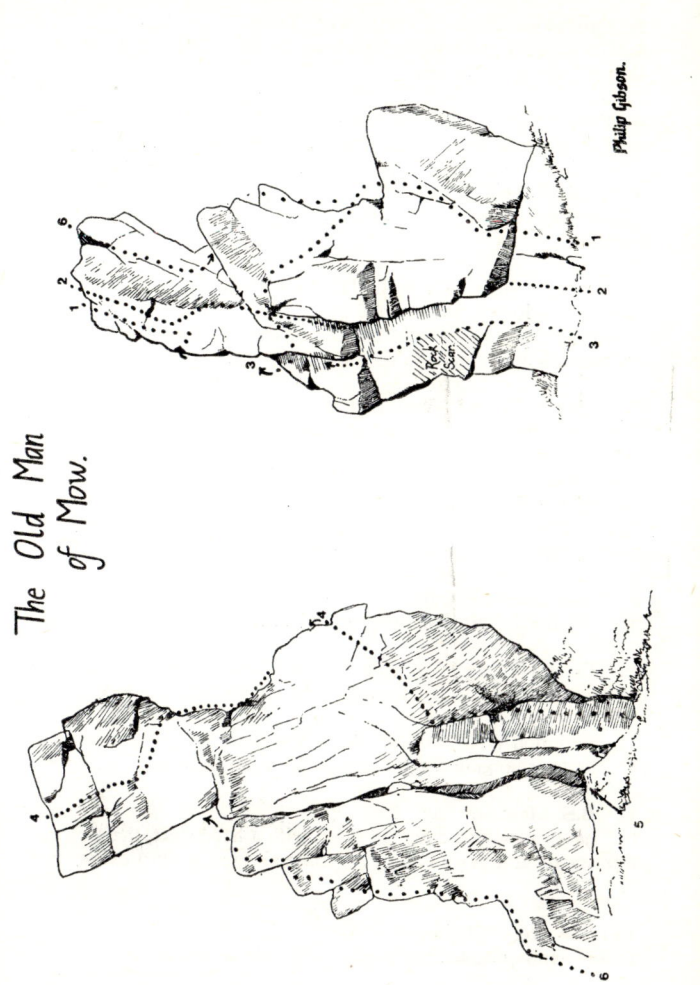

The Old Man of Mow.

Philip Gibson.

**5  Cambridge Crack**  35 feet   Very Severe  ★
4c. The obvious overhanging crack on the back face to a small slab. Finish up any route.

**6  Piton Route**  55 feet   Hard Very Severe
5b. The series of steps on the arete to the left all the way.

## THE OLD MAN'S QUARRY
The quarry adjacent to the pinnacle has 2 routes worthy of mention.

**7  Route 1**  30 feet   Very Difficult
Start at the lowest point of the quarry. Up a short wall to a ledge. Climb the front of the buttress to an overhang. Go over this and up the wall above or take the slab on the left, Hard Severe.

**8  Route 2**  30 feet   Very Difficult
The wall a few ft right. The top is delicate and loose.

## THE FOLLY CLIFF
This is directly below the castle and has a prominent arete. Recent landscaping has affected the next few routes and made them easier.

**9  Cioch Groove**  30 feet   Very Difficult
The obvious leftward slanting groove at the right end of the wall.

**10  Crystal Voyager**  30 feet   E1
5a. The steep slab 10 ft left joining the groove near the top.

**11  Initiation Wall**  40 feet   Very Severe
4b. The overhanging crack and wall 10 ft left. Loose.

**12  B.S. Mow**  60 feet   E1
6a. The once-pegged crack 10 ft left with a hard start, then rightwards up the wall above. A loose alternative start exists just right.

**13  The Arete**  70 feet   E3
5c. The sandy peg-scarred cracks in the prominent arete.

**14  Man Mow**  70 feet   E1
5a. Start just left of the arete. Gain this and swing up right to a ledge in the centre of the face. Go directly up past an inverted spike.

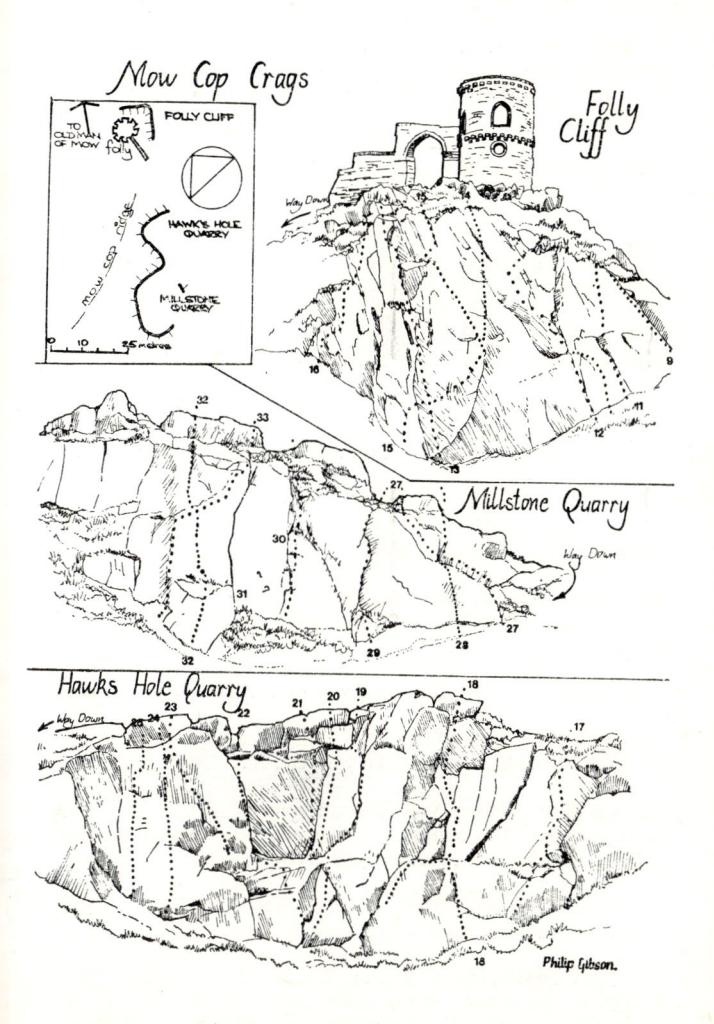

MOW COP 263

Mow Cop Crags

Folly Cliff

Millstone Quarry

Hawks Hole Quarry

Philip Gibson.

**15 Folly Berger** 75 feet Hard Very Severe
5a. As for Man Mow to the ledge. Go diagonally left to the arete then step right and up directly to the top.

**16 Right Tot** 60 feet Hard Very Severe
4c. Start on the right of the scoop left of the arete. Climb the wall to the traverse line. Go left for 10 ft to a flake. Climb this and the wall above.

**Rot** and **Tot** are on the wall to the left; both are outstandingly loose as is the Girdle Traverse.

HAWKS HOLE QUARRY
The hole-like quarry to the south of the castle. In the upper part of its right wall are 2 V-notches.

**17 Double Vee** 40 feet Hard Severe
4a. From the floor of the quarry, go up through notches to the top.

**18 Three Steps** 50 feet Severe
The stepped broken corner left of, and starting up, Double Vee. Another start is up a small corner to the left. Hard Very Severe, 5a.

The overhanging wall just left provides the dynamic duo, **Batman** and **Robin**, both of which are A2.

**19 Hawks Hell** 60 feet Very Severe
4c. The back righthand corner of the quarry starting up a huge flake.

2 cracks start from the ledge part way up Hawks Hell. These are:

**20 Right Eliminate** 30 feet A1
**21 Left Eliminate** 30 feet Very Severe, 5a.

**22 Vee Diff** 50 feet Very Difficult ★
Start just left of Hawks Hell. Go diagonally leftwards to the large ledge. Continue up the arete or slab above.

**23 Square Buttress** 30 feet Hard Severe
4a. The centre of the square buttress 15 ft to the left.

**24 The Captain's Blood** 25 feet E2
Left of Square Buttress is a scooped face.
6a. The blank-looking righthand side of the scoop.

**25  Captain Skyhook**  25 feet  E1   ★
5b. The centre of the scoop stepping right at the top.

MILLSTONE QUARRY
This is round to the left. Starting at the righthand end are:

**26  The Reach**  35 feet  Hard Severe
4a. Climb the right arete until a step left leads to a groove and the top.

**27  Carbonel**  60 feet  Very Severe
4c. As for The Reach for 15 ft. Step left and follow the obvious diagonal traverse line to the top.

**28  Silent Scream**  45 feet  E3
Above the traverse of Carbonel is a short corner.
6a. Climb the wall directly to the corner. Finish up this.

**29  Bow and Arrow**  50 feet  Very Severe
4c. The disgusting bird-limed crack 10 yards left.

**30  Special Branch**  55 feet  Hard Very Severe
Just left is an even more disgusting line and left again is:
5b. The vague crackline 10 ft left of the gully.

**31  Castle Crack**  60 feet  Very Severe   ★
4c. Gain the conspicuous wide crack, just to the left, from below and climb it to an easy finish.

**32  Crystine**  60 feet  E2
5b. Climb the wall just left to a good ledge. Climb the wall 10 ft left of Castle Crack to easy ground. Go directly up the arete above.

**33  Arete And Slab Climb**  85 feet  Severe
Climb the vague line 10 ft left again, by-passing a tricky section on the left, to gain the line leading right. Follow this until directly above Castle Crack. Finish direct.

There are numerous problems in this huge quarry, notably the small vandalised slab (without using the hands). The rest are not described and are left for those with a bent mind.

NICK I' TH' HILL   O.S. Ref. SJ 881607
There are several quarries along the crest of this ridge 2½ miles north-east of Mow Cop. Many overlook gardens, all look dangerous. The furthest from Mow Cop appears to be the most interesting.

# ADDENDUM

## DOVEDALE—TISSINGTON SPIRES

**24a  Manna Machine**   120 feet   Very Severe   †
4c. Start at the same point as Silicon. Climb the obvious cleaned slab above, first slightly right and then slightly left, to a huge tree. Step up then move left and go up to a niche. Climb the crack above to the col.


## THE ROACHES

**95a  Trebia**   40 feet   E2   †
Start on the ledge 10 ft left of Round Table and below its left arete. Climb the overhanging arete to a niche below the roof. Climb the roof direct.

**36a  Swan Bank**   70 feet   E3   †
5c. Start 10 ft right of Mincer's normal start. Pull over the bulge as its Superdirect and join Mincer. Step up then undercut left to the end of the flake. Climb slightly left to join The Swan at its crux and finish up The Swan.